ATHINA ONASSIS IN THE EYE OF THE STORM

ATHINA ONASSIS
In the Eye of the Storm

An insider's story

By

Alexis Mantheakis

KIBOSS PUBLICATIONS

"To live well you must live hidden"
Henri Roussel to his son Thierry

"Rich people are not poor people with money"
AM

Sections *of this book previously appeared in Greek in an edition of Periplous Publications, Greece (©.2002), in Portuguese in an edition of Francisco Alves, Brazil (©.2004), and in French, Editions Favre, France (©.2005)*

ISBN-13: 978-1479304899

The Guardian – *Jon Henley and Helena Smith: "Alexis Mantheakis is the author of the only inside account of the heiress, "Athina Onassis in the Eye of the Storm..."*

CNN LIVE Today: *Daryn Kagan, Anchor: "Our next guest is a former spokesman for the Onassis family, and the author of Athina in the Eye of the Storm. And Alexis Mantheakis is joining us from Athens, Greece..."*

USA TODAY – *Jeannie Williams: "Alexis, you are the best source of this story on Athina..."*

CNN Student – *"Alexis Mantheakis, author of Athina in the Eye of the Storm (book cover shown) speaks to us about Athina Onassis..."*

Point de Vue (France) *Dorothee Lalanne: Interview with the author- "Athina Onassis – "Her biographer Alexis Mantheakis is the witness: For years he was part of her inside circle. He paints an intimate portrait of the heiress in Athina Onassis in the Eye of the Storm."*

NBC The Today Show – *Live from Athens. "Alexis Mantheakis, author of Athina in the Eye of the Storm* tells us about what the heiress and her Olympic Medalist... "

The History Channel – *"The Heiresses" – Interview with the biographer of Athina Onassis*

L'Illustre (Switzerland) *Cover Story – "The Hidden Face of Athina Roussel. Laurent Favre: "For five years Alexis Mantheakis participated in the life of Athina Onassis and her father Thierry Roussel. In his book Athina Onassis in the Eye of the Storm he reveals the terrible struggle of Athina ..."*

TA NEA (Greece) *"...exclusive pre-release of the most important chapter of the book Athina Onassis in the Eye of the Storm, written by Alexis Mantheakis about the Onassis heiress.*

QUEM (Brazil) *"We interview Alexis Mantheakis, the author of Athina Onassis in the Eye of the Storm, who maintained a close relationship with Athina, her brother and sisters and with her father. He gives us details about the life of Athina, her family relationships and how she manages her fortune."*

CONTENTS

A Sable Coat at the Hotel Particulier

Scorpios – Mon Royaume Pour un Cheval!

Acknowledgements

I would like to thank my wife Dimitra, who bore the brunt of the legal and media attacks by Athina Onassis' and Thierry Roussel's enemies against me with fortitude when I was the Roussel family representative and their close friend. She spent years and many sleepless nights, without pay, researching legal archives and preparing documents to help Athina and her father in the battle for the Onassis billions. I, and others, owe her a debt that cannot easily be repaid.

Thanks to my old school friends from Rhodes House at the Prince of Wales School in Nairobi, Dr Mike Lawrence Brown, OA, of Perth, and Alan "Nala" Smith of Auckland, without whose encouragement and support this book could not have been published.

Thanks to my daughter Marina, who uncomplainingly saw Athina often take precedence over our family affairs and endured with patience the round-the-clock intrusion of the local and international media into our lives.

Thanks to Athina Onassis, to her father Thierry Roussel, and to gentle Gaby Roussel for opening up their homes and yachts and sharing their family life with me as their guest on numerous occasions in Greece, Switzerland and Spain when we broke bread together during the difficult years when I was their "Man in Greece".

Thanks to Ares Kalogeropoulos, the founder of the "I am Greek, I want to Go Home" Parthenon Sculptures campaign, who kindly designed the book cover.

Thanks to my Greek publisher and friend Dionissis Vitsos for his patience and encouragement.

Seven biographies have been written about Athina Onassis, the last surviving member of the legendary Greek shipping dynasty. Six of them by writers who have never seen or spoken to the heiress.

Revised and updated in 2014 "Athina Onassis - In the Eye of the Storm" is the seventh book - the only inside story about Athina, what she is really like and about the people closest to her. Alexis Mantheakis spent several years as the press representative and adviser to Athina's father Thierry Roussel and was a close friend of the family. His book describes times spent with Athina and her family in Switzerland, as their family holiday guest in Ibiza at Athina's stunning hillside mansion with its eight swimming pools and its secret discothèque. In Greece he stayed on Scorpios Island with the heiress and her father. In Paris he visited the Onassis apartment at 88 Avenue Foch where Jackie lived when Ari was carrying on a turbulent love affair with Maria Callas, the opera diva. He sunbathed on yacht decks with the young Athina in Greece and in Spain. He and the Roussels attended each others family parties.

He was present at meeting after meeting with her lawyers in Switzerland, Paris and Greece. For six years Mantheakis was at the centre of a whirlwind of court cases across Europe involving the Greek former employees of her grandfather who ran the Onassis Foundation and who turned against Athina and Thierry. Later he watched a new Athina emerge from this struggle to embrace and then to shake off her Greek past. A bitter father-daughter conflict developed after her coming of age with the entry of the older and charismatic Brazilian horseman Alvaro Affonso de Miranda Neto into her life. Five tragic deaths followed almost immediately supporting the theory of an "Onassis Curse' on the fortune she inherited.

It is the first time that the English language reading public will have a chance to share the life of the reclusive Onassis heiress and get to know the characters and intrigues of a legendary dynasty through an anecdotal and first hand account of how they live behind closed doors.

Author's Note

Anybody involved with the Onassis family and its conflicts in any capacity quickly discovered that along with the undeniable magic that the dynasty held for the initiate and the outsider it was impossible to avoid enemies springing up as in Jason's field of Dragon's teeth. The complicated interests, stemming primarily from the vast amount of money and power involved and who would control parts or all of it, spawned hostility as well as deep friendships. Shifting loyalties, financial, amatory, political, sexual, and workplace intrigue led to some of the highest profile conflicts reported by the international media since World War II. Often the conflicts came from inside the family itself, the family here including the Roussels and, more recently, the de Mirandas of Brazil.

A surprising number of enemies of Athina and her father soon made their presence known to me after I started to represent them. Enemies in the courts, in Greek Parliament, in the European Parliament, in the media - both Greek and international - and often even among ordinary people in the street. But Athina and her father had the ultimate weapon: the use and claim to the legendary Onassis name, revered in Greece and known throughout the world.

I had chosen for sentimental and historic reasons, but also because I believed they were right, and for the challenge it presented, to accept Thierry's invitation to represent him and his family in the days of the most intense conflict with the Onassis Foundation and Athina's Greek patrimony administrators, appointed with Thierry Roussel to administer Athina's money until her coming of age. Unpredictable events and sea changes occurred weekly, reminding me more of a le Carre novel than what was on the surface an inter-corporate conflict, albeit one over a billion plus dollars. Those enemies I personally made, by default, continue to spring up from time to time while the vociferousness of some of this book's reviews, a minority it is true, almost always by people who have not reviewed other books, make me smile in the knowledge that the same old battle is still going on somewhere, out of the limelight, but still going on. One issue I had to deal with when I wrote the book was that of referring by name to famous or notorious people I have known - name dropping - as it is disparagingly known. For this I make no apologies since it would be a contradiction in terms to write a celebrity biography about people I know without revealing their names, nor do my readers expect anything less!

This book is a series of stories, incidents and anecdotal descriptions about Athina and the Onassis and Roussel families. It is not a journal written according to a calendar timeline but a collection of stories where the reader will share my own experiences with the Onassis-Roussel family and read of other incidents recounted to me by immediate family, Onassis relatives, family friends, former associates of Ari Onassis, Scorpios Island staff, Onassis Foundation employees, embittered former lovers, jilted wives, and of course bodyguards on both sides of the conflict who, human nature being what it is, switched loyalties each time the balance of power shifted and a new winner in the struggle appeared to be about to finish the fight and control the legacy.

The dynasty has come to a halt with Athina, the last Onassis. Married for years now to handsome

Brazilian horseman and Olympic Champion "Doda" Affonso de Miranda Neto, she has not produced an heir nor has her money been freed from the trust in which it has been safely held since she was 18. Will she shake off the Onassis Curse that has taken so many lives? And what about the Onassis Love Triangle curse whereby two generations of Onassis women, Athina's mother Christina Onassis and her grandmother Tina Livanos Onassis, suffered the presence of other women with whom their husbands maintained long standing affairs, some lasting for years?

The birth of a new heir or heiress and the release of the Onassis fortune when the trust elapses, or with Athina's possible adoption of husband Doda's teenage daughter Vivienne, making her the Onassis fortune heiress, will once again bring about unforeseen developments in the Onassis saga…

Preface

I have been fortunate in often finding myself in places where historic or interesting things were happening. Kenya at the end of the British colonial era, California where as an undergraduate at Stanford University I observed the sea change in American political and social awareness prompted by the Vietnam war, London where I lived as a young actor in the exuberant ferment of Swinging London, Greece where I witnessed optimistic crowds celebrating the return of democracy after a series of increasingly repressive military coups which had led to the shootings at the Athens

Polytechnic in 1974 a few months before. A film set at the ancient Greek theatre at Dodoni, where at 22 years of age I was in front of the cameras next to Orson Welles and spoke my lines, watched by great, and not so great, Hollywood film legends. The Greek Orthodox Church of Nairobi when I stood next to Archbishop Makarios as his 11 year-old assistant while the revolutionary Cypriot leader, just released from British exile in the Seychelles, made his first public speech speaking for the right of subjugated peoples everywhere to assert their independence from colonial masters.

As a child I lived through the Mau Mau rebellion in East Africa. It was a time when foe was no longer discernible from friend. Kenya then was a country enveloped by a strange pervading silence which engulfed everybody as they went about their daily routine always listening for that one – different - sound which would mean the difference between life and death. One morning the fighting stopped and Kenya became paradise once more.

My family had come to East Africa (originally to Tanganyika) at the turn of the century when my father arrived there as a 14 year-old stowaway from the island of Crete. He had a vision of making his fortune, and he did, in what was then still unexplored German East Africa. I grew up in a Greek household near Lake Victoria in British East Africa on a sisal and sugar plantation. I finished boarding school in Nairobi when the sun was finally setting on the British Empire.

My next three years were spent at Stanford University where I studied English literature, learned more languages and took an intense interest in what was happening in California. Realizing a youthful ambition I left Stanford to become an actor for four years, appearing on television and in several films in England and in Greece. When I was 23 I was invited to the Berlin Film Festival as the lead in a participating Greek film made by a noted award-winning director. It was a promising start to an interesting career, but I was restless and one day I shuffled the pack and dealt myself a different card. I finally settled, in a manner of speaking, in Athens, where I married and became a business consultant. I found though that fateful and historic events continued happening in places to which I was travelling, so I began writing about them.

Half a century earlier when my father had escaped the slaughter in Asia Minor another ambitious young refugee, Aristotle Onassis, embarked for South America.

Onassis' daring character and unique ability to spot a business opportunity helped him make a vast fortune, while his jet-setting lifestyle, his legendary luxury yacht 'Christina' in Monte Carlo and his numerous affairs with glamorous and famous women later made him into a twentieth century legend.

In Athens I saw Onassis several times in the gloomy bar of the Grande Bretagne Hotel and at the noisy *bouzouki* clubs we both frequented. Onassis was then near the end of his life, I at the beginning of mine. Whenever we passed each other on the street, or rubbed elbows at *Zambetas* bouzouki club in Fillelinon Street neither of us knew that fate would bring our families together a quarter of a century later.

The media clamoured after Onassis and begged for details of his extravagant lifestyle. The Onassis legend took root and the tragic family events that followed made the Onassis myth even stronger. One after another the members of the golden family died or were killed by hands unknown. Of all the Onassis family only one person survived - Athina - the daughter of Christina Onassis and Thierry Roussel, Christina's French fourth husband.

On the 15th of March of 1975 several small groups of Greek villagers in the Ionian island hamlet of Nydri stood quietly discussing the death that day in Paris of Aristotle Onassis, reputedly the world's richest man. Across the narrow stretch of cobalt-coloured water boats were busily coming and going to the wooded private island of Scorpios. There, hushed staff were making preparations at a small whitewashed chapel for the funeral of the shipping and airline tycoon. 13 years later Christina, Onassis' only surviving child, was buried in a white marble tomb in the same modest chapel next to her 24 year old brother Alexander and her father Aristotle.

On the morning of the 29th of January of 2003 Christina's reclusive 18 year old daughter Athina Roussel inherited half the Onassis fortune while trying to ignore the crowds of journalists, international television crews and paparazzi waiting outside to report on the handover of one of the world's great fortunes.

The Greek tycoon's only living descendant was growing up in a Swiss village surrounded by ex-SAS commando bodyguards when I first started to hear about her.

Chance was to draw me into the center of the Onassis saga soon after. In November 1997 my wife was watching television in our apartment located in a wooded northern Athens suburb on the slopes of Mount Penteli. Bored by the usual fare of Greek soap operas and political talk shows she switched channels. There, on Antenna TV, four members of the Alexander Onassis Public Benefit Foundation Presidency, all former employees of Onassis, were giving their side of the events involving the arrest of a team of former Mossad agents in Switzerland and in Israel. The agents had been involved in an alleged kidnap operation against the Onassis heiress. I decided to watch the interview. It was a decision that changed my life.

I was surprised by what I heard during the interview that evening. My immediate reaction was to sit down when the programme was over and write an article which I gave to an Athenian newspaper. I followed this up a week later with another article. The kidnap story by now was all over the international media so I moved on and wrote about other events, forgetting the Onassis episode for the moment.

Three months later, on January 27th, 1998 I received a call from a newspaper editor saying a fax had come from Switzerland asking for information about the journalist who had written about Athina. Neither I nor the editor had heard of the company or the person sending the fax. I presumed it must be from the Onassis Foundation which had its base in Liechtenstein.

"Mr. Mantheakis, we would like to discuss your articles" said the woman who answered the telephone when I dialed the Swiss contact number on the letter.

"Are you from the Onassis Foundation?" I enquired, prepared to defend what I had written, and to ask a few questions of my own.

There was a brief pause. "No. I am the private secretary of Mr. Thierry Roussel, the father of Athina. He would like to meet you."

I had not read good things in the press about the former husband of Christina Onassis. The media had repeated accusations made by the Onassis Public Benefit Foundation presidency that Athina, the heiress, was growing up as a virtual hostage. There was much more. The accusations were so intense that I was now sceptical and was curious to meet the man and his daughter. I suspected that things were not as they had been presented by their opponents. I accepted the invitation to go to Switzerland and at five thirty the next afternoon I was looking out of the window of a Swissair plane as it banked over thick woods and small, pristine patchwork fields with red-roofed matchbox-like farmhouses as we approached Geneva airport. I did not know what I would find in Switzerland but I was excited at the prospect of my first contact with the legendary family of Aristotle Onassis.

This book tells the story of Athina Onassis, the Golden Heiress, as I got to know her from then on, from a privileged position close to the family.

***

Athina had been pestering Thierry for a long time to allow her to go to Belgium where she wanted to enroll in the Nelson Pessoa riding academy. Athina was obsessed with horses and show jumping and what had started as a hobby in her spare time now took precedence over all her other extra curricular activities. Thierry liked horses and the family had theirs at a nearby stable. Athina,

Thierry and Sandrine were the riders in the family. Erik, Athina's half-brother was allergic to them and kept well away from the equine companions that his sisters admired so much.

Thierry had seen changes in Athina recently. After her sixteenth birthday tensions were building up in the family. Athina was changing from the docile, cheerful and shy teenager seen hanging onto her father's arm whenever they were in public together, into a brooding, introverted girl with many things on her mind. The conflict with the Onassis Foundation, public scrutiny and criticism of the heiress and her lifestyle, tensions created by the court cases, her father's five year prison sentence in Greece and a kidnapping scenario in Switzerland, plus the pressures of being the last bearer of the Onassis name made Athina look for something that would keep her away from public attention and allow her time on her own. She found refuge in the privacy of her stables and the freedom she felt when she was riding one of her favourite animals. Here she could have a sense of achievement as she coaxed her steeds over ever higher jumps.

Thierry was not an easy man to get on with. I had observed him at home and knew that his family was expected to do what he said. The extent of this control and his view that he would always be in charge of Athina, and by extension of her affairs, financial and social, were apparent to those close to the family. An incident at Athens airport made it even clearer that Thierry was not prepared to let go. He still saw Athina as the little girl she no longer was. When Thierry stepped out of the arrivals lounge where I had been waiting for him two Greek television reporters approached us and started asking about Athina. Thierry's answers were well rehearsed and expected until one of the reporters asked him "Does Athina have a boyfriend?"

Thierry thought for a moment. "No, of course not, she is only fifteen."

The answer took the reporters by surprise. It was clear that he was unaware or unwilling to accept that his daughter was now a young woman and that it was the most normal thing in the world for her to have an interest in boys of her own age.

As the pressures of puberty and of growing up as an Onassis started closing in on Athina she began losing her former interest in her lessons and turned her attention to her horses. At the same time she started putting on weight because of an indulgence in chocolate and cakes. Thierry, who had exercised all his life and was on a permanent diet, was proud of his slim, muscular body and thick blond-highlighted hair and he was not pleased to see Athina's recently expanding figure. It reminded him of her mother Christina's ballooning figure after binging on chocolate and Coca Cola, something she followed with crash slimming diets boosted by handfuls of prescription pills and amphetamines. The ghost of Christina Onassis with all the accompanying stories of sexual excess, emotional instability, drug use and incapacity to forge lasting and meaningful relationships hung heavy in the Roussel family home. The situation was made more complicated by the realization that no matter how fairly Gaby, Athina's Swedish stepmother, treated the children Athina was always going to be something different. She could not escape the fact that she was the child of a problematic, tragic and absent Greek woman who had willed her whole fortune to Athina and Thierry, allowing the Roussels and Athina to have a lifestyle of luxury that was the envy of the world and the secret jealousy of their friends. Athina had to cope with the rumours and gossip she heard and read about her mother and her grandmother Tina whom Truman Capote had called 'a whore', and also with the knowledge that Gaby had stolen Thierry from Christina. Christina's death and the repeated news items referring to it as part of an Onassis 'curse' must have weighed heavily too on young Athina as she prepared to make her way into adulthood. For Athina the situation was not made easier by statements in the press that Thierry had cynically married an unattractive and dumpy Greek heiress for her money. Christina Onassis became an object of love but also of shame for her teenage daughter. Christina's photos were one day taken down from the mansion outside Geneva that she had given to Athina. Things came to a head one evening at the dinner table in Lussy when Athina asked for another piece of bread and Thierry exploded, saying "You are just like your mother, putting on weight all the time with chocolates and food!"

The dinner table insult was perhaps the turning point for Athina about whom the press was speculating as to the cause of her increased weight. One television station in Greece, during a programme dedicated to the heiress, had put the question of Athina's weight gain to a psychologist who pronounced that the gain was not normal and that it indicated, in his view, psychological problems Athina was having. I tried to defend the heiress and her public image when journalists called me about it, saying that it was not unusual for teenage girls finishing high school and faced with exams to wind down on exercise and to acquire some "puppy fat" from eating more. It was plausible, but I too had started to wonder about what was really happening with Athina and whether the wild rumours and gossip about her father Thierry, added to all the other pressures, were having an effect on her. She was not helped by the fact either that her father was spending more and more time away from the family home at Lussy, dividing his time between the mansion at Boislande just 20 minutes away, the Avenue Foch Onassis apartment in Paris, a home in Morocco, his 58 bedroom family chateau at Sologne, the mansion estate in La Jondal in Ibiza or wherever else his work and fancy took him. There was little time left now for his family.

Thierry did attend all the family birthdays as Gaby had proudly told me, calling him a "wonderful father" during our first interview, but he was away more and more. An accident in Ibiza when two young East European girls riding a jet-ski belonging to Thierry were killed in a collision with a yacht skippered by a German added fuel to media speculation with one scandal sheet going as far as to claim that Thierry had been playing host to eight young East European women at the time on his yacht. He made himself an easy target for malicious gossip because of a model agency he had operated from one of the Onassis apartments in Avenue Foch. An appearance at a Geneva disco with some of the models had to be explained for what it was, a professional outing, when friends of Sandrine mentioned seeing Thierry there. His detractors never proved anything but the rumours did their damage. It was perhaps, as a Greek friend said, the price that Thierry Roussel had to pay for being too good looking, too rich and too aristocratic, qualities inevitably destined to cause envy among those of more modest means, inferior social standing and everyday looks.

As time passed Athina again demanded to go to Belgium to train at the Pessoa Riding School. This time Thierry realised that he could not continue refusing his daughter because in a year's time she would be in charge of her multi-million dollar Onassis patrimony and Thierry wanted to continue managing the money for her. It stood to reason that if he caused a rift with his daughter she would in all likelihood take her money and leave the day she turned 18. The Onassis women were known for their rebelliousness and Thierry could not take the risk. One day Thierry summoned Athina and announced to her and the family that he was going to send her to Belgium to become a professional standard show jumper. Athina put her arms round her father's neck and kissed him, beaming with happiness. But there were conditions, Thierry said. They would rent a house in Brussels where Athina would have her own apartment with her maid, Erik would be on the middle floor and Thierry would be living on the ground floor apartment to be able to keep and eye on who came and went in order to protect Athina. Thierry was also adamant that Athina should not abandon her studies and would have to enroll in a school in Belgium to get her Baccalaureate.

Athina was ecstatic. After arrangements were made and a suitable house was found in the Belgian capital for Thierry, Athina and Erik, they left with her personal maid and other staff for Brussels, leaving behind Gaby, Johanna and Sandrine at Lussy.

When they arrived in Brussels Thierry took Athina outside the capital to Nelson Pessoa's country riding school and enrolled her there.

It was a decision he was to bitterly regret for years to come. Unknown to Thierry Roussel a tall, good-looking, unsmiling Brazilian Olympic silver medalist show jumper named Affonso Alvaro de Miranda Neto who was also enrolled at the riding school was to steal Thierry's daughter's heart and redirect the Onassis fortune.

Three men were of pivotal influence in Athina's life, all older than herself - her French father Thierry, her Dutch riding coach and co-founder of the Global Champions/Athina Onassis International Horse Show, Jan Tops, and her Brazilian husband Alvaro "Doda" de Miranda. Each had a special place in Athina's life and each was to put his stamp on the Onassis story.

When Athina moved to Belgium with Thierry, he confided to me that he was unhappy with Athina's passion for show-jumping because he considered it a dangerous sport. Athina was so passionate with riding and dedicated to her training at the Pessoa Riding School that all Thierry could do was to keep an eye on her and to accompany her to the riding academy whenever he was not travelling. What he did not know was that Athina was starting to get emotionally involved with her fellow rider Alvaro Affonso "Doda" de Miranda Neto. De Miranda was 12 years older than the teenage heiress and had been living with a Brazilian model, Cibele Dorsa, with whom he had a 4 year old daughter, Vivienne, in Sao Paolo.

Athina was struck by the tall, dark, Olympic medalist who lavished attention on her and before long the impressionable 17 year old heiress and her fellow rider were a couple. They initially kept their affair a secret from Thierry. Athina knew her father would have objections when he found out, but for her the man in her life was now Doda. It was a repetition of the Onassis story where in every generation the heiress took up with an older man and their first marriage had as much to do with getting their own way as it did with love.

Athina's grandmother Athina 'Tina' Livanos, the daughter of one of the richest Greek shipowners shocked her family when she declared that she would be marrying the brash shipping upstart Aristotle Socrates Onassis. Tina was 17, Onassis 47. Tina and Onassis own daughter Christina ran off to marry a grey-haired middle aged American real estate man she met at a hotel swimming pool in the Riviera when she was 19. It was a marriage that was to infuriate Onassis who did everything he could to end it. Now it was the turn of another Onassis heiress to declare her love for an older man. Doda was 30 and a man of the world. When Thierry got wind of the affair he was incensed, but knew he would have to handle the situation carefully. He was nonetheless shocked by his daughter's decision to leave home and stop her studies in order to be with Doda. At the same time Roussel was concerned, knowing very well how susceptible young heiresses were to good-looking men. Thierry knew it from his own relationship with Christina who had been a plaything in his hands and would do almost anything Thierry wanted of her. He knew nothing of Doda and understandably had fatherly concerns that his daughter's new lover could be a fortune hunter. It was a label that he himself had had to endure after his marriage with the inordinately richer daughter of Onassis. Thierry knew that it would be a matter of time before the media caught onto the story and he wanted to protect Athina and his family from what would follow. He also wanted to see how serious Athina was about her new boyfriend and above all he wanted information about who Doda was, what his financial situation was and anything else that would help him meet the challenge from the newcomer. His lawyer in Paris sent letters to request copies of all press articles referring to Doda and Athina. Thierry wanted to know what was happening with Cibele, who had learned of the affair and was about to go to the media. Athina put her foot down. It would be Doda, whatever Thierry or anyone else said. She did not care if Doda had money or not, if he had children or not, it was he she was in love with and she would follow him to Brazil or to the end of the world.

I was driving along the newly opened Attiki Odos motorway in Athens to the new airport of the capital near where I was building a house when my mobile phone rang. It was a journalist who worked for one of the Athenian tabloids wanting to know if I knew anything about an affair or about Athina getting married in Thailand because a wedding invitation had circulated that afternoon in the Greek media. I denied knowing anything about the story and said I would call Thierry to see if it was true. I knew it would soon be in the public domain and there would be a lot of misinformation and probably attacks on Athina and her new beau if answers were not readily forthcoming to put the record straight. Thierry confirmed the liaison and we agreed not to say anything yet to the press. The affair suddenly became public when Athina left with Doda to go to Thailand and the couple was photographed by a Greek tourist who recognised her. Soon journalists from around the world were calling anyone they thought could confirm the Onassis heiress sighting in Bangkok with an unknown man.

Half an hour later, having spoken to Athina's father I told the journalist that the story about a Thailand wedding was bogus and the invitation that was faxed to the journalist was a fabrication. It was in fact such an amateur effort that I had to laugh because Athina's name was spelled incorrectly as was the location of the supposed wedding. The reality was that Athina was in Thailand, she was with Doda and the story was out. The media also got wind of the fact that Athina had left home and spoke of a rift in the family. I refused to comment when I was called about this.

Not long afterwards Doda's companion, a Brazilian beauty called Cibele Dorsa – it was unclear if she was in fact married to him - gave a scathing interview about Doda and Athina. She said that Doda was only interested in the Onassis money because he himself had none, he did not even own a car, she said, and quoted Doda as having said in the past that there was nothing going on between him and Athina who was "like an elephant". Thierry and his family were distressed at the turn things had taken. They were in contact with Athina but the relationship with Thierry was becoming more strained by the day. There was another cause of concern for Thierry. Athina in a couple of months would be 18 and half the Onassis fortune would be under her total control with Doda at her side. The idea was not appealing to Thierry who had other plans and who considered his daughter unready to handle the huge fortune without his help. It did not take much imagination to guess what Thierry's felt. He had brought up his daughter over the years in a very protected environment, had endured endless battles and attacks from his Greek fellow administrators of Athina's fortune, had seen his family humiliated and had sat accused in a criminal court in Greece for months as a result of actions he took to protect, as he felt, Athina and her Onassis Foundation legacy. A whole office in Gingins in Switzerland was filled with dossiers of court documents and media articles referring to the Onassis fortune battle between Thierry, who was Athina's guardian, and the Four Greeks, his co-administrators of Athina's fortune. Another office, in Upper Engaddin in Switzerland, belonging to Athina's lawyer, Nuot Saratz, was wall-to-wall with Athina Roussel's Swiss case files, while more than sixty large dossiers packed with media articles and press releases, court documents and property deeds and Onassis wills from Swiss, French and Greek jurisdictions took up a bookcase in my study in Athens. After millions of dollars spent and years of conflict having elapsed where Thierry had stood up as Athina's champion, aided by his legal teams and the Athens office, it appeared that everything he had fought for, including his daughter, was slipping through his fingers.

The press was reporting that the heiress had fallen into the hands of a fortune hunter and this argument was given extra weight by Cibele's statements in Brazil. When it became clear that Doda was Athina's choice I realised the distress Athina must be in to hear these attacks on her loved one. It was time to respect her choice. The truth was that Athina was a tall, beautiful, charming and well brought up young woman with a sense of humour and could, money or no money, attract almost any young man. There was no proof that Doda had gone after her for her money.

Cibele's statements about Doda's lifestyle in Brussels where he had been for several years did not reflect the presence of money despite the stories that were circulating about the de Mirandas being a wealthy family with insurance companies in Brazil. Public records showed that Doda's father Ricardo Lima de Miranda and two business partners had financial and legal problems stemming from a violation of Social Security law no. 95 that resulted in their receiving summons from the prosecutor regarding a company called Pamcary Administracao de Servicos. What was surprising was that the amount in question was quite small, equivalent to around 20,000 CHF in 1995. This raised even more questions about the reported wealth of the Brazilian family.

Doda had made his personal choice and would have to live from now on with constant suspicion and public distrust regarding the difference in his and Athina's financial situation. Thierry himself, though from a much wealthier family than the de Mirandas of Brazil, and an aristocratic one at that, had never been able to totally free himself of accusations that he himself had been a fortune hunter too. Few men indeed have turned down the chance to marry a woman with more money than themselves because of pride and ego, and neither Doda nor Thierry had said no to a bride with the Onassis millions.

After Athina returned from Thailand with Doda she left for Brazil where she bought a 1,100m2 duplex penthouse overlooking Ibirapuera Park in São Paulo where the couple set up their love nest, dividing their time between Brazil and Belgium.

After much wishful thinking by the media word came that Athina and Doda were getting married in Brazil. Speculation began immediately as to who would be the best man, would Archbishop Christodoulos of Greece marry the couple, what would happen with Athina's father with whom she had fallen out, which Greeks would be invited to the wedding, would the happy couple have their honeymoon on the Onassis island of Scorpios where Athina's grandfather, who had created Athina's fortune, had married Jackie Kennedy? The questions never stopped. Everything the international and Greek media asked boiled down to one issue - would the wedding be an Onassis affair in the grand tradition or one dominated by Brazilian equestrians and local Sao Paolo celebrities. When details concerning the wedding became known it was clear that this wedding would be like no other.

First came confirmation that Archbishop Christodoulos had not been invited to preside over the ceremony. When asked about it he replied that he had not received an invitation, even as a guest, adding magnanimously that he wished the couple happiness and health in their married life. "May God be with you Athina and Doda" was his message to them. The archbishop in 1998 had ignored considerable opposition when he agreed to receive Athina and Thierry in Athens. He had at the time publicly stated his support for

Athina, blessed her and assured the frightened 13 year old heiress that everything would work out for her.

The wedding was not to be held in a church like previous Onassis weddings but Hollywood-style under a marquee. There were no Greeks in the guest list when it became public except for the name of the best man Nikos Kotronakis and one young female relative of Athina. As soon as it was made known that there would be 750 guests attending the first question asked by the press was whether Thierry and the rest of the Roussel family had been invited. A string of calls followed from leading media organisations and journalists from around the world and from Brazil to ask if I myself had received an invitation, something that the press considered a foregone conclusion since most editors and reporters were aware that I had been Athina and Thierry's "Man in Greece" when the legacy battle with its intense legal and media confrontations with the Onassis Foundation was at its peak. As more information became known about the wedding arrangements the stranger the whole affair was beginning to look.

The only expected decision by the couple was to exclude the media from the wedding. At first it was leaked that the ceremony would take place in the presence of a photographer of Athina and Doda's choosing, something normal for celebrity weddings but still a far cry from Aristotle Onassis' and Jackie's wedding when Ari had gone outside the Panagitsa chapel on Scorpios and upon seeing the camera crews and paparazzi in a flotilla of hired fishing boats standing on decks in the rain waved to them to come ashore, some of them diving into the water fully clothed to get to the chapel first to photograph the wedding of the century for Greece. In Sao Paolo there was to be none of this spontaneity or Ari Onassis' empathy for those doing their job. The press would be kept out of Doda and Athina's wedding. Even so as the big day approached a Greek journalist who had covered Athina and Thierry's visits said that his paper was going to pay for him to go to Brazil and stand outside the wedding venue gates to see and report on the couple and their guests as they arrived. Other journalists were already on their way from the US and Europe in the hope of talking to the couple. It was to be a wild goose chase. After the wedding it was announced that no photographs would be released in keeping with the couple's wishes. A press report put this down to a tantrum by Athina because there had been a recent negative report about her mother Christina in the press somewhere.

Thierry at the time of the wedding was not speaking to Athina, though she herself had maintained some contact with her Roussel siblings. A few days before the wedding I got a call from Yves Repiquet, Thierry's lawyer and childhood friend in Paris, to say he had been with Thierry who wanted to know if I had been invited to the wedding. I had not yet received an invitation, I told him. I understood from the nature of Yves' enquiry that Thierry too had not been invited to the wedding. I thought at the time how ironic our exclusion from the wedding was after the criminal and civil court and media battles that Athina's father and I had waged for years for Athina with Papadimitriou and his co-administrators until the Swiss authorities gave her the Onassis millions. A Brazilian newspaper ran a half-page story on Athina and noted her omission of a wedding invitation to her father and the family's "Man in

Greece". It was all more strange because this was unlike the young Athina I had known, the one we had shared holidays and jokes with, the same Athina who would listen to what I had to say when we were alone in Greece or in Ibiza and laugh with me on numerous occasions. Was this the same young girl who had written me her first letter, on of several, after I sent her a tank top for Christmas –

"Cher Alexis,
A thousand thanks for this wonderful top. It gives me great, great pleasure. Hoping you and your family are well.
See you soon, Athina."

There was another letter later at the height of the conflict between her, her father and the Greek former Onassis employees running the Onassis Foundation. This now well-known "Dear Alexis" letter made every wire service and hundreds of newspapers around the world because it was the first declaration of the Onassis heiress regarding the Onassis Foundation. It was written on pale yellow paper with a delicate flower border and said:

"Dear Alexis,
I would like to thank you very much for the letter you sent to the members of the Onassis Foundation on (the) behalf of my father regarding me. Now I do hope that the board members of my grandfather's foundation will stop the attacks against me. Best Regards from all the family and best wishes to my friends in Greece.

A.Roussel"

I recalled her amusement as we chuckled conspiratorially during dinner at a family wedding when she was surrounded by young admirers who hovered like moths around our table, several no doubt sent by ambitious mothers hoping to link their sons with the Onassis dynasty. The Roussel family then was closely knit and snippets came back when the marriage took place without Athina's family. I remembered young Erik, grown now and rivalling his father Thierry's good looks, to whom I sent a bottle of after shave, a token present, when he was entering his middle teens, telling him it would work wonders with the girls of his age. Erik had replied to me with youthful enthusiasm:

"Dear Alexis,
I wanted to write this letter to tell you how glad I am to have this parfum. I wanted it, but my mother would not buy it for me, so what a marvelous surprise that you gave it to me. Like you said in your letter 'Good luck with girls' you were right, it works! It is like a love potion this parfum! Thanks so much, Best Regards, Erik".

I thought back to Doda's arrival in Athens for the Olympic Games the year before when I had left a message at his hotel and with his trainer, welcoming him to Athens and leaving him my mobile number. He never replied to me or to others. Loyalties and interests had shifted, as they always did in the Onassis family and it was to be expected.

As more information surfaced it became plain that the wedding was to be an esoteric Brazilian gala with the equestrian Olympian Doda showing off his beautiful and very wealthy Greek young trophy wife to the domestic CARAS set.

The media had a lot to write about, Athina had ordered a Valentino wedding dress and there would be six best men! Invitations had been sent to the Roussel family, though I still am not sure if Thierry was ever invited, and I never brought it up after the wedding in order not to embarrass him. Athina's half-sister Sandrine was appointed to go to the nuptials as the Roussel family's representative. This token participation made it even more obvious to the world that the breach between the heiress and her husband with her family was deeply felt by the Roussels. I had expected Erik to be at the wedding. Erik was the Roussel child who had always been closest to Athina; they were of the same age and I had observed how proud he had always been of his dark-haired Greek half-sister. Sandrine who went to Brazil was Nordic in appearance, icily beautiful, serious, a Roussel through and through, and a truly gifted rider. I was surprised when I was informed that it was she who would represent the family because I had always felt that because she lived in the shadow of Athina that this bothered her. I had sensed as much during a paparazzi frenzy over Athina during our yacht visit to the island of Hydra when I had looked back from where I was walking next to Athina to see the then 11 year old Sandrine take out a brush to once again comb her long, shiny natural blonde hair trying to look her best in the crowd milling around us. In Brazil she would again be in the shade as all eyes and the spotlight would be, as always, inevitably on her wealthy and famous Greek half-sister.

Some of Aristotle Onassis' immediate relatives in Greece were invited but only Alexandra, the granddaughter of Aunt Kalliroi, Onassis' half-sister, attended. The reason that the other relatives were not there I understood was the high cost of accommodation and travel to Brazil. Alexandra's mother, Marilena Patronikola, who had been close to Christina and Athina stayed behind, as did her other children. The invitation protocol was a far cry from the Onassis family's hospitality where planes were always chartered and laid on for friends, guests and relatives for weddings and parties. Athina's mother Christina had her pilot on 24 hour call for her friends as had Onassis for his guests too. The Brazilian wedding was in this respect a PYOW – a *Pay Your Own Way* affair. Athina must have known that most of her invited Greek relatives could not all afford to come and would not therefore be at the wedding. I could not but compare the wedding hospitality with a christening in Monte Carlo to which I and my wife had been invited by a Greek associate. He had invited over 200 people from Greece and chartered a commercial Jumbo jet for his guests who included the Archbishop of Greece who was to preside at the ceremony. My friend had supplied chauffeured cars for his guests upon their arrival in the principality, put them up in Monaco's best 5 star hotels for the three days of celebrations and taken care of every imaginable need they had.

On the day of the wedding the Greek journalist who had gone to Brazil to cover the wedding from the entrance gate of the Romero Foundation got a call from Athens.

"Did they let you in when you told them you had come from Greece for the wedding?"

"You must be joking," he replied. The place is crawling with suited gorillas keeping us all away. The hosts haven't even put out a table with water for us in this summer heat let alone any drinks or snacks. Not even a glass of water!"

According to people who were at the wedding a thousand bottles of the best champagne were opened for the guests, friends of Doda and his family. Athina's friends, if there were indeed any at the wedding, were thin on the ground. None of her childhood friends from Switzerland, except Nathalie Jakobsson, were reported to have attended the event. Athina had cut herself off from childhood friends and family and was in a new world now of her own choice.

I had attended several events where the media were excluded but there was usually provision for drinks and for some shade for the press corps outside. At the Romero Foundation gate the press was not welcome. How differently the media would be treated in a few years time when Doda, Athina and her very favourite trainer and special friend, Jan Tops, set up the Global Champions Tour and the Athina Onassis International Horse Show. Sponsors who demanded media exposure were sought out by Doda and the same press that was so despised by Athina was welcomed to these equestrian events and given special passes, and of course, they took them. It was, as always, money in the end that talked.

The sponsors with the money wanted the press to be at the GCT and at the Athina Onassis

International Horse Show and of course the press got in. Interesting too was the reverse sponsorship as it appeared on Doda's cap during the Global Champions Tour event in Doha in 2012. The logo on his cap was that of Julius Baer Private Bank, coincidentally the same bank that Thierry had chosen to put on the board of Athina's trust in 2003. With so many hundreds of millions placed under the management of Julius Baer it would have been bad manners for the normally secretive Swiss wealth managers to refuse to sponsor the husband of the patroness (who was also their Trust Beneficiary) on his world riding circuit. The Onassis name, legally adopted by Athina who was until then known as Athina Helene de Miranda (formerly Roussel), was used on all the Brazilian advertising and international media promotional material, banners, signs, logos, internet websites, press handouts, during interviews by participants when referring to the Global Champions Tour events held in Brazil and in numerous other applications when the event there was christened the Athina Onassis International Horse Show in 2007. The Greek shipping dynasty name's power to act as a magnet for sponsors' money and venue ticket sales was put to practical and effective use. Those who had made the fortune and handed it down to the Golden Heiress were far away in peace in the white marble tombs of the Panagitsa Chapel in Scorpios, never to be visited by the Brazilian couple to light a candle, as is the Greek way of honouring dead family members. Nor were the couple to say a prayer on Scorpios for Athina's mother and for her grandfather Aristotle Onassis after the fortune was handed over in 2003 to the heiress.

Rumours came and went of Jennifer Lopez being paid a million dollars to sing at the wedding reception, but these and other stories went up in a puff of smoke on December the 3rd when Doda and Athina's guests started arriving at the wedding venue. Neither Lopez nor any other famous singer was to be seen. The only international celebrity there was the Greek bride. After that it was Brazilian glitterati and local TV serial stars, businessmen and athletes so driven by a desire to attend an Onassis wedding in Sao Paolo that, according to a report in Britain's Guardian newspaper they agreed to have their mobile phones and cameras banned and to be issued with photo id's in order to enter a parking lot where they had to leave their cars and be ferried under escort in rented Audis to the reception area. Hundreds of Brazilians came dressed in their best clothes, curious to see the Onassis heiress at close quarters. What they saw, apart from the couple, were some footballers, Doda's riding friends, his family and relatives, minor TV celebrities and sitcom players along with hundreds of security guards. The guests in their finery and best jewels, the Guardian wrote, agreed to be screened by metal detectors while those with cameras had them confiscated for the duration of the wedding. It was surprising how much personal humiliation Brazil's café society and local celebrities would endure in order to be cleared for entrance to the wedding of the Greek heiress and her local Olympian horseman.

In Greece a television station invited a panel of guests to comment on the wedding as it was taking place. While the ceremony was in progress a helicopter hovering above the wedding tent managed to photograph the couple through a clear plastic section of the roof. Live footage of the ceremony showed a fair-haired man standing next to the bride. Immediately there was a media buzz since it appeared that Thierry had gone, after all, to Brazil to give his daughter away. I phoned Thierry to see where he was. He told me that he was in Morocco with Gaby and Erik. A photo published the next day confirmed this, showing a rather forlorn and publicly and unfairly humiliated Roussel family standing together next to a Moroccan beach. It was indeed a sad way for the Roussel family, which had raised Athina and given her a happy home, to celebrate her wedding.

The religious ceremony was unusual too. A Middle Eastern Orthodox priest without the traditional Greek Orthodox cassock and stove pipe hat read the wedding rites together with a Catholic priest. Six best men stood around the couple.

After the wedding the couple left to go on their honeymoon to Uruguay's Punta d'Este resort, not, as had been expected, to Athina's island paradise of Scorpios.

A long chapter in the Onassis family closed with the Sao Paolo wedding and a new one had opened in South America. The message to Greece and to Athina's Greek relatives and supporters was clear – there was a new sheriff in town. Doda was "in charge" now.

After a snowstorm in February of 2004 that aborted Athina's trip to Athens I started feeling that six years after meeting the Roussels and being close to them something was starting to go wrong. Someone was trying to keep those closest to Athina away from her. For me it became apparent when I got a call one afternoon from Yves Repiquet, Thierry's personal lawyer and friend in Paris with whom I had been working closely as liaison with a group of Greek law offices I had appointed for Athina and Thierry.

"Alexis, Athina will be coming to Athens with Gaby next week. She said she does not want anyone to be at the airport or at the hotel with her." I said nothing. He continued "Something else, she wants to use your security people in Athens. Can you give their phone number to the secretaries in Boislande?"

The request was contradictory and did not make sense. It certainly did not sound like the Athina I knew. My relationship with Athina had been one of trust and I had never let her take second place to anyone, including my family, during her visits to Greece. There had been a tsunami of hostile press and public opinion when six years earlier I had been invited to defend what looked like a lost cause when Thierry was indicted and in danger of going to jail here in Greece. At the same time the whole Onassis fortune, including Athina's inheritance was in the hands of the Onassis Foundation administrators led by Stelios Papadimitriou. In fact there was doubt as to whether Papadimitriou would actually hand over the fortune to the heiress on her 18th birthday as Christina Onassis had ordered in her will. He had stated that he himself would decide if he would hand over the inheritance to Athina or not on her 18th birthday.

I had been close to Thierry and Athina from 1998 when their fortune and Thierry's freedom hung from a thread. Attitudes changed slowly after we got the campaign going.

I had been Athina and Thierry's only material witness in numerous court cases in Greece when no one else would go to defend them. For three years I had the doubtful honour of personally being dragged through the courts by Papadimitriou and the Onassis Foundation after helping Thierry win a 15 million dollar court case that had been brought against him. The tide of public, press, judicial and political hostility had been turned bit by bit by a synchronized press and legal campaign managed for the Roussels until Athina was voted in a magazine poll as the person who would be the most influential individual in Greece in the next ten years. As for her father, from being an object of media scorn, we managed to change Greek public attitude towards him to the point where a senior public prosecutor who saw me in the hallway at the Athens Appeals Court building said 'I have to admit that perhaps your client was not in the wrong after all." Thierry, despite his opponents attempts to denigrate him, I quickly found out was extremely intelligent and able to size up a developing situation in a split second and take evading action, as I noticed on numerous occasions when we walked into press scrums where potentially damaging questions were asked.

Oprah, Dan Rather and Larry King and other TV stars asked me to arrange interviews with Athina, which she nearly always declined. The situation improved as was evidenced by a man who recognised Thierry in an elevator at the Athens Hilton and burst out "Mr. Roussel I want to congratulate you for what you have done for Athina," whereupon he grabbed a startled Thierry by the shoulders and planted a wet kiss on both his cheeks. Thierry flushed red as a beetroot, but the incident was indicative of the sea change that had taken place in the public's perception of Athina and her father.

The struggle in Greece had its rewards. A venerated law professor hired by the Onassis Foundation sent his assistant during a recess in yet another criminal defamation case brought by the Foundation against Thierry to tell me, "The Professor has seen what is being done for Roussel and his daughter. Don't think we have not noticed." It was perhaps the ultimate compliment for a job that I had undertaken, not just professionally. For a Greek the opportunity to do something for the only surviving member of the tragic and iconic Onassis dynasty was an emotional as well as a national matter, and I was happy and indeed privileged to have been chosen.

Thierry moved like the fox he is, managing to take over control of Athina's fortune after she inherited it on her 18th birthday. It was cleverly done. Some years previously, before meeting the Roussels, I had written an article suggesting that the solution to the dispute with the Onassis Foundation would be for a trust to be set up to be managed by prestigious private asset administrators. I had suggested Julius Baer, the oldest private bank in Switzerland, Bank Leu, and some other financial institutions in Switzerland, saying that they should be in charge of her patrimony until Athina "got to know the ropes", After this the heiress would be able to take over her fortune and that of the Onassis Foundation. The article had been the reason Thierry invited me to meet him in Switzerland. What I did not know was that Thierry had squirrelled away my formula and set up a trust with friendly professional trustees and him on the Board of Trustees so that Athina would not be managing her money upon inheriting it. It was a major coup for Thierry. He pulled the plan out of his memory chest and during the turbulent first weeks when the conflict over Doda had begun he told Athina that her money must be safeguarded. Athina in order not to aggravate their relationship further, agreed to have her patrimony put into a trust, as Thierry had suggested to her. It made sense at the time for both sides. Athina could prove thus that Doda was not interested in the fortune because she had his approval for the trust, and Thierry would be happy to be in the driver's seat once again after having been thrown out illegally from the Onassis patrimony board by his Greek co-administrators, and later legally, in 1999, by the Authorite de Tutelle of Upper Engaddin in Switzerland which appointed KPMG to manage the patrimony until the heiress's coming of age.

My information regarding the trust was that Yves Repiquet had prepared a power of attorney for Athina to sign allowing Thierry to establish a trust to be managed by four private banks and by him. Thierry had also got Athina to agree to settle amounts of money on her Roussel siblings from her Onassis inheritance. The presence of the banks on the board was a guarantee to Athina that Thierry would not be in sole charge of her money and the involvement of these respected bankers was a further guarantee for the safe and conservative management of her fortune. Doda, who was a new fixture in Athina's life knew of the objections of Athina's father to their relationship and was understandably keen to keep himself out of any inter-Roussel family dispute about the management of the Onassis fortune. He had enough public image problems of his own not to be called a fortune hunter by the father of his new-found love so he wisely kept his distance waiting for a more convenient time to assert his position.

On the 29th of January, 2003 amid massive press speculation Thierry got Athina to sign the powers of attorney allowing him to set up a trust with Julius Baer Bank of Zurich, Rothschild, Citicorp and HSBC. Thierry was the fifth trustee. He was now in excellent and reputable financial company and was working with the most trusted names in private banking in the world. Not bad for a former playboy and "useless clown" as Papadimitriou had called him in the infamous press conference that took place at the Onassis Foundation headquarters in 1997 in Athens! Thierry could always be counted on to pull a rabbit out of a hat to confound his friends and enemies. His worst enemy though was often his own impatience, a symptom of an over-privileged upbringing, and his impetuousness, as noted in a dry comment in a letter sent to him and me by his Zurich lawyer, Marc Bonnant, a former president of the Swiss Bar Association, who had referred to Thierry's "charactere eruptif".

When Athina came of age she inherited Christina Onassis' vast personal fortune that include the apartment at no 88 Avenue Foch, the islands of Scorpios and Sparti in Greece, the Pogorroi Bay mansion complex "La Jondal" in Ibiza, 140 offshore companies, a prime seaside Onassis plot in Glyfada, scattered properties in Switzerland, Greece, Spain and France as well as a substantial portfolio of shares, bonds, cash, precious metals, Impressionist paintings, the 20 million Euro Onassis chalet 'Villa Crystal' in St Moritz", a stunning collection of jewellery that had belonged to Christina and to Athina's grandmother, Tina Livanos-Blandford-Onassis-Niarchos, and numerous other valuable items. With the passing of this fortune into her hands Athina voluntarily gave up control by agreeing to put her assets into the trust.

Thierry had pulled off a major coup. As a father working to protect his young daughter's fortune he could not be faulted. He had taken the entire Onassis fortune inherited by Athina out of her hands and was once more a trustee managing the fortune as he had been after the opening of Christina's will. This time there was a basic difference, Thierry Roussel did not have rivals as colleagues - as the Greek dominated Papadimitriou board had been - instead he had willing, and no doubt appreciative, partners pleased to have been invited by him onto the Athina Onassis trust board. These institutions and their directors were valuable to Thierry who were a bottomless mine of information regarding the management of important private fortunes.

Thierry now dropped from the media radar in keeping with his father's advice that to live well one must live "cache" – hidden. His business affairs, as Papadimitriou kept reminding everyone, were somewhat sketchy. Few knew what he was up to and I was perhaps one of those, but I never knew what his purpose and eventual goals were. There was a small boatbuilding facility in Morocco and a house in Casablanca. He had also set up a sheep farming operation with 5,000 animals in partnership with a Moroccan princess. Both of these ventures reminded me of what a relative of his had once said. "With Thierry you never quite know what he is doing professionally - he is a bit here and a bit there." To be fair to him when he was getting 2.4 million dollars a year from Christina's will (inflation indexed from 1988) he did not need to earn a living or to prove himself to anyone. The Italian saying "dolce fa niente" would have been perfectly acceptable for a person of his social standing given the income he had for life from Christina's estate.

The Moroccan ventures were not businesses that would make him millions but Thierry all the same seemed to enjoy having a Moroccan base and perhaps these businesses occupied his spare time and offered him more than just the prospect of increasing his income. Morocco was a secluded playground for the very rich and famous from early in the twentieth century and it was a place where they could enjoy themselves in the privacy of an exotic, film-set atmosphere, primarily in Casablanca, with an unlimited supply of cheap servants, sybaritic pleasures on hand and a chance to be away from the rules and strictures of bourgeois Europe. Many celebrities and high net worth individuals had played out their fantasies there. Their stories are legion and during Thierry's time in Morocco there were rumours circulating regarding a European neighbour of Roussel's nicknamed "The White Pasha of Casablanca". Local urban legend has it that this eccentric playboy in his late fifties liked to sit on a carved throne dressed in an embroidered black caftan while twenty attractive young hand-picked Moroccan girls danced in a circle in transparent oriental veils in front of him in his exquisitely decorated Moroccan palace-style throne room. As each girl passed in front of him the White Pasha liked to lift the silk veils and stroke the bodies of whichever dancers took his fancy on that day. The story goes that the attractive young women were recruited by a salaried "mother hen" and were permanently on call whenever the Pasha was in residence in Casablanca. There were other colourful characters too. The servants of a glamorous European couple were amused to hear the couple's children referring to their parents in the kitchen as "Bonny and Clyde". "Clyde's" car would be seen on occasion cruising the Bois de Boulogne at night where the chauffeur had been instructed to pick up one or two prostitutes to take back to the Ritz whenever his employer was passing through Paris. Whether apocryphal or not these stories are of less importance than the fact that Casablanca can still spawn gossip to tickle the imagination of those who do not live there.

To return now to Athina's visit to Athens. Stefanos was unhappy sensing that something was wrong and that I was covering up someone's tracks. I had organised the details of the visit. Cars were hired, guards booked, coordination with the authorities done and unmarked patrol cars were supplied to us by the directorate of the anti-terrorist department while experienced VIP protection guards who had looked after President Clinton and Prince Charles were assigned for Athina's protection. The VIP lounge was booked at the airport and special staff put on call for the arrival of the Onassis heiress and her stepmother. I had made sure there would be no media at the airport or at the Grande Bretagne Hotel when Athina arrived there. Everything was in order when Gaby and Athina stepped off the Swiss flight. As soon as they entered the VIP room at the airport I got a call from a worried Stefanos.

"Athina is asking where you are and was looking around for you. She expected to see you here. What is happening?"

Athina clearly knew nothing of Yves Repiquet's call asking for her not to be met at the airport or at the hotel. Yves had not been honest with me. Doda I was sure would not have become involved in something like this and the finger pointed to the shadow of Thierry behind Yves at the Cabinet des Avocats on Rue Mozart.

I was on standby throughout Athina's trip in case she would need me in an emergency. She appeared next to her step-mother Gaby; Athina now a stunning, mature young woman with perfectly coiffed blonde-streaked hair, immaculately tailored clothes and the poise of a princess when she came out of the hotel's front entrance to go to dinner with Aunt Kalliroi, Onassis' half sister. All was not well though. I saw signs of a disturbing change in Athina.

Coming out of the hotel Athina was greeted by several of the young women TV journalists who had spoken to her at my daughter's birthday dinner in Vouliagmeni, had slept in café chairs all night to cover our yacht visit to Hydra island in 1999, had spent hours in flimsy boats off Scorpios in choppy waters when we went to the island for the memorial service for Christina and had become familiar faces and names to Athina. Athina, on seeing them put her head down, looking at her mobile phone as if looking for a number to call while the reporters greeted her in English and in Greek. As I watched the scene on TV I could hear the press corps girls welcoming calls "Hello Athina!" "Welcome to Greece" "How was your trip?" "Did you have a good flight?" "Yassou Athina!" Athina kept her head down ignoring the greetings and did so even when Alexia Koulouri who had been to the Roussel home in Lussy and knew her asked her how Doda was.

The car with Gaby, Athina and the driver drove off through the small group of press reporters followed by the security cars and made their way to Aunt Kalliroi's apartment nearby. I was the recipient of several phone calls by annoyed reporters who said that Athina had not even made eye contact with them and had ignored their welcome messages. It was true, and indicated that the heiress had started on a one-way journey into a world of press and camera phobia, something that had not been discouraged by Thierry who in the past had reason to control all photographs of his daughter and access of the press to her.

A few weeks before Athina's Athens visit I received a phone call from a Greek journalist telling me that a relative of Aristotle Onassis had asked for my phone number. I agreed and an hour later my phone rang.

"My name is Olga Onassis. It is very important for me to meet you as I want to contact Mr. Roussel or Athina."

I had no idea what she wanted and she did not want to tell me over the phone. When we met she told me her story. She was a cousin of Athina's grandfather Ari who had given her and her husband a monthly allowance as he had done for several relatives and those working for him. Olga Onassis was a distinguished looking woman in her eighties who looked younger with her dark hair. She explained that her allowance had been paid to her by Christina unfailingly until she died and the payments had continued when Papadimitriou and the administrators were in charge of Athina's patrimony. Olga had no other income and her two sons were unable to help her as they had little income of their own. As soon as Athina came of age Aunt Olga's income was cut off as were monthly payments made to family cooks and staff whom Onassis himself had arranged to be supported when he was alive. Thierry was on the board of Athina's trust so I sent a fax to Boislande to inform him of the situation. When there was no reaction I told Yves Repiquet who promised to bring the matter up with Thierry when he was back in Paris again from Morocco.

Olga Onassis called me every ten days or so to say she had no money at all and could not work because of her age. Inevitably when nothing happened the story that Athina had cut off her aged aunt's income leaked to the press from a relative of the old lady. It was a damaging story and apart from the human tragedy that was unfolding unnecessarily the public had started commenting on Athina's indifference.

I had in the past, when asked to describe the sensitive and shy Onassis heiress said that she had another side to her that would become apparent, in my view, after she became 18 and was free to do as she liked. I was quoted in a Swiss weekly "L'Illustre" saying that young Athina was a "Poupee d'Acier" - a doll made of steel. I believed that under the shy exterior she was as tough as any Onassis and my prediction of how hard she

60

was going to turn out came true in a manner that I would never have hoped to see.

Athina and her people in Switzerland ignored the plight of Olga who phoned me again to say she had heard that Athina was coming to Greece. Could I arrange a meeting for her with her niece? I explained that Athina would almost surely not agree but may respond if Aunt Olga Onassis left a letter for her at Athina's hotel. It was still a mystery for me why Athina had not attended to this since it was only a matter of a thousand or so Euros a month. The allowance would allow a fragile and proud old lady to live out the rest of her days in dignity and security.

Olga Onassis told me she would go to the Grande Bretagne Hotel and ask to talk to her niece regarding the allowance. The short visit by Gaby and Athina to Athens was to show up a different side of Athina, one that the world had not seen, but that I had hoped was not there when I had spoken three years before of a doll of steel.

Two Onassis aunts were associated with Athina's visit. Kalliroi, the wealthy half-sister of Aristotle who was expecting Athina and Gaby for dinner and the pathetic, poor-as-a-church mouse, Olga Onassis who had made a great effort on that day to be well dressed for her hoped-for meeting with Athina.

Stefanos called me early in the evening to tell me that reception had informed him that a woman was in the lobby of the hotel who claimed to be Athina's aunt and wanted to speak to her on the phone. Did I know the woman, Stefanos asked, and should he tell Athina?

"Her name is Olga Onassis, Athina's aunt," I explained. "Ask Athina if she wants to speak to her."

"Okay," said Stefanos, ringing off.

At about 11p.m. I had a call from Olga Onassis from the hotel reception desk.

"Athina did not respond to my request to talk to her. I will wait until she comes back and if she doesn't want to talk to me I'll leave a letter for her. "

Olga, wearing a balding fur coat and a once elegant dress sat in the hotel lobby until almost 1a.m. When Athina had finished dinner with Aunt Kalliroi and was back in her room Olga realised that she would not be able to see her niece, so she left her letter at the reception desk with a request for it to be given to Athina the next morning. Athina never responded to Olga's letter. What happened next was not a happy development. A front page story of an Athens tabloid revealed soon after that an Onassis aunt was observed every day in a long line at Ayios Nikolaos church among the homeless and destitute patiently waiting for her turn to receive a plate of warm food from the church's charity kitchen volunteers. The story was, unfortunately, true.

Soon after this Athina was reported on October 22nd of 2003 by O Globo newspaper of Brazil to have bought a prize cow for her fiancé, Doda, for R920,000 (230,000 USD). The purchase of a Gulfstream jet to ferry the heiress and her horseman husband from riding venue to riding venue also put into stark contrast the lifestyle of the Onassis/de Miranda couple and Olga Onassis.

Help, albeit temporary, came to Olga Onassis from Thierry. In November of 2004 I met him at the Noga Hilton in Geneva where I was staying. He handed me an envelope of his own money to give to Olga on my return. There were several thousand dollars enclosed and when I met with Olga, her son, and Dionissi, a journalist friend in a tea room in Maroussi, a suburb of Athens, the old lady was delighted when I explained that the envelope was Thierry's present to her so that she would have a Happy Christmas.

On the evening that Olga Onassis had been waiting in the lobby of the Grande Bretagne Athina and Gaby were having dinner with Aunt Kalliroi and her daughter Marilena. It was to be the last time that Athina would choose to see her beloved aunt. Kalliroi called Athina aside and asked her if she was sure of Doda's sentiments.

"You must be careful Athina," she said, "because many men will approach you for your money."

The words of family advice from an aunt who had been like a doting grandmother to her were not received well and neither Athina nor Doda ever visited Kalliroi again. When Kalliroi died a short time afterwards I was at the funeral with members of the family. Everyone from the Onassis family was there and the Onassis Foundation had also sent one of their presidency members to the funeral in Piraeus. Expecting Athina and Doda to show up at any moment all eyes turned towards the entrance of the cemetery whenever someone entered. When the burial service was over and we were taking part in the traditional Greek coffee and brandy ceremony it was clear that Athina was not coming. Athina had sent flowers instead. The snub to her aunt and her close Greek relatives was apparent to all. No one commented openly on her absence. It was sad that she had not come to say her last farewell to Onassis' half-sister who had stood by the heiress at difficult moments in her life, even during the height of the conflict with the Onassis Foundation when it was responsible for giving Kalliroi her annual allowance from her brother's estate. Kalliroi had put her Lagonissi seaside estate at the Roussel family's disposal during their visit there in July of 1999 for Kalliroi's grandson's wedding. Athina and Kalliroi had exchanged numerous visits over the years in the Alps where Kalliroi's chalet was close to Villa Crystal, the chalet that Athina inherited from Christina in St Moritz. Their bond had been very close until the evening when Kalliroi spoke to Athina about being careful about any suitor's financial motives.

Neither penurious Olga Onassis nor her doting Aunt Kalliroi Onassis-Patronikola had in the end escaped the icy cold shoulder of the Onassis heiress. Olga Onassis suffered terribly because of her poverty for a while, and then I heard that the Onassis Foundation had stepped in to give her a monthly allowance. It was not their obligation, but it was a welcome act.

"I have more money than you."
Rumoured to have been said by Thierry Roussel to his daughter Athina during a heated argument.

When Athina came of age on January 29th of 2003 and inherited her Onassis fortune Thierry seemed unready to accept that the daughter he had acted for and brought up was now an adult. Athina had been receiving a small amount of pocket money over the years, amounts in keeping with that of a middle class family, not those of the richest teenager in the world. Through the trust Thierry set up with Athina her allowance was increased to several thousand dollars a month and any extras that were needed were met by the trustees on a case-by-case basis. Boislande, where Thierry had his financial services and property company, SGFC, took care of the details and Thierry's staff was available to Athina.

Thierry told me that when Athina wanted to buy Doda a horse that cost 50,000 USD the money was immediately released. It was a reasonable amount for a horse but when a demand came in for a multiple of this sum for another show jumping equine Thierry was not happy and communicated this to Athina. Again the money was given since it was, after all, Athina's own money.

Soon afterwards Athina needed some funds when her monthly allowance had run out. She called Boislande and asked for the money to be wired to her account. The secretary in charge of payments to Athina told her dryly "You have drawn all your allowance for this month."

This was the last straw for the heiress. Athina, furious, told Doda what had happened. According to reports from a source close to the heiress she contacted several of the banks where her money, estimated at hundreds of millions was in accounts in her name. Account after account was said now to have been found empty. It transpired that Thierry had transferred the money from the banks to the trust set up by him with the agreement of Athina. His motive for setting up the trust was to protect her inheritance until she was older, Thierry explained to me over lunch at the Noga Hilton in Geneva in 2004.

The offhand remark of the secretary from Thierry's office precipitated a chain of events that was to cause a deep rift in the family and cost tens of millions of dollars. Those close to Athina supported her, saying that she was the Onassis heiress and nobody could talk to her like that. Athina was trapped. Her money was in the trust where her father, as a co-trustee had a say, while she had none. When she checked to see if she could break the trust and get her money back she was informed that Switzerland's trust laws were among the most watertight in the world and unless gross mismanagement or violation of a will could be proved there was very little room to do anything.

The fracas proved that Thierry had grossly miscalculated his current influence over his daughter, thinking that Athina would carry on now that she was an adult as she had when she was the frightened and shy little girl hanging on his arm. He thought too that she would be content, as before, to live within her allowance as she had done when she was a minor. Her frustration now, and the realisation that as the Onassis heiress she had acquiesced to blocking access to her own money caused her to blow up. Advised that she could not break the trust she turned to Baker and Mackenzie, a top UK law firm and put the matter into their hands, apparently at the suggestion of Doda. Thierry told me that they investigated him and his management of her patrimony for months. But, he added, he had increased the value of Athina's trust portfolio 12.5% in two years and he had the letters from his co-trustees, the bankers, to prove it. Of course, he explained, there was a clock ticking at the side of the team of lawyers Athina had hired. I estimated the fees to have been around 600 pounds sterling per hour for each lawyer from the UK law firm. A similar amount was reportedly charged by Allen and Overy, the law firm Thierry hired to protect himself and prove that he had carried out his fiduciary duties diligently. Thierry told me that the total cost of Athina's anger and determination to expose him was 30 million dollars. 20 Million was paid to Athina's lawyers and Thierry paid 10 million to his own legal team. It was one of the most expensive father/daughter spats in history. While we were having coffee at the Perle du Lac restaurant at the lakeside in Geneva Thierry explained the aspects of the dispute and its result. He was in a good mood, having just finished lunch with five international bankers where, as I learned later, they agreed to support Thierry in his plans to register a hedge Fund of Funds in Luxembourg, to be run from his Swiss offices, now at Nyon.

He told me now that the only expense that he had paid over the years as an administrator of Athina's patrimony that was not accepted was a bill for 250 Euros for some phone calls he had made. After the investigation Athina had no grounds to sue her father as she had threatened to do when the dispute began. Though both father and daughter backed off for the moment it was clear that the rift was too deep for Thierry to be acceptable as a trustee by Athina. Athina, probably with the agreement of Doda who was not on good terms with his future father-in-law, who perhaps saw too much of himself in the Brazilian rider, looked for another way to dislodge her father from the management of her fortune

I asked Thierry if Athina was aware of the pain and humiliation that he had been through for six years in his battle with the Papadimitriou group. Was she aware of what he had done for her and her fortune as a father, I asked him? Thierry thought about it and asked me to intercede with Athina. Could I write a letter from the heart to be presented to Athina, describing all the humiliations I had seen Thierry suffer in Greece, the months he had spent in Athens criminal courts, the attacks by the Onassis Foundation presidency on him personally, the destruction of his reputation and his health that this had resulted in. It had been a father's battle, as I would explain, for his daughter's rights to control her fortune and to establish her inalienable right to become president of the Alexander Onassis Foundations upon becoming 21.

I don't know what happened after I sent him the letter to give to her, but the feedback I got was that Athina soon after said "Take it all, I am not interested in the money." At that point those on her side apparently did a quick double-take in horror and told her to retract immediately! I had acted, I thought, as a bridge maker to bring together an estranged daughter and her father and was not aware until a little later that there had been a financial issue involved. I was stunned to learn from a third party that Athina, moved by the description of her father's privations on her behalf agreed to settle 85 million dollars on her father for him to leave the managing board of her trust and to close their dispute. His net profit from the dispute with his daughter Athina and its subsequent settlement came to 75 million dollars after his legal fees were subtracted. I had to grudgingly admire, though not condone, Thierry for his absolute mastery when it came to hard-ball financial bargaining. It did not matter whether it was with business associates or with his own flesh and blood; he was the Master of the Game. I, for my part, was not proud to have unwittingly helped to bring about this settlement, if indeed my letter had played a part in moving Athina. My willingness to help father and daughter in their *rapprochement* made me feel as if I had been scaled!

I voiced my objections, for what they were worth, to Thierry and to Nuot Saratz, his Swiss lawyer. Thierry of course took no notice and took off to Nyon on Lake Leman to establish his hedge fund called GMT Multi Strategy Fund of Funds at 6a Chemin de Joran, with the prestigious support of Banque Privee de Edmond Rothschild as the custodian and agent for GMT. Of course the fund did well, at least for the three years that its performance was posted for non-subscribers on the web. Thierry Roussel had finally achieved what he had craved all his life, to be a respected businessman and financier. He was at the top of the tree now and had finally shaken off the stigma of the failed strawberry farms and the Guyana timber project. His small inflatable boat venture and the sheep rearing farm in Morocco were peanuts now. Thierry was among the financial big boys: and ones with great prestige at that. He could now finally live as he wanted, and he did. Cache – hidden from public view.

A year or so previously I had been in contact with a leading lawyer in Vaduz to whom I had set out the question of Athina's right to the Onassis Foundation presidency. He had seen the deed of charter signed by the board, which had included Papadimitriou, several Onassis relatives and Christina Onassis who was the first - and by general admission - very successful Onassis Foundation president. The founding deed of the stiftung, or Foundation, stated clearly that an Onassis descendant would always be president, without the need of election upon becoming 21. It further stated that the deed's articles relating to the presidency could never be modified. There was a clear cut case for Athina to become president of her family-financed Foundation with its fleet of super tankers, Manhattan skyscraper, Nash Terrace real estate, and numerous multi-million dollar assets around the world. Papadimitriou and the Greek board members of the Foundation had come out regularly against Athina's automatic right to the presidency as described in the Deed of Charter. They did not want Athina as president - that was clear. The Lichtenstein lawyer who saw the documents was amused to see that on the board of the Foundation was a man called Peter Marxer who, a lawyer himself, had been prime minister of the tiny principality.

"A very shrewd move by the Greeks," the lawyer said, "to put a former prime minister and head of one of the leading local law firms on their board!"

Thierry had always spoken about how his battle with the Onassis Foundation and the Greek co-administrators of Athina's patrimony was to assure her of her rights and to protect the Foundation. It was, he had always maintained, a battle for her right to become head of the Onassis Foundation. When in 1999 the hold of the Papadimitriou Four on Athina's patrimony was broken by a series of legal decisions in Switzerland and the patrimony was assured of passing into her hands on her coming of age, the second issue of the Foundation presidency loomed large and needed to be addressed. Some time later I started looking into the issue and finally had what I needed when I had finished preparing the thick Onassis Foundation file with hundreds of documents, depositions, legal decisions, wills, interpretation of laws and it was up to Athina now to take what was hers according to the deed of the Onassis Foundation.

I arranged a meeting with Thierry and Yves Repiquet at Yves' Avenue Mozart offices in Paris, not declaring over the phone, for reasons of confidentiality, what the subject of our meeting would be. I booked my plane tickets and hotel and flew to Paris with a file I had prepared for Thierry and a briefcase full of documents. He was a man who loved papers and wanted everything laid out clearly for him with a covering note or letter to explain what was being presented each time. He had demanded and received a fax from me almost every day including the weekends for the years I had acting as his spokesman, media advisor and coordinator of his legal offices.

Yves and Thierry were waiting for me in the elegant conference room at Yves' legal partnership's offices. The large room was similar to other law offices I had seen in Paris, with its *decappe* bleached oak wall paneling and bookcase lined walls. The muffled buzz of early evening Paris traffic filtered through large double-glazed windows. Thierry was in a jocular mood, heavier than the last time we had met, again wearing his favourite dark blue suit, white monogrammed shirt and Tod's driving loafers. He had come to the meeting from the heavily gilded ornate Onassis apartment at 88 Avenue Foch which was his Paris base, just a step away from the Arc de Triomphe. Thierry smiled at me and said, somewhat impatiently "Yes, Alexis. What is it?" It was a stance I had seen on other occasions when Thierry had made arrangements to go somewhere else immediately after a meeting, usually after business hours.

I handed a copy of the thick Liechtenstein file to Thierry and to Yves and began my introduction, starting to explain that everything was ready for Athina to instigate a legal process in Vaduz for the presidency of the Alexander Onassis Business and Public Benefit Foundations. This had been our object for years and we had fought together in courts of law and in the world's media for Athina to get what was her Onassis birthright and to be able to play a public role that had been provided for her by her grandfather Aristotle and her mother Christina. Sixteen legal offices had represented the heiress and her father and I had been a go-between for most of them because someone was needed who understood the briefs in their different languages and jurisdictions and could organise what documents would be presented to which lawyers and in what courts.

Thierry closed the file, pushing it away from him.

"Alexis, Athina has her money now. She has enough not to care about the Foundation. We are not interested."

With that he stood up, checked his heavy gold sports watch, glanced at his reflection in a pane of glass, fixing a wayward lock of blond hair and came round the table to shake my hand.

"Thanks Alexis, for coming from Athens."

I picked up my files, put them back in my briefcase and took a photo of Thierry and Yves as was my habit as proof that the meeting had taken place. I left in the elevator, as the office door closed behind me, leaving the two old childhood friends to get ready for their evening outing. They had been together from their teenage years, sharing tents when camping, girlfriends when older, and experiences during the difficult years. They had now put behind them, for the moment at least the matter of the Onassis Presidency for Athina.

What was equally strange was something Thierry said to me in 2004 when we were having lunch on the first floor of the Noga Hilton in Geneva. Erik, Athina's half brother, was now a mature and handsome young man with a soft-spoken manner about him. He told me he was working for a bank as an intern. I congratulated him on hearing this and said "Erik, after we help Athina get the presidency of her grandfather's Foundation it will be nice for her to have her brother with her now that you are getting banking experience. You will be able to do great things for the Foundation and for Greece too."

Erik clearly had not thought of being with his sister on the Onassis Foundation board and he looked interested at what I had suggested, but Thierry immediately interrupted, waving a hand, saying, "No! No! It is not for Erik."

His categorical statement made me wonder. Why would Thierry not want his son to be on the board of a prestigious international foundation and one that had been established by Athina's mother and grandfather with the Onassis family in mind. Did the same apply for his daughter? Thierry called for the waiter to bring the bill, making it obvious that he did not want the conversation with Erik to continue.

After the meeting at Yves Repiquet's Paris office I wondered if the whole conflict had boiled down to a matter of "enough money'. Was this the only thing that now interested Athina? What of the Onassis dynasty and its obligations? Was she afraid of starting a new conflict? Was Doda and her horses all that her life and ambitions had come to after five years of an army of people in her and her father's employ working to prepare the way for her accession to the presidency of the two Alexander S. Onassis Foundations of Lichtenstein and to that of the Alexander S. Onassis Foundation in New York? Had she, in the words of Shakespeare's King Richard II exchanged her "Kingdom for a Horse"?

I recalled what Thierry had declared, when he was choking back tears of anger and frustration as we walked through a crowd of paparazzi and a bank of TV cameras in the Athens courtroom just after the sentence of five years imprisonment had been handed down to him for perjury, defamation of the Onassis Foundation and false accusation. Standing there defiantly before the massed media he had declared to the Swiss correspondent of the Tribune de Geneve and to a French radio station that was broadcasting live from the courtroom *"It is Athina's great responsibility to her grandfather to serve the Onassis Foundation whose money built the Foundation. If I have to I will go to every court in the world to defend her right to the Foundation".*

In the now empty office building's old fashioned elevator memories flooded back of what Thierry had said in the court late that night when the sentence had been handed down. We had spent 42 days in court, Thierry in the dock and me one row behind him for support and to deal with the ever present media. Images flashed by and I remembered all the visits to and by the Roussel family, of anxieties shared in close family circumstances across Europe with Thierry, Gaby and Athina. Images of stressful days with Thierry and Gaby in hostile law courts, of late night half-hour calls from Thierry, of nights alone poring over court and police depositions in French, German, English and Greek, of Thierry calling from Switzerland to say that Athina was in hysterics because Papadimitriou had had a confiscation notice for their properties served at Boislande, of me going to talk to people in all walks of public life to explain why we were campaigning so hard on behalf of Athina and Thierry, of three years I had sat in court, falsely accused by the Foundation, before I won the case with a unanimous decision by the three judges.

I stepped out into the street to take a taxi back to my hotel near the Louvre. The coloured lights of Paris flashed by the cab window as the young driver zipped in an out at speed from lane to lane along by the banks of the Seine and I felt empty. Had everything been just for the money for Thierry and Athina? Had the Onassis dynasty been forgotten?

I wondered too about a board meeting of the Onassis Foundation where they had altered the statutes of the Foundation regarding the rights of Onassis descendants to the presidency. The statutes had been changed, taking away Athina's automatic right to the presidency despite the Deed of Charter saying that none of the clauses referring to the presidential rights of Onassis descendants could be altered. I wondered too why the Onassis Foundation governing committee had met in Lausanne, just a kilometer or two from where Thierry and Athina lived, a place so far from Greece where the Foundation members lived, but just round the corner from the Roussel residence at Lussy sur Morges. Had there been a meeting between the two sides? It remains one of the few unsolved mysteries of the Onassis story for me even today.

The long confrontation between father and daughter had other repercussions. Thierry had enthusiastically supported a proposal I made for three leading construction firms in Greece to submit tenders and plans for a joint venture proposal whereby they would develop the Onassis property Athina had inherited in the choice Athens seaside suburb of Glyfada. The companies offered to build two apartment buildings in the acre and a half plot giving the larger independent luxury apartment block to Athina. Her building would have its own land, and entrance. The buildings were to be of the highest standard with indoor, outdoor pools, expensive marble and the best imported wood for the floors of the buildings. It would have cost Athina nothing and would give her an exclusive block of 300m2 apartments and office space for her staff plus a landscaped garden just off the most expensive seafront real estate of the Greek capital. I had just received the plans and computer drawings of the elevation of the buildings and was entering a fish restaurant in the suburb of Halandri to attend the birthday party of my old school friends from Kenya, Jimmy Zibbaras, when my phone rang. It was Thierry.

"Forget about the Glyfada project, Alexis. It is over! Doda is in charge of everything now. He even picks up Athina's phone for her when we try and call her. That is the situation."

With that he rang off and I wandered into the taverna not delighted by the news of so many months of work going down the drain because of a family squabble. I now had to explain to the architects who had spent weeks preparing plans that "Doda was in charge". The plans, in their elegant large black zip folders are still somewhere in the back of one of the closets of my office. The plot, instead of offering a prestigious income producing base for the Onassis descendant and her husband on the land that had belonged to her grandfather, was sold off by tender by a lawyer appointed by Athina's new advisors, as were her mother's personal jewels that were sold at auction. These were the same jewels that Christina Onassis had adored and that had touched the skin and the fingers of Athina's adoring and tragic mother when she had been alive. This sale shocked many who could not understand the sale of such personal heirlooms when they had come from Athina's adoring mother. No one could believe that Athina had done this because of a financial shortfall and wondered at her real motive. It will be up to her one day to tell her family and the surviving Onassis relatives why she did this.

Thierry himself in a late night call to me said in desperation that Athina had changed in character, was being isolated by the Brazilians and that Gaby too had commented on her altered behaviour after accompanying Athina to Athens to see Aunt Kalliroi.

The minivan with its "Green Wheels" stickers stopped on the side of the Swiss country lane in Gingins, a hamlet populated mainly by affluent businessmen and a concentration of diplomats working at the various international missions in Geneva, 30 minutes to the south.

Three athletically-built young men and a girl wearing cycling gear climbed out of the van. They unloaded their mountain bikes and conferred briefly among themselves. A fourth associate stepped out of the front of the vehicle and joined them, showing them a map. The leader of the group, who called themselves the Green Wheels, looked up and pointed to a distant group of houses. The cyclists put on their helmets, mounted their bicycles and set off in the direction of the mountains looming like a grey wall five kilometres to the north. They rode their bikes at a steady pace, leaving behind them the man in the minivan and the sound of traffic on the busy Geneva-Lausanne highway.

It was cold that day: the weak winter sun was unsuccessfully trying to take the chill off the thin air to coax the first reluctant buds of spring from the dormant fields. The group rode in single file past flat fields and parallel to the hardy hedges that shielded the occasional grey mansion in the bleak winter landscape.

The cyclists stopped at several houses on their way, telling the residents that they were a group of environmentalists called the Green Wheels, and that they had come from far away to learn more about the environment of the village and about its residents. The

Swiss whom they talked to were pleased to see these four well-behaved young foreigners who showed such sensitivity to the environment and had an interest in the local inhabitants.

Some of the village residents were happy to contribute money when the cyclists asked them for a donation. One old lady who lived in a cottage outside the village found the young men and the girl particularly affable and feeling sympathy for them gave them five hundred francs. The group had shown such an interest in Gingins, and seemed very impressed that the home just up the road from the old lady belonged to Athina Roussel, the 12 year old daughter of Christina Onassis and Thierry Roussel.

The cyclists wanted to know all about the Roussel family, when were they at the house, what did they do, did they have guards and where did the bodyguards sleep. The old lady, proud of her famous neighbours, told the Green Wheels everything she knew. She told them, when they asked, that Athina was not seen often here, but that she could be spotted quite often roller-skating in the village of Lussy-sur-Morges, twenty minutes further north, near Lausanne, where the Roussel family had another home.

The cyclists mounted their mountain bikes again and made off up the gentle slope towards the Onassis mansion with its extensive grounds nestling behind large trees. The environmentalists took a left turn onto a narrow uphill lane, passing a field and a grey house on their left. At the next turn they came to a low wooden gate bordered by hedges surrounding the Onassis property. From where they stopped, in front of the gate, by stretching up on their toes they could see a winding drive inside the wooded setting.

On the left of the drive was a small guard house, just as the old lady had described it, and on the opposite side, partly concealed by a mass of bushes was a two-story mansion with a sloping shingle roof. The house had been designed by its architect to blend tastefully into the country setting. It was in keeping with the absence of any external ostentatious features of the homes in this wealthy neighbourhood.

On the wooden gate there was a nameplate which identified the mansion as "Boislande", the famous last home of Christina Onassis. It was where she had lived with her husband Thierry and Athina before she died. It was here on a stormy winter night that she had summoned Stelios Papadimitriou and his three associates as well as the manager of her shipping office in Monte Carlo, David Banfield, for a hurried meeting.

It was said that the day she summoned them Christina had had a row with Thierry who had previously divorced her and gone off to live with Gaby Landhage, the Swedish beauty with an MBA, a soft-spoken and charming former model and multinational company executive who later married Thierry. Thierry's fiery outburst against Christina that day was to cost him millions of dollars and trapped him in a web of court cases and a public squabble with Papadimitriou and three Greek colleagues from the Onassis Foundation that would take up the best part of five years.

Christina had originally "stolen" Thierry from Gaby, and now that he was again with her Christina had tried desperately to get Thierry back, offering him financial and other inducements. He refused. She lowered her sights and asked him if at least he would agree to give her another child. Thierry was adamant, it was over.

It was after this row that the four Greeks had found Christina in a desperate mood, and they quickly and - according to an unsuspecting Banfield whom they left behind at their hotel - secretly went to Boislande. There they met a distraught Christina, who rewrote her will in haste in their presence. It was a will of just four pages. Strangely there was nothing in it about her daughter, except that she was to get the bulk of the estate. Nothing about any last wishes, only some brief financial instructions which would cause problems for everybody in the coming years. Problems for Thierry, for the Swiss authorities, even for the 4 Greeks , and most important it would be the document that launched years of unhappiness and insecurity for Christina's daughter Athina, making her the centre of a worldwide publicity and legal battle that seriously affected her happiness and curtailed her freedom.

The Green Wheels cyclists rode around the boundary of Boislande that afternoon, taking photos, making a video of the mansion and its surrounding approaches, and later they went back again for a second look. There was no sign that the family were there. What they did not seem to know was that Boislande was being used as offices by Thierry and that Athina was not there.

They hid their van and entered the grounds carefully. The cyclists were not what they claimed to be. These polite young men and the girl were part of a hardened Israeli team comprised mainly of former Mossad and Shin Beit agents carrying out reconnaissance for a mission which was scheduled to take part in June that year. One of the men, Rafi Pridan, was an electronics expert who boasted that he had laser equipment capable of eavesdropping on the family conversations inside if he could have access to a window pane from which to bounce off his laser beams. Christina Primsit, who accompanied the team later, revealed that she worked for a security company, the ISC group that had offices in Athens, Tel Aviv, Geneva, and in Columbia. ISC was headed by Moshe Lan, a former general in the Mossad.

Another member of the Green Wheels group was Benny Bayl, an independent security consultant in civilian life. He was engaged by ISC to take part in the mission against Athina and her father.

The Green Wheels group spent several days in Switzerland. They went to the residences of the Roussel family trying to locate Athina and Thierry to find out what their daily schedules were. Their main contact in Switzerland was the ISC representative called Ronen Ballulu. It was Ballulu who was instrumental in coordinating what was to be known as plan A of the operation. The proposal for Plan A was detailed in a contract sent to the financiers of the operation.

Plan B, the main object of the operation was to take place in June, but was never committed to paper.

The activities of the group came to the notice of the Swiss police. An arrest order was put out for them. Some were apprehended in Switzerland, one in Milan and the rest in Israel. When word leaked out that the object of their operation was Athina Roussel and her father, the press and wire services went into high gear.

A media frenzy followed as stories leaked to the press of a possible kidnapping operation. Some accounts identified the father as the object of the group, yet others said it was the daughter who was to be "lifted". For some days there was no information from the police. Then Juge Delieutraz, the investigating judge, subjected in the meantime to enormous pressure by journalists, called a press conference.

"Certain foreign nationals have been arrested for planning an illegal operation on Swiss soil. The operation in question was a planned kidnapping, though at this moment we do not yet know whether the victim of the kidnapping was to be Athina Onassis-Roussel or her father."

The statement was a bombshell and was transmitted worldwide by Associated Press. It was picked up by hundreds of newspapers, radio and television stations, all of which clamoured for more information.

The Onassis name once again was a magnet which attracted the public's interest. Journalists and TV reporters besieged the Roussels and the Swiss police for a follow-up. There was nothing at this point to reveal who was behind the attempt, if indeed it was a kidnapping attempt.

A second bombshell dropped only hours later. Stelios Papadimitriou, president of the Onassis Foundation and his three associates, all co-administrators of Athina's enormous patrimony, made a public announcement that the Israeli commandos were working for them. It was not a kidnapping, they insisted, but a security operation demanded by Lloyd's for the protection of the little girl.

It was a mess. Athina and her family were terrified. Her security staff – former SAS commandos - were put on extra alert and the moves of the family were restricted for safety reasons. Erik, Athina's half-brother, began having nightmares and Sandrine, Athina's half-sister shook with fear at every sound. Only little Joanna, the youngest of the Roussel children, was oblivious to all the activity going on around her. The house of the family in the village of Lussy-sur-Morges became a fort. Because it was located on the edge of a forest the guards were exceptionally vigilant. Every few minutes one of the guards would scour the tree line with his binoculars to look for signs of any suspicious activity.

Athina attending a public high school in keeping with her father's wishes for her to grow up in normal surroundings with normal everyday friends was for a while not allowed to skate to school or take the bus, but was driven by an armed chauffeur and accompanied by her bodyguards.

As the investigation proceeded the Israelis admitted under questioning to being part of an operation against Thierry Roussel. In a sworn statement to the Israeli police, the leader of the group said:

"Our company head in Athens, Moshe Peri, called us to meet one of his clients, the president of the Onassis Foundation for whom ISC was already engaged in doing security work. We were summoned to the Onassis Foundation headquarters in a Neo-Classical building opposite a Roman arch in Athens; there we were met by Mr. Stelios Papadimitriou, a Mr. Ioannides, and a lawyer called Theodore Gavrielides. Papadimitriou explained in detail that under the terms of Onassis's will half his money went to his daughter and this would in turn go to his granddaughter Athina Roussel. Papadimitriou explained that Roussel had been appointed as one of five co-administrators in Christina's will, and also received personal money due to him according to the will. It was Papadimitriou's intention to withhold any payments due to Roussel, and to have him lose custody of his daughter, over whom Roussel had a strong influence."

Those interrogated gave versions of the above. They also said that Papadimitriou wanted in the first instance for them to follow Roussel, investigate his private life and the suspicions that Roussel was a drug dealer who held orgies in the presence of his 10 year old daughter and there was even worse to come in one of the depositions, where it was implied, without proof, that Roussel had done more. Papadimitriou wanted information about Roussel's businesses and financial affairs. He wanted the Roussel family investigated in Switzerland, France, Spain, Portugal, England and the US. Everywhere they had homes or contacts.

The Israelis would admit to no more under questioning. The Swiss police did not give up so easily. There were too many loose ends for them. Also the reputation of Switzerland as a safe haven for rich foreigners was in doubt if rumours persisted that the authorities could not guarantee the safety of those in the financial bracket of the granddaughter of Onassis. The Swiss government sent investigating officers to Italy, England and Greece as well as to Israel to follow leads and speak to witnesses. Security inspectors Pahud and Mottet interviewed suspect after suspect and followed every lead that came up. The family was told to increase their security after the police interviewed a witness called Patrick Chastagnier.

In February 1998, when the investigation was in full swing I was sitting in the VIP lounge of Athens Airport with the Roussel family. Athina was very quiet and introspective. The lack of noise in the private lounge was in startling contrast to the media stampede that she had been exposed to for the duration of her two-day stay in Athens. Athina was sitting just opposite me, still holding an olive branch given to her on the Acropolis by a young girl admirer. Four bodyguards hovered a few feet away. Outside the door of the VIP lounge there was a group of anti-terrorist police ordered by the Greek government to guard Onassis' granddaughter and her family.

Thierry was sitting next to me when I leaned over and asked him "Has there been anything new in this kidnap story from Switzerland? Papadimitriou and his people say it was a Lloyd's mandated security check and that you are making it all up." I spoke quietly so that Athina would not realise what we were talking about. Thierry looked concerned.

"Alexis" he said "It seems worse than just a kidnapping. A man called Chastagnier, if he is to be believed, confessed scary things to the Swiss police".

Hearing the word police, Athina who had been petrified since the kidnap story had broken, looked up at me and her father with an expression of concern. We halted the conversation and only took it up later after Athina, her brother and sisters and Gaby had boarded their plane for Geneva. Thierry had stayed behind to wait for the departure of the flight to Zurich fifty minutes later. As I sat with him, the two of us alone in the lounge, he let me know that there was new information from the police who had questioned Chastagnier.

The following document is an extract of that deposition -

Canton of Geneva,
11ᵗʰ December 1997
POLICE DEPT – SECURITY 105

Declaration made to Inspectors Mottet and Pahud

"My name is Patrick Chastagnier, I was born on 25.10.1953 at Angouleme, France, and I am a hotel employee and married.

... I recognize the photo you are showing me of the man you call Ronen Ballulu. Three weeks after our first meeting he asked me if I knew people in the Belgian "milieu". I know a bar in Belgium where mercenaries gather. He then asked me if I knew of anyone who could neutralize a person. I asked him to explain what he meant by "neutralize". He told me that he was looking for a "killer" (he said the word in English).

Three days later he (Ballulu) asked me whether I had thought about his request. It was then that he told me that he was part of a team of agents from Mossad, the Israeli secret service. He explained to me that they intended to kidnap Athina Roussel, and kill her, because in the event that the minor disappeared her father could not inherit (her fortune) and that the Onassis Foundation, which was managing her fortune, would become the beneficiary.

He asked me where the best place to hide a hostage in Switzerland was, and if I was able to locate a hideaway. I answered that a farm in the canton of Fribourg would do best for this purpose.

I had children of my own and replied that I had no intention of getting involved in this operation.

In order to convince me he said that if I found an assassin I would personally receive $400,000.

I have nothing further to add.

Signed,

Patrick Chastagnier.

Ballulu was Papadimitriou's personal security chief in Switzerland and a member of the ISC group in Athens which worked for the Onassis Foundation. The testimony as it appeared at that moment was chilling and naturally terrified the family. There was more to come before the matter finally cleared up and the Swiss authorities put the matter to rest.

Athina's Administrators Reply

The Greek administrators said that ISC and its agents were hired to do a standard security check for Lloyd's. The kidnapping story had another side to it. On the one hand Israeli News Service quoted a police official in Tel Aviv who said that there was no kidnapping planned by the Green Wheels and their employers at the Onassis Foundation. The official explained that according to the arrested operatives there had been an operation designed to make Thierry lose custody of Athina. This, if it had been successful meant that she would have been deprived of the happy home in which she had grown up with her half-brother and sisters.

This story was only an example of the conflicts between the Greek administrators and the Roussels. Thierry, as Athina's father, and the first on the list of the five administrators appointed by Christina to look after Athina's money had considered it his right to know what was going on with his daughter's money. This view was not always shared by the co-trustees.

Papadimitriou and his colleagues became agitated when Thierry discovered that 130,000 dollars had been sent by them from his daughter's personal account to an obscure Panamanian company called Samoa, an Onassis Foundation company which was being managed by the Greeks. They refused to say who had received the money after it was paid out by Samoa. When this question came up in Thierry's defamation trial in November of 1998, one of the four Greeks when asked where Athina's money had gone said that he would not answer. Papadimitriou followed suit. "I will only answer to Athina when she grows up." The court allowed the question to go unanswered.

There was more. A sum of 600,000 dollars taken in cash from Athina's account at Citibank in Piraeus by one of the trustees was paid by him to parties whom he would not identify, either to the father or to the courts. When Thierry wrote to the Citibank branch to ask for an explanation of monies moved in and out of the branch in his daughter's name, and who had taken the money, the manager replied -

"We have conferred with our legal department regarding your daughter's accounts, and would like you to know that it was their opinion that you are not entitled to have this information".

Later Citibank officials came to court as witnesses for Papadimitriou in the slander trial. Papadimitriou incidentally had been a legal adviser of the bank for several years.

These incidents show the level of tension between Thierry and his co-trustees.

As the Swiss police investigators dug deep into the kidnap scenario Juge Delieutraz went to Israel to interrogate the arrested Israelis. No further evidence was forthcoming regarding an illegal operation.

While the former agents were in prison, the Onassis Foundation presidency - Papadimitriou, Ioannides, Gavrielides and Zambellas - called a press conference at the neo-classical mansion which houses the Onassis Foundation at 56, Amalias St. opposite Hadrian's Arch, on a busy street junction. The Foundation building decorated with Onassis family paintings and bric-a-brac housed the so-called "Onassis Museum", a couple of rooms with furniture and items belonging to the heiress.

Representatives of the domestic and international press now crowded into a wood-paneled room with floor-to-ceiling curtains. At one end there was a long table for the speakers. Blinding klieg lights illuminated the room while a jumble of cables lay across the floors, tripping up careless reporters who sought somewhere to sit in the rows of folding chairs brought in to accommodate them. A bank of cameras was set in the second row of seats. There was a buzz of anticipation in the air as the Foundation Four filed in and took their seats with Stelios Papadimitriou, always the protagonist, nodding to familiar faces in the crowd and making joke asides to reporters closest to the podium. I watched the screen as the Foundation Four took their seats and shuffled papers in front of them

At the center sat Stelios Papadimitriou, a short rotund man with a loud tie and a thin mustache. His brown eyes were large and darted back and forth, while his heavily gelled ginger-and-white hair was slicked sideways in tightly scalloped waves. He reminded me of a well-to-do Levantine businessman and I expected him at any moment to pluck a set of worry beads from his pocket and start fiddling with them. At that moment I did not suspect that what was to follow would drag me into the monumental conflict between these four people and the heirs of Aristotle Onassis. In coming months I would come to know a wealth of detail about the Foundation directors, their characters and the way they functioned.

On Papadimitriou's right sat a man who introduced himself as Pavlos Ioannides, he was the only tall man among them. Thin, bald and narrow-shouldered, with a white military-style moustache, he was smartly dressed in the passé manner of ex-India Army British colonial planters. He sat ramrod straight in his chair and moved his head and torso simultaneously when he wanted to look round, swiveling from the waist upwards as if he had a stiff neck. Ioannides was clearly the 'aristocrat' of the group. Later I found out that despite his lack of a university education he was the son of two upper middle class Athenian doctors and had grown up in the wealthy Athens diplomatic suburb of Psychico before becoming a pilot.

The crowd of journalists at the press conference could not decide when the press conference should start. There was banter about what language would be used. The foreign correspondents preferred English. The Greek TV crews wanted to go out live on the 8 o'clock news and wanted the interview in Greek. A compromise was reached as we watched the discussion. A third member of the Onassis Foundation Four at the press conference was Apostolos Zambellas who some years before had been responsible for the Onassis Cardiac Surgery Hospital tenders. He was some years later to turn against his colleagues when internal disputes in the Foundation came to a head.

On Papadimitriou's left sat Theodore Gavrielides, a pale, bespectacled man. He was the newcomer to the group, a lawyer who had entered the Onassis Foundation stable after the others. I later got to know him and found he was an affable and decent man who had had a successful career as legal adviser to some of Greece's largest companies.

"Gentlemen of the Press," announced Papadimitriou, "We are here to give you details about a situation which I will describe as 'The Announcement of a Pre-Decided Entrapment Conspiracy'. I will describe this to you."

Papadimitriou went on to say that Thierry Roussel's lawyers in Switzerland Maitres Bonnant and Saratz had conspired with two Swiss judges, Messrs. Joos and Delieutraz to arrest the Greeks by linking them falsely with a supposed attempt to kidnap Athina Roussel. As proof he produced two letters sent by a Roussel lawyer to a colleague saying that they should be ready with their media reply for when the arrest of the Greeks was to take place.

Papadimitriou did not say how he received these confidential communication letters between two lawyers. He said only that the letters were the originals. He then went on to describe how much he respected Switzerland which is "a big country", but that he was going to sue some corrupt judges and lawyers there.

The whole story of the kidnapping was a fabrication, he said. What had happened was that the four, as part of the administrative group for Athina's fortune (the fifth member was the father), had an obligation to protect her patrimony. Because of this an insurance policy against kidnapping was taken out on the child. It had been a requirement of the policy that security checks had to be done.

"For this purpose," continued Papadimitriou, "we contacted a respected company, ISC, serious people, with many clients and offices in Greece and in other countries. It was not a kidnapping. This story about a kidnapping was a fabrication by the father who wanted to discredit us, to have us thrown off the board of his daughter's administration so that he could get his hands on the money."

"Who were these Israeli commandos, and how long did your check take place?" asked a French reporter.

"They were not commandos, this is Roussel's nonsense. They were employees of ISC, serious people. The security check took place over a period of three months." Papadimitriou replied.

"Who would have an interest for Athina to be kidnapped or to be killed" asked a reporter who was close to the Foundation.

"Roussel," he continued, "was a man who had financial problems; he was always asking for money, he had lost large amounts in two business ventures. He would be the beneficiary."

We were stunned. A father setting up his daughter up to be killed?

"You see," said Papadimitriou, "we were worried about the little girl's security. There had been stories of Roussel taking her on his motorbike, and getting away from the guards. Also there was a story in the New York Post that Athina had a premonition of dying. That she would be writing a will to make him the beneficiary. All these stories made us worry."

The reaction to his statements was those of surprise, certainly for me and more so perhaps for the wider Greek public watching the prime time interview.

Papadimitriou continued, demonizing Roussel, driving a wedge between him and his daughter's interests, negating him as a father. Papadimitriou described himself and his three colleagues as close and trusted confidantes of Onassis and Christina.

Something was wrong, I thought. Could strangers have a child's interests more at heart than her own biological father? A father who was living with his family and who appeared to adore his children?

The outburst of Papadimitriou against Roussel in front of such a large audience stunned me. At some point during the interview he lapsed into street slang. It was not what I expected from the head of a major international public benefit Foundation speaking before the international media in a formal press conference.

"You will see," continued Stelios Papadimitriou, "that in the Foundation there is not just one Papadimitriou, we are a board of fifteen people. We are serious people. The brains are here in the Foundation, and we work. *Those who have no brains are in the other camp!*"

A Greek paper, To Vima, had previously printed an article titled "Sons of the Fathers" in which questions were asked about the management of the Foundation by the four Onassis employees. The article made much of the fact that the administrators had put their own sons on the board. It further questioned the behaviour of the four and said that the Greek public should know what was going on behind locked Foundation doors because it was in the national interest. The article and the medium had cast the first public doubts on the Foundation and its managers and Roussel was to follow up with his own accusations.

Soon after their press conference at the Foundation's headquarters in Athens the Four Greeks appeared in a panel discussion on Antenna TV. There Stelios Papadimitriou and his three colleagues, under pressure from the interviewer and the recent events in Switzerland made certain revelations which stretched my credulity and caused me to look more closely at the dispute.

When asked by the interviewer what Athina father had to say about the kidnap insurance which the Foundation had taken out on Athina, Papadimitriou replied "*We did not allow him to know because the insurance policy specified non-disclosure to third parties*". The interviewer's calm demeanour changed for a moment, registering incredulity.

"Mr. Papadimitriou, surely the Foundation and not Athina's father is the third party?" countered the interviewer. "Would it not be normal and expected for a father to know if other people were taking out life insurance on his daughter's life?"

Papadimitriou answered that Roussel was untrustworthy, immoral and an unfit father. Papadimitriou, feigning shock at Roussel's alleged amatory transgressions never mentioned why he had agreed to work for Onassis, a man well known for carrying on numerous adulterous affairs and who once in a notorious incident had exposed his genitals in Maxim's Restaurant to a paparazzo to get rid of him.

Papadimitriou was asked next about the letters from Roussel's lawyers. The obvious question for the viewer was how had these letters to Roussel from his lawyer - if indeed they were genuine - come into Papadimitriou's hands? Had someone stolen them, had an unknown party tapped the lawyer's fax in Switzerland or was there another possible explanation? It was, replied Papadimitriou, quite simple. A package containing two letters referring to the kidnapping plot had dropped through his letter box late one night at his family apartment building.

Viewers were expected to believe that Mr. Papadimitriou, under investigation by the Swiss authorities, and by his own admission connected to the arrested agents, had been helped by an unknown party who had flown to Switzerland, risked imprisonment by breaking into Roussel's lawyers office or by setting up a monitoring device at Roussel's lawyers' house to intercept the faxed letters, had then hopped on a plane from Geneva to Athens, at his own expense, taken a taxi from the airport to Mr. Papadimitriou's home, waited until dark before popping the package with the letters into the president of the Onassis Foundation's letterbox, and then quietly disappeared into the night, content in the knowledge that he had helped save little Athina Roussel's fortune from the scheming Swiss judges and the immoral Mr. Roussel. Another possible explanation was that a Roussel secretary had decided to take the letter and fly down to Greece to put it in Papadimitriou's letterbox.

The next day I sat down and wrote an article in which I expressed disbelief at some of the things I had heard in the Onassis Foundation interview.

Negative public opinion worldwide as a result of Papadimitriou's attacks on Roussel family up till then was such that the article questioning the behaviour of the Foundation officers was one of the first to dispute statements made by the president of the Onassis Foundation and his allegations about Roussel.

Athina's Return to Scorpios, November 1998

I held on tightly to the handrail of the heavily loaded Bertram cruiser as it crashed and slewed over each successive wave of the black sea. Ahead of us loomed Scorpios Island, a dark tree-covered mass barely distinguishable from the dark sea and the low grey rain clouds of that November evening.

Athina and Thierry were standing just in front of me, looking silently ahead, while the bodyguards who had found seats among the piles of luggage made their best to avoid the lashing streams of sea spray. As we approached the island where the Onassis family were buried the tension in the boat was palpable. Athina had just a few hours ago left her school in Switzerland and her cheerful place among the Roussel family, of which she was an integral part, to find herself suddenly an Onassis.

Athina who had not been to Scorpios for several years was understandably apprehensive as we approached the place where her mother was buried. I saw her move closer to the reassuring figure of her father as we rapidly approached the dark place where her Greek mother Christina was interred in a small private chapel with three other members of the Onassis dynasty. A few minutes later we pulled alongside a large jetty. There old Onassis-family retainers had come to welcome back the heiress and owner of the island. For me it was a relief to be at the end of our journey since the trip had not been an easy one.

Earlier we had been flying in an 18 seat chartered Olympic Airways Dornier from Athens.

"There is a storm ahead," the captain had announced thirty minutes after take-off. Accompanying Thierry, Athina and me were eight worried-looking journalists whose colour became ashen as we started losing height.

"Why are we descending?" asked Thierry, leaning into the aisle.

"The clouds are getting lower," the pilot explained "We need to get under them to retain visual flight rules".

Just then there was a nasty jolt. The plane bucked, then banked and dipped suddenly to the right. In front of us all I could see through the cockpit windscreen were clouds, less than half a mile away. We descended hurriedly to perhaps a thousand metres above sea level before the captain eased the plane out of the dive and levelled its wings. Below us the crinkled surface of the grey sea appeared immobile like a photograph. We crept along now with reduced power, hanging just under a brooding ceiling of dark clouds that seemed almost to be touching the roof of our plane.

Just then the pilot saw a break in the cloud bank and sharply veered the plane's nose up and to the left, aiming it at the chasm of clear sky between what looked like two huge perpendicular cliffs but were in fact steep cloud formations bearing in on either side of us. The captain gave power to the props and started a full throttle ascent. The noise and vibration inside the small cabin of the Dornier was almost unbearable for the passengers. Through the open slice of sky between the two cloud banks a looming mountainous mass - the Peloponnese peninsula - was approaching us at an alarming rate.

I held my breath until we cleared the mountain obstacles and then asked the co-pilot why we did not go over the clouds.

"We have no oxygen or pressurization system" he mimed over the din in the cabin.

The plane was bouncing now, once again buffeted by clouds into which we had wandered. It felt like an age but must have been only minutes before we broke clear again skimming over white cloud tips into a dazzlingly blue sky with the sunshine reflected off tiny almost horizontal glistening trails of water on the outside of the cabin windows.

The girl reporters in the plane were unusually silent. I turned in my seat to see a row of anxious faces. Alexia from Sky TV, a pale, freckled girl with a white skin, more Scottish than Greek in appearance, had a deathly pallor. Noticing she was gripping the armrests I teased her, in an attempt to cheer her up, but with little success. Eftichia, from Star, a slim girl in her late twenties was calmer. I could see that their personal videocams had been put away and the reporters were silently watching Athina who was in the single seat immediately behind me. The SAS bodyguards, all muscles, balding heads and wide shoulders seemed reassuringly relaxed. Athina had dozed off to sleep. A photo of her grandfather Aristotle Onassis, the founder of Olympic Airways, was staring up at his granddaughter from the open page in the complementary flight magazine in her lap. Athina looked totally relaxed. She was calm in adversity. A true Onassis, I thought.

A few minutes later when we entered the clouds again, Thierry stood up, agitated. The plane was completely enveloped in cloud now and the interior of the cabin became dark. Outside I saw that visibility was no more than ten or fifteen metres.

"They are not allowed to fly in cloud," Thierry said to me, more anxious for Athina than for himself. "I am going to talk to the captain."

He peeked through the door to the cockpit and then turned back, his tall frame bent almost in two because of the low cabin ceiling. He nodded to me as he sat down. "They are on IFR now." We were both relieved to see that the plane had the necessary instruments for flight in cloudy conditions.

After a while the plane suddenly lost altitude once again. The pilots explained that the cloud ceiling was lifting and they could fly now by sight, which meant going under the clouds. After flying below the low cloud ceiling for half an hour we started to descend. Below us there was a fertile coastal area with flat emerald green fields. Then we saw the airport runways. In minutes we touched down and after coming to a halt we were met by the airport director. A row of taxis and Mercedes cars were waiting for us in front of the small country airport building.

Thierry and Athina rode in the car ahead of me, following a patrol car which had turned on its rotating blue beacon. Behind us a convoy of taxis carrying press and security personnel jockeyed for position. My mobile phone was ringing constantly, reporters wanting to know where we would stop. Associated Press called to ask if the rumor that Athina was going to Scorpios was true. I could see Athina and Thierry in the car in front. At that moment she turned and smiled at me. I confirmed that Athina Roussel was indeed on her way to Scorpios. In a few minutes Associated Press had put the item on world-wide release.

A few minutes later CNN rang, then three paparazzi in quick succession, and then Thierry rang anxiously asking where I was, as he could not see my car. I told his driver on the mobile to slow down because two press vans had wedged themselves between us and I had lost sight of him. To add to this confusion three hired cars came alongside with cameramen hanging out of the windows, their heavy professional video cameras pointing at us. The reporters were travelling parallel to us, in the wrong lane of the narrow winding country road. Over the car radio I could hear a Greek station giving a live broadcast of the pending arrival of the Onassis heiress at Scorpios. A mile from Nydri, the island resort opposite Scorpios I had a call from an unofficial representative of the paparazzi asking whether we would bypass Nydri and get into a boat to avoid them and go straight on to Scorpios Island.

"No, we are arriving now" I reassured him as we entered Nydri. The village was strangely deserted. I wondered where everyone was. The answer came when we turned off the main street into a narrow passage between some shops and turned out again along the quay in front of a row of tavernas and folk art shops. Just ahead there was a crowd of perhaps five hundred people - villagers and journalists - waiting for us. The whole village was there.

Athina stepped out of the car and took her father by the arm after the bodyguards had taken up their positions, Thierry motioned for me to approach and then we were engulfed by the welcoming villagers. A gap opened and directly in front of us there stood a line of local officials. The mayor of Nydri, Mr. Gazis was there, while next to him was Father Apostolis, the sprightly octogenarian priest who had baptized Athina and had presided over the funerals of three members of the Onassis family. In a moving reversal of roles he bowed his tiny frame and kissed Athina's hand.

Eftichia from Star, a streetwise reporter not normally one to be sentimental whispered to me. "I am in shock, I am in shock!" Her eyes had misted over as she looked at Athina standing just in front of us. At that moment the teenage heiress was standing in for Aristotle Onassis, her uncle Alexander and for her mother Christina. The occasion was no longer a private visit. It had assumed all the formality of a minor state occasion.

I was now directly behind Athina, less than a foot away. The image of the last Onassis, this tall dark young beauty in her immaculately cut charcoal two-piece trouser suit, being respectfully received by the village was one of the most moving moments of my life. I felt goosebumps on my arms and an involuntary shiver went down my spine. There are no words to properly describe that moment. It was local history in the making, the return of the Onassis dynasty from the dead. All of those present, including me and the camera crews felt the symbolism of the moment while a strange hush fell over the crowd.

One would have expected this slim, dignified 13 year-old girl to be bewildered by the thronging reception. More so since the officials and the villagers addressed her one by one in Greek, a language she did not understand. I stepped forward and stood next to her in case she wanted a translator, but I saw in her eyes that she knew exactly what the mayor was saying and understood what was happening. The Onassis family had risen from its ashes but for how long would be the question that people would come to ask in a few years time.

There was an immediate almost fairytale feudal rapport between Athina and the villagers. The legendary family was here again, in the flesh.

"Life in this village stopped ten years ago when your mother, Christina Onassis died," said the mayor to Athina. "Today life has returned to Scorpios and to us. Welcome home, Athina."

Three awed schoolgirls stepped forward and shyly gave Athina a large bouquet of daffodils, irises and red roses.

Athina had been an awkward and homely little girl when she last visited the island four years previously. Today the chrysalis of death which had trapped her family had opened and a beautiful butterfly had emerged. The spell was suddenly broken when one of the Scorpios employees stepped forward into the barrage of flashbulbs and tugged at Thierry's sleeve. "The boat for Scorpios is ready," he said.

The Bertram cruiser carrying us, the bodyguards, and a mountain of luggage was bumping noisily over the waves as the sea became choppier. Scorpios, heavily wooded, had loomed in front of us when we turned round a headland and before long we tied up at the large jetty Onassis had built to hold his 340 foot yacht the "Christina". Captain Anastassiades, the former yacht captain was waiting with a row of cars for us. He motioned for us to enter the first vehicle, but Thierry had other ideas. He was not a guest here. He took the keys of the two white Mini Mokes, famously featured in photos of Onassis wedding to Jackie. He tossed me the keys of the second Moke. "Alexis, drive that one," he said authoritatively, making it plain to all there that the owners were back on their island.

We were met at the Pink House by Mme. Olga who had been the housekeeper from the time Christina and Thierry had lived on the island. She was crying as she spoke to Thierry saying how happy she was to see the family back at last, but I noticed that Thierry and Athina were being no more than polite in listening to her. The reason for their reserve I later learned was that Olga and most of the staff had allied themselves with the Papadimitriou group of the Foundation and some of the staff had even given critical press interviews about the family. The fact that they were being paid their salaries by Athina and owed her their loyalty escaped them. For the Onassis descendant this did not go unnoticed.

What surprised me when we entered the villa was how perfectly at home Athina was. She walked straight in, looked briefly round the room and collapsed on a sofa, stretching her legs out. It was the same sofa that her grandfather Aristotle had specifically had made for the Pink House so that he could stretch out on it and catnap in front of the fireplace.

Thierry sat next to Athina and lit a cigarette, loosening his tie. I left them to chat and went with the housekeeper to a villa a hundred yards further up the road. This was the Hill House, the simply furnished villa where Onassis himself lived when he was on the island and not sleeping on his yacht. Below the villa, down some twenty steps in the garden were the kitchens and staff quarters where our two English bodyguards had installed themselves in one room while Emilios and Petros, the Greek guards, took the adjacent one.

After unpacking I went back to the Pink House and asked Emilios who was outside now, where Thierry was.

"He went down towards the chapel on foot" he replied. I decided to follow Thierry, in order not to leave him alone. I walked for about half kilometer along the paved road past olive groves and a densely planted pine and cedar wood. Along the roadside there were rows of white and red oleander trees leading to the chapel near the bottom of the road on a bend where it approached the large dock.

I saw no sign of Thierry in the main room of the chapel. I then looked in a room to the left that contained the tombs of Aristotle and Artemis, Onassis' older sister. There was nobody there. Passing through a small arch into a chamber to the right I saw Thierry standing in front of Christina's white marble tomb with his back to me. His head was bent and his hand was resting lightly, gently stroking the polished marble surface of the raised tomb. He had not heard me approach and was deeply absorbed in his thoughts as he looked down at where the remains of Christina lay. For a while he stayed like that, and I made no noise or movement to disturb him.

It was strange for me to see to see this much-maligned man, accused of not caring for his first wife, of being a man with few feelings, here in this chapel, praying in private and obviously communicating in his own way with his dead wife and mother of his child. They were intensely private moments and I felt like an intruder. For anyone who could have witnessed the scene in the chapel there could be no doubt that he still harboured feelings for Christina. Suddenly, as if awaking from a trance he turned and saw me. There were tears running down his cheeks and his eyes were bloodshot. I stepped back to light a candle for each of the four of the Onassis family members who were buried in the chapel and followed Thierry outside.

We walked back without exchanging a word. Thierry only spoke when we reached the Pink House, asking me to come in. I told him I wanted to take a shower and change at the Hill House and would see him later on.

As soon as I entered my room the phone rang. It was the chef who wanted to know what I would like for dinner. This service was one of the pleasures of Scorpios. A guest could order anything to eat from the chefs who were on duty day and night. The five villas on Scorpios Island offer their guests the support facilities of a luxury hotel. There are professional standard laundry rooms, large kitchens and stores, a twenty-four hour telephone operator when guests are on the island and a large machine room and desalination plant on the south west corner of Scorpios. Additionally there are stables for horses and a farm which formerly housed cows to produce milk and cheese, while 36 staff kept the island running smoothly. When we arrived we saw no trace though of the Scorpios-bred pheasants, apparently they had flown off or been shot by members of the staff. On a later trip I was happy to see the pheasants were back in large numbers. The cost of maintenance of the island and its services ran to in excess of a million Euros a year.

Thierry and Athina went across by boat to Nydri for a dinner I had booked for them at a fish taverna. Though I was a friend of the family I decided that while we were on Scorpios it would be better for me to stay out of sight of the television cameras and the paparazzi because the occasion of our visit was Christina's memorial. It was, and had to remain, a strictly family affair.

When I had showered and changed I went down to the Pink House, the villa that Jackie had spent many months and a very large amount of Onassis' money to refurbish. It was her home for weeks at a time when she was on the island.

Dinner was grilled sea bass, a salad of Scorpios-grown vegetables and an exquisite fruit flan. The quality of the cooking was expectedly on a par with that of a Michelin three-star restaurant since the chef was the same one who had cooked for Onassis, Jackie, Maria Callas and all the famous and demanding guests who had been on the "Christina".

After dinner I settled on a couch and switched on the television. Our arrival at Scorpios was on every station. Three channels had live coverage of Athina and Thierry dining at the restaurant in Nydri. There was even an interview with the owner, who explained that Athina's mother used to eat at his taverna whenever she came to Scorpios. It wasn't exactly true, but it sounded good and no doubt brought him a lot of extra business the following summer.

At eleven fifteen Athina and Thierry returned, exhausted from their long day. Athina with a sigh of relief plopped onto one of the couches in an adjacent lounge. Thierry went to the bar asking me to join him for a drink. I noticed a row of bamboo chairs stacked against the wall behind the bar and remembered hearing that this was all that remained of Jackie's refurbishing of the villa. Jackie, soon after marrying Aristotle Onassis had remodeled and redecorating several of the Onassis properties, just as she had done at the White House after she married Jack Kennedy. Christina had thrown out everything that reminded her of the former first lady of the US whom she despised, saying that Jackie was only interested in her father's money and had brought bad luck everywhere she went.

Thierry and I sat and spoke for a long time. He told me about Christina and what their life had been like. He recounted stories of their stays on Scorpios and how different things were now.

"The island's facilities were quite basic, even primitive in some aspects, when Onassis had it, but he liked it that way," explained Thierry, "Christina had different ideas. I remember, Alexis, how surprised I was when I first came here and saw that the main bathroom had a half-tub, the ones you sit up in. Christina later upgraded the island houses and added "Main House" where we lived. The pool came later."

I had heard that Onassis never wanted a pool because he considered it excessive to have such fine beaches and the turquoise Ionian waters at one's feet and swim instead in recycled chlorinated water.

"Christina built most of the roads and put in the luxury touches," Thierry said. "We were happy here, but it did not last. There was too much pressure on us from people who had interests in the management of the fortune. None of Christina's marriages survived these attacks from the outside."

I asked him about Athina. Did she know much about Christina?

"Now that she is older I have started to tell her more about her mother. Tonight I will show her a letter her mother wrote before she died. She had asked me to give it to Athina when she grew up. There are things in it......" His voice trailed off and I saw him thinking about the woman he had once loved. It had been a doomed love. Christina, deeply troubled from her teenage days followed a lonely road after her divorce from Thierry, often begging him to go back and sometimes hurting him with her behaviour. It was a road that finally led her to Buenos Aires in 1988, to die kneeling next to a bathtub. Alone.

I finished my drink and left Thierry with his memories, making my way up the winding path towards the Hill house. Outside the door I saw the reassuring and vigilant figure of Emilios standing in the dark, keeping watch over the house where Athina was with her father. As I passed the kitchens and staff quarters further up the hill I heard the voice of men laughing and glimpsed the British bodyguards relaxing with the chef and his daughter. In front of them on the kitchen table a neat row of empty beer and whiskey bottles signalled the signs of an end to their career as Onassis bodyguards. I shook my head and went up to my room.

I was woken by the sound of the shutters banging. It was dawn and a strong breeze had picked up across the sea, forcing its way over the island, bending the oleander bushes almost flat along the edge of the lawn while low rain clouds hung in the sky. I decided to take a Mini Moke and went on a drive round the wooded island, stopping at various places along the way to admire the scenery and some of the 250 types of exotic trees Onassis had imported from around the world. The lawns surrounding the villas were from seed brought from Cape Town. On a later trip I was surprised to see the sheep and goats on the island had not chewed up the lawn and asked the gardener about this.

"Ah, Mr. Alexis," he replied, "Mr. Onassis chose this lawn because it is bitter and animals will not eat it". The genius of Onassis I thought, and how these details showed a man set apart in his thinking from other men.

I stopped briefly at the large jetty below the chapel to meet Stefanos Dianellos, the young journalist from "Ta NEA" newspaper and a female photographer he had brought with him to take photos of the memorial service. Thierry had been adamant about not having press on the island. He did not want Athina exposed to the media at anytime on Scorpios and especially not while praying at her mother's tomb. He had promised this to Athina. On the other hand I explained to him that for historical importance, and for Athina herself, the return to Scorpios and the attendance by Thierry and Athina at Christina's memorial was too important an occasion, both for the Onassis family, and for Greece, not to be on record. He reluctantly agreed with my logic and spoke to Athina. We both made a promise to her that there would be no interview and no photographer in the chapel.

When I returned Emilios told me that Mr. Roussel was waiting for me for breakfast at the Pink House. I entered and I saw Thierry dressed somberly in a dark suit and tie, while Athina was wearing a charcoal grey suit and a white blouse. I was shocked at the change in their appearance from the night before. Thierry's eyes were red and his face drawn. Athina's eyelids were swollen and her eyes too were bloodshot. There was no doubt that the hours they had spent alone had been a time of great emotional strain as Thierry told Athina much more about her tragic mother. Thierry took me aside and said "I spoke to Athina about Christina last night. I read her the letter her mother wrote to her...» He had spoken at great depth to her about the woman who had died a few years previously and was buried in the chapel down the road.

Athina had obviously been crying for much of the time when Christina Onassis and her tragic life story was unfolded for her, sentence by sentence, by the man who had known her mother better than anyone else. Thierry carried a message across time and from beyond the grave to his daughter. I could see this morning that Athina was a changed girl and that she was ready and prepared to participate in the memorial service at the tomb of her mother.

There was understandably little conversation at breakfast; Thierry drank coffee while Athina pecked at a croissant. When it was time Athina went to fix her hair and Thierry took me out onto the rear terrace of the Pink House on the side that faces Lefkada Island and the village of Nydri three miles away.

"I didn't sleep at all last night," said Thierry, "Athina was upset about her mother. There was so much to talk about."

Athina came outside asking her father in French if it was time to go. Thierry nodded to her and they left by the stone steps, descending towards the drive that leads to the chapel. They were followed by Emilio and Petros. I had asked the guards to keep a discreet distance from the Roussels because of the media. I did not want bodyguards to appear in any shots of the memorial service for Christina. Leaving to go up to my room I saw the two ex-SAS guards standing outside, taking photographs of each other with the Pink House as background. I informed them that the Roussel's had already left and they had better get a move on if they were to catch up. Thierry later confided to me that he was going to replace the security team with a younger group when they returned to Switzerland because he was not happy with their recent performance.

Looking down the wooded slope I could now see a row of fishing and day boats anchored about fifty metres offshore. Their decks were tightly packed with paparazzi and television camera crews. Telephoto lenses pointed at Thierry and Athina as they walked towards the chapel. These distant shots were all the media would get because the entrance was on the other side of the chapel, facing away from the sea and from the journalist's hired boats.

I went back inside and waited for Athina and Thierry to return from the memorial service presided over by tiny Father Apostolis. I sat down once again and fielded a series of telephone calls from the press for the next hour until I heard the crackling of walkie-talkies and the sound of shuffling feet on the steps outside the house.

"It was a very good ceremony" said Thierry, "but we had a problem with the photographer. Athina was very upset."

"What happened?" I asked, surprised.

"She came very close and photographed Athina during the ceremony. Athina was distracted by the sound of the shutter clicking all the time and became very distressed."

I had specifically given instructions to the photographer not to approach to a distance of less than thirty metres in order to avoid just such an occurrence. For the young female photographer the temptation of having a world exclusive of the Onassis descendant bowing in prayer over her mother's grave was too much. The photographer had gone right up to the open chapel door to record the service inside.

"Come, let's go for lunch," said Thierry, suddenly cheering up.

Father Apostolis walked by my side, wanting to tell me all about the ceremony. He spoke no English and asked me to translate his words for Athina and Thierry who were walking next to us.

We entered the cavernous reception room of the Hill House where the staff of Scorpios had in the meantime laid out a series of dishes on a long buffet table. The main item was a whole sea bass boiled in herbs and served with home-made mayonnaise, steamed new potatoes and young carrots. Fish is the traditional dish served at Greek Orthodox memorial services and is associated with early Christian times when a fish symbol was the secret sign of recognition among Christians. Today boiled fish is still eaten in Greece after memorial services in honour of the souls of the departed.

We served ourselves and sat at one of the round tables next to the open doors leading to the terrace. The sun was out again but it was too bright to sit outside, something not unusual in Greece even in November. Father Apostolis dressed in his black cassock and sprightly for his eighty-odd years was fascinated by young Athina, seeing how much she had grown since he last saw her. She had been an infant then and he had baptized her here in this same room.

"I can see her mother in her" he said to me, and then addressing Athina in Greek "I remember your baptism here, when the whole family were present. It was a happy occasion".

He turned to me "Don't tell them this, it is not the right time, but Athina's godfather, George Livanos – Christina's uncle - did not give Athina and Thierry the support which his duty to them demanded."

Later Father Apostolis bravely made this same statement on camera for the eight o'clock news, knowing that the four administrators in the Onassis Foundation and Athina's uncle would be displeased by anyone coming out in public to support Thierry or his daughter.

After lunch the four of us went out onto the terrace to admire the view.

"This is the beauty of Scorpios" said Thierry "It is how I remember the island. It is so green and the sea on a calm winter day like today is just like blue glass. Christina and I used to sit here in the evenings and watch the moon come up from behind the hills over there." He pointed to a row of granite mountains wrapped in a mantle of silver-blue haze on the other side of a wide stretch of the sparkling Ionian Sea in front of us.

Athina wandered back inside the house to choose some out-of-season cherries from the buffet table leaving Thierry and me alone with the priest. Thierry took out a bulging white envelope from his jacket pocket and gave it to Father Apostolis.

"Ask him to give it to a needy family in Nydri," instructed Thierry. I translated the request.

The priest was visibly moved. "Thank them both dearly from me," he said and added "The gift will do good. I assure them of that."

A bodyguard came out onto the terrace and discreetly pointed to his watch, letting me know it was time for us to leave for the airport.

We returned to Athens on the midday commercial flight from nearby Aktion airport. There was a minor panic because of a delay in take-off which put Athina in danger of missing her Athens connection to Geneva. This was taken care of when the captain radioed ahead to the control tower at Athens airport. A patrol car was waiting on the airport runway to lead our minibus across the tarmac to the runways at the Olympic terminal at the East International Airport where the Swissair plane was waiting for its last scheduled passenger. Athina kissed her father goodbye and hurriedly went up the steps of the plane with her bodyguards, relieved to have caught her flight because she had an important exam at school the next morning.

I dropped Thierry off at the Athenaeum Intercontinental Hotel. He too had an important, though less pleasant, appointment the next day. He had to be in courtroom number 9 for the resumption of his defamation case.

Two months later, when Thierry was back in Switzerland and the visit to Scorpios was well behind us I received a letter -

Nydri, January 3rd 1998
Dear Mr. Mantheakis,

Please thank Mr. Thierry and Miss Athina for their very kind help. We are a family of five children between 3 and 12 years old, without a father. Our mother finds it difficult to make ends meet. Father Apostolis gave us the money and we have bought new clothes, school books and some furniture for our house, as well as a heater. I am now able to go to school again.

May Miss Athina, Mr. Roussel, and all their family have happiness and health in all their life. May God be with you! With gratitude and respect, and many thanks from my mother, my brothers and sisters and me.

Christos M.
12 years old

Onassis– Summer, 1974

Lost in his thoughts, the tanned man in his late sixties sitting in the director's chair stared into his whisky glass, gently swirling the pale malt whisky to make it catch the bright reflection of the overhead sun.

The man made a habit of coming to this particular spot whenever he could, choosing on these occasions to sit alone on the terrace in front of the roughly plastered whitewashed cottage built years ago by some long forgotten Greek fisherman. The cottage itself was just a few feet from a white pebble beach in a heavily wooded cove, the same spot where the anonymous fisherman used to beach his rowing boat and spread his nets to dry; suspending them from poles planted next to the bright blue painted windows of the cottage. That was the myth of the cottage; the truth was that the building had formerly been a pig sty. It was cleverly converted to look like a fisherman's cottage. Now in its new guise its unglamorous history was forgotten and it was what it pretended to be – a simple and charming Aegean-style island dwelling.

From what he told his friends it was the privacy of the location that had first attracted the pensive man, allowing him to escape the pressures of the business empire he had created and the emotional demands of his family whenever these became excessive. This man, whose face was known the world over, was the Greek known as Ari to his English-speaking friends, as Telis to his intimate Greek circle and as Aristotle Socrates Onassis, or "The Golden Greek", to the rest of the world. His favourite title though, and the one that he had cultivated carefully with the media, was that of "the Richest Man in the World". Onassis chuckled at this description in private because he knew that it wasn't true. Once he had received a phone call from a bemused Greek shipowner from London who had said "Ari, what is all this nonsense about you being the richest man in the world? You know very well *that I am*."

"Yes," Onassis had replied «but I don't take the late night economy flight to London. I use my jet..."

This was the essence of Onassis. He was a man who had made a fetish of conspicuous consumption in an age when the world was recovering from a world war and Europe was locked into a period of privation when Onassis had made his name known to the public. People hungry for stories of success harboured an escapist hope that their own lives might one day be better. Onassis to them was more than just another millionaire. He created a myth which brightened their lives and offered them the hope that they too would have a more prosperous future. For others it was the thrill of reading of glamorous lives and loves, and perhaps the reassurance and secret satisfaction that even the gilded lives of the most privileged and wealthy of citizens are not exempt from personal tragedy.

On Scorpios Island pine and cypress trees and dense juniper bushes hugged the shoreline of the tiny bay. On this particular morning Onassis watched a loose group of yellow butterflies flitting along the water's edge, diving and rising up and diving again. A pair of the butterflies stopped to rest briefly on a glistening pink-veined marble pebble before taking off again, ascending in a meandering drunken-like flight. Then they headed landwards to seek nectar droplets on the stamens of wild flowers growing in the century-old grove of gnarled silver-grey olive trees on the hill behind the white cottage.

It was late June. The cicadas were now out partaking in a deafening chorus. For the three previous days there had been a persistent easterly wind skimming the tops of the waves and turning them a brilliant white as if a giant hand holding a gargantuan whisk had whipped the surface of the blue sea into frothing rows of white topped waves. Ari Onassis observed now with pleasure that the wind had died finally down, and the sea was once again totally still. The water was like a transparent sheet of green glass.

A small school of silver-backed brown fish swam in tight formation just below the surface of the sea, their disciplined progress suddenly interrupted when the tycoon tossed a twig, making them scatter. Seconds later they returned, cautiously, to gingerly nibble at the floating stick to test whether it was edible. Disappointed they regrouped, and moved off once again in tight formation to scour for something more suitable for eating.

It was these opportunities to observe nature coupled with the sensuality of the enveloping summer heat which Onassis claimed to his confidants gave him a sense of tranquillity. It was a feeling he could not experience in the harried world of his offices in Olympic Tower, his Manhattan skyscraper or in his gilded dwellings with their impressionist paintings, heavy damask curtains and antique furniture in London, Paris and Monte Carlo. Scorpios, his private island hideaway, lying across the cobalt-coloured straights from the ancient Ionian island of Lefkada was near where, in prehistoric times, dazzled by the same pristine sparkle of the Ionian sea among the small group of wooded islets hugging the purple-hued cliffs of the west coast of mainland Greece ancient Odysseus, the eternal traveler, had finally found his own safe haven and a waiting Penelope to soothe his troubled soul and tired limbs. It was here at the rough stuccoed whitewashed cabin that the tycoon, who saw himself as a latter-day Odysseus, said that he was happiest.

Onassis had made his own destiny, reaching great social and financial heights, but there were signs now that his body was giving up. Disobedient eyelids hung like half-lowered sun blinds over his tired eyes while the appearance of age blemishes on his forearms were an intrusive reminder that there was an aspect of his life which Onassis could no longer control. He perceived these changes as warning signs. A red flag to caution him that he was approaching that point in life – the inevitable terminus - where all men and women shed all their trappings, their achievements, their failures and their families, to meet one another and their Maker with only their souls to bare.

Normally Ari wouldn't have given a damn about the onset of old age or his own mortality, but he had always expected to hold the tiller of his life and his businesses tightly until the end of the mortal journey. He was a man who had fearlessly stood up to powerful enemies and to the Gods, and he had almost always won, but in the past two years he had started inexplicably to lose control over certain aspects of his life. The recurring loss of control over his body and the implication of this regarding his destiny was a totally alien sensation for him.

These incidents of physical weakness had been accompanied by a creeping claustrophobia, an unfamiliar and unacceptable sensation that he was being swept away by a tide that was flowing faster than he could swim against it. Several times recently events had bettered him and solutions had slipped through his fingers, something he had never allowed to happen before. He had until now planned his life well, having long ago put aside questions that others often worried over such as where their lives and careers were going. Unlike most of the people he passed in the street who had worries about their future, or about themselves, Onassis had always known who he was and what he expected to reap from his life. From his driven and ambitious teenage years his goals had laid out a series of milestones. He had reached and passed them at regular intervals, amassing money, fame and notoriety along the way.

He finished his drink and snapped fingers impatiently over his shoulder. From inside the dark interior of the cottage an attendant in crisp naval whites, one of his yacht's crew, stepped out into the sunshine and took the now empty whisky glass, asking his famous master if he wanted anything else.

Onassis looked down at the blue dial face of his gold Patek Phillipe watch, "Call Captain Anastassiades to send the launch in half an hour, and tell Yves to have the helicopter ready. I have to leave for Aktaio airport to fly to New York."

The steward retired to the cottage to phone the yacht's captain and inform the French pilot to be on standby. Onassis stood up and lit another cigarette. He thought for a moment about the changes around him and considered his options. What had set him apart from others was that Onassis had always been The Boss. He gave the impression that he bowed to no man. He hosted statesmen and movie stars on his fabled yacht, the "Christina". Lavish and well-publicized parties at Monte Carlo, in the Caribbean and at Scorpios, now known the world over as a destination where he and his privileged guests set the tone for the cult of fame that was to dominate the western world for years to come. His parties and guest lists in the fifties and sixties shared the glamour of the sybaritic and heady Roaring Twenties while looking to the future. Onassis to many was the John Gatsby of the post war era. The difference was that at Onassis' parties he, rather than the guests, was the star attraction.

The rich and famous beat a path to his gangway. Women of all ages, often in the presence of their husbands, threw themselves at him. Everyone wanted something from Ari. He knew it and enjoyed the power it gave him. What he particularly liked, when suddenly tiring of a pompous guest, was to act the boor, and then apologize innocently, saying "Excuse me.... my manners... I am just a simple peasant". It was his way of deflating the affected, sycophantic and freeloading guests who craved his generous hospitality. Even Jackie Kennedy was not immune to this occasional charade. His claim of being a peasant was of course a front.

Onassis came from a wealthy Greek merchant and banking family from Asia Minor where they had lived until they were driven out by the Turkish massacre of the Greeks in 1922. The Turkish government, whose policy at that time was to rid the eastern shores of the Mediterranean - the Ionia of ancient times - of its oldest Christian communities, had found that ethnic cleansing was an effective way of quickly imposing permanent political change on troublesome provinces. "Turkey for the Turks" was the official cry of the Young Turks and their leader Kemal Attaturk. The Armenians had experienced this national cleansing in 1915 at a time when the world was too involved in World War One to care. The Greeks soon after shared the fate of the Armenians, as did other ethnic and religious minorities in the new Turkish Republic. It was against this political backdrop that Onassis lived his early years.

The Asia Minor debacle had been a time of extreme turmoil for the Onassis family who were lucky to have survived at all. Onassis favourite uncle, Alexander, died in a Turkish prison, while Ari - 16 years old at the time – and his family escaped to Athens. Soon after Onassis, with little money, emigrated to South America to seek his fortune. This though was not the end of the Asia Minor chapter. Some years ago I had heard a rumour that an Onassis girl aged twelve had been dragged from her mother's arms by a Turkish officer for his harem as the family prepared to step into one of the fishing boats evacuating Greek refugees from the harbour of blazing Smyrna, under the neutral gaze of warships belonging to the Great Powers.

I first heard rumours of this Onassis tragedy in 1975 from my mother who knew Onassis' sister

Artemis, but it was not until 1999 that I finally found another Onassis family member prepared to acknowledge the story of the missing girl, and to tell me what had happened. We shall see what happened and the unraveling of this mystery further along in the book.

The women who circulated like gilded flies round Onassis were a permanent fixture of his later life. They hoped for an expensive gift, or for the publicity that association with his name would give them. Some females, the adventurous ones, wanted to test the depths of his dark Levantine sexuality, to see what it held for them. The more ambitious among the female admirers dreamed of being the next Mrs. Aristotle S. Onassis. Of the many who offered themselves, only two succeeded - Tina Livanos and Jackie Bouvier-Kennedy.

Onassis through his successful and often daring business dealings lay down the economic Foundations for his family to become a great dynasty. It seemed that nothing could stop the passing of wealth from generation to generation. Perhaps Ari should have heeded what the Ancient Greeks said - that tragedy came to those mortals who became too powerful and provoked the Gods. It was the sin of Hubris. Perhaps Ari had committed it by summoning the world to witness his success.

A year before this summer day at the "fisherman's" cottage on Scorpios the golden surface of Onassis' life had suddenly cracked wide open when his only son and projected heir, Alexander, had been killed in a plane accident at Hellinikon Airport in Athens, under mysterious circumstances while accompanying a new pilot on a flight to familiarize him with the handling of the family's amphibious Piaggio plane. Onassis was convinced his enemies had murdered his son. He appointed a private investigator when the state investigation left the case open. The private detective named Halkiadakis, one day announced to the press that he was on the trail of the saboteurs, and he would make damning public revelations soon. A few days later on the Athens-Thessaloniki highway an unidentified truck hit his car and forced it off a bridge. Halkiadakis was killed. The official verdict: an accident.

On the 10th of March, 1975, Onassis was flown from his sister's house in Glyfada to the American Hospital in Paris, and five days later, on the Ides of March he died of myasthenia gravis, the debilitating neurological disorder that had caused him to progressively lose muscle control. This was the official story and no one questioned it except those who put forward theories that there was a conspiracy to kill the whole Onassis family so that the shipping empire could pass into the hands of others.

Over the years there has been much speculation on how accidental the mysterious deaths of Onassis two children had been, but no one had really put forward any evidence that Onassis himself had not died of myasthenia. I myself started having doubts about Onassis death when I met a well-known shipowner who suffered from the same disease as Onassis for five years. His son told me that their doctors said he could live for another ten years. In February of 2001 I spoke to a neurosurgeon who expressed his own doubts as to Onassis quick death, saying that it was unusual for myasthenia to bring the sufferer to such a quick end. The neurosurgeon said he was personally mystified and felt something else had killed Onassis.

The first evidence came when Onassis personal doctor of thirty years gave an interview to *Tachidromos* magazine in Athens in the summer of 2001. Professor Nikolas Christeas, Onassis doctor, a highly respected practitioner and a Fellow of the British Royal College of Surgeons was categorical that Onassis had not died of myasthenia. Christeas told the interviewer that Onassis had suffered from a gall stone for 12 years, but that beyond occasional painful crises there had never been any immediate danger to Ari's life. Christeas recounted how in 1975 he was urgently summoned by Jackie (who was in the process of being divorced by Onassis) to see Onassis who was having another gall-bladder crisis.

Professor Christeas told Jackie that Onassis should under no circumstances be operated on because his liver was irreparably damaged owing to his penchant for whisky. Jackie then brought in her American doctors. They held a medical conference with Christeas present and insisted that Onassis should undergo surgery. Christeas made it clear that he disagreed with his colleagues. Jackie and her doctors decided to go ahead anyway with the gall bladder operation. Christeas revealed in his interview Onassis never recovered from the operation and died a few days later.

In his final few days Onassis was attended to by a distraught Christina and by Maria Callas who loved him to the end. Jackie, at the time of Ari's death, was in New York entertaining friends. Under Greek law she stood to inherit a part of his fortune. She later settled for 26 million dollars.

This was not the end of the deaths in the family. Within three years both Christina and Maria Callas had also died. By 1988 the only surviving member of the immediate Onassis family was little Athina Roussel.

The Division of the Inheritance

The Onassis fortune after Ari's death was divided into two parts, his son Alexander's share went for the founding of the Onassis Foundation, with Christina as its president. The other half of Ari's fortune went to Christina. After her death in 1988, it passed in its entirety to a trust to be held for her daughter Athina until her majority at 18. It was these two successions in the fortune that were to cause the bitterly fought battle between the family and four Onassis employees, one of whom — Stelios Papadimitriou - had been entrusted by Ari as a co-executor of his will. The rest of the executors were almost exclusively members of the family.

Athens. Saturday, 21st March 1998

The kidnapping story concerning Athina kept cropping up in the press in 1997 and 1998. Conflicting statements were made by both sides and the matter became more and more confused as the Swiss police investigation went on. The information I received from Thierry was disturbing. The public in the meantime became more and more curious about the teenage Onassis heiress who had only been seen in some television telephoto footage when she had made a brief appearance in Greece four years earlier to Scorpios Island.

Saturday afternoons in Athens are normally quiet. After the shops close at 2.30 p.m. traffic fans out past the base of the rock of the Acropolis in a slow crawl towards the sea and north along Kifissias Avenue as tens of thousands of shop owners inch their way home after counting the morning take and tidying up their premises.

By contrast, in the avenue lanes going towards the centre of the city one sees only a light smattering of cars, mostly driven by *xenichtides* – nocturnal Athenians who have just woken up after spending yet another night out at clubs and the *bouzoukia*. Their primary thought is to find friends and a table at one of the crowded and fashionable cafés in the environs of Kolonaki Square. *Da Capo*, known for its aromatic espressos and for the corner table the owner keeps empty as he scours the faces of passing pedestrians looking for a celebrity to seat at the table, is the favourite. For the less well-healed and for the younger crowd on an allowance the object of desire is an outside barstool at *Everest*, the sandwich and *tiropitta* hangout opposite the Trussardi store in Tsakalof Street, just fifty metres from Kolonaki square. Grey Mercedes, blue Audis, silver Porsches and overpowered Peugeot Rally 305s in jewel-like colours jealously occupy every available inch along the yellow no-parking lines running next to the pavements of the narrow streets. Groups of garrulous designer-clad teens and languid twenty year-olds drift from café to café, looking for a table, hoping that its occupants, generally older Athenians living in the area, will get up and go. They know better than to expect the same of the small groups of expensively coifed blonde Greek women who have drawn up a chair or two on which to place large shopping bags with the names of exclusive boutiques and international designers embossed on them in gold or black letters.

At the same time, in thousands of apartments in the city, the traditional Greek lunch table is being set. Casseroles with *dolmades,* oven trays with lamb and potatoes, grilled *brizola* steaks, chicken in tomato and garlic - or lemon and oregano sauce - accompanied by no 6 spaghetti are ready to be served. Slow burners keep the food warm as families get together to have their late Saturday lunch. The meal traditionally begins at around three in the afternoon. Many career women, breaking with tradition, will have ordered a pizza or perhaps made sandwiches and a salad. On television the face of a familiar announcer with his reassuring electronic monologue will keep the family company for the weekend, telling them every hour or so what is going on in the city and in Greece in general. On the weekends that is sensibly very little. A football game, a political wedding, perhaps a change in the ambient temperature.

The weekend is also quiet for those working in the media. Only a skeleton staff remains at newspaper offices and at the five major television stations. Heads of news departments and well-paid star TV anchors leave behind long weekday work hours to visit their holiday homes or those of wealthy moguls on nearby islands.

One breaking news item is enough to shatter this routine.

Just after midday on Saturday 21st March, 1998 the rumour of the impending and unannounced arrival of a 13 year-old girl at the east airport terminal of Athens sent television station owners and managing editors scrambling for their mobile phones while journalists desperately tried to get return bookings on ferry boats or planes in order to get back to their studios and newspaper offices in the capital.

After years of absence from Greece, Athina Roussel, or Athina Onassis as the press and public called her, the granddaughter heiress and only surviving descendant of Aristotle Onassis was due to land at Hellinikon airport in Athens at 2.55 p.m. aboard a Swissair flight.

I had been at the airport since 1.15 p.m and was one of the few people who had no doubt about whether Athina and her family were coming to Athens since I had made the arrangements for their visit. As I approached the arrivals gate I saw a frustrated policeman engaged in an agitated discussion with a group of noisy reporters who had blocked the exit of the arrivals lounge.

The milling crowd of journalists and television camera crews had quickly formed themselves into an impenetrable wall of bodies, tripods and camera equipment outside the glass exit doors of the luggage claim lounge. Some of the reporters were now trying to barge into the arrivals area. The exasperated policeman was unsuccessfully trying to clear a passage for exiting passengers and their loaded baggage trolleys. The confused new arrivals, brought to a halt by the mass of reporters and blinded by a bank of klieg lights tried to comprehend what the huge fuss was all about.

Careful not to get caught in the tangle of black electric camera cables I pushed my way through the group of jostling journalists and forced my airport pass into the hands of the policeman. The reporters, recognizing me as the representative of the Roussel family assailed me with a staccato barrage of questions. Hands, seemingly out of nowhere, clamped themselves firmly onto my jacket sleeves in an effort to keep me from getting away before I had confirmed whether the rumour that had brought them hurriedly to the airport was true.

"Will Athina Onassis be here?" "Are the Roussel's really coming?" "Where are they staying?"? I noticed the tiny red light on two of the television cameras light up, indicating that I was being filmed. "Why are they coming?" "Will all the family be with Thierry?" "Is Thierry alone?" "Why is Athina coming?"

A TV anchorwoman who is a household name in Greece asked me why I was going into the ordinary arrivals area and not into the VIP lounge. "Are you misleading us so that Athina can leave through the VIP exit?" she asked suspiciously.

With the help of the policeman who had in the meantime been joined by two more colleagues I managed to disentangle myself from the octopus-like mass of arms. I told the reporters that I would answer all their questions later and quickly went through the glass doors into the cavernous passenger arrivals and baggage claim area beyond.

Two planes had landed within minutes of each other and the lounge was full of passengers pushing trolleys or waiting by the luggage carousels. In contrast to the cacophony outside the hall, inside there was only the hum of hushed conversation and the squeak of wheels of loaded baggage carts. As I went forward I was startled by the sudden grunt and squeak of carousel no 4 as it began turning its scuffed black rubber scales to receive and deliver neatly labeled cases removed from the belly of an Airbus that had arrived from Frankfurt a few minutes previously.

The overhead display confirmed that Swissair flight number 333 from Zurich had just landed. I made my way to a vantage point at the far end of the lounge next to the staircase leading up from passport control on the lower level. I knew that in a few minutes the normal weekend calm in Greece was about to be shattered, at least for the media.

A group of Swiss tourists and Greek businessmen were now coming up the escalator. At the back of the ascending line a tall blond man in a blue suit stood out. He was looking around somewhat anxiously. When he reached the top of the steps he saw me and smiled in recognition, extending his hand to me. It was

Thierry Roussel. I ushered him to a row of PVC bucket seats opposite the carousel to wait for the rest of the family while the four Greek bodyguards I had hired waited at a discreet distance, scanning the room and checking the faces of the passengers in the lounge.

Thierry and I talked, catching up on recent events and filling in time as we waited for Gaby, his Swedish second wife, to arrive on the flight from Zurich with Athina and the three other Roussel children, Erik, Sandrine and Johanna. The Roussels, for security reasons travelled on separate flights. There have been too many premature deaths in the Onassis and Roussel family for Thierry to tempt either fate or his enemies by flying with Athina in the same plane.

I took the opportunity now to inform Thierry about the arrangements I had made for the family stay in Athens and to ask how Athina viewed the trip.

"Athina hates the media. You know how they badger her," he said and continued "Everyone was against this visit, Alexis, but I trust you and I took the decision for us to come."

Athina and Thierry had not come to Greece for several years owing to the acrimonious and very public battle which was taking place with the Greek members of the Alexander Onassis Foundation. These men were four former Onassis employees who had been named, along with Thierry, as co- administrators of Athina's multi-million dollar fortune in Christina's last will. Because it was the Onassis fortune that was involved and the accusations on both sides so bitter in the ensuing fight for control of the fortune, the international and domestic press was following every twist and turn of the battle with immense interest, happy to feed a voracious public interest in the Onassis family saga.

Some weeks previous to the visit to Athens in March 1998 Thierry had told me in Switzerland of his desire to bring Athina to Greece again. He wanted her to see her Greek relatives here and visit the country of her mother Christina who had died so tragically at the age of 38. Thierry complained to me that the Foundation 4 had made life impossible for the family in the last few years, and added that Athina and Gaby were frightened to come to Greece as a result of the kidnap revelations. I told Thierry that if he trusted me, took my advice and brought the family to Athens as he wanted to, he would have a huge and very pleasant surprise. Above all it would be good for Athina, I reassured him.

On Wednesday, February 11th 1998 I had received a phone call late in the evening. It was Thierry.

"I am coming, Alexis. With the children. On Saturday. Make all the arrangements and send me a schedule. I will also speak to selected media."

The next three days were busy. I needed to organize the visit with the precision of a military operation. Cars, bodyguards, hotel rooms, schedules and visits had to be booked and arranged. For security I planned alternate travel routes and fallback plans. It was my responsibility to see that what I had promised would be done. All without any leaks to the press.

On Saturday as I was getting ready to leave for the airport from my apartment bordering the pine forest on Mount Penteli in the north of Athens, I got a call from a reporter at a television station. Someone had broken the news to him of the arrival of Thierry, though nobody as yet knew that Athina would be coming. By the time I reached the airport the reporters were already there, on the Onassis trail.

'There they are" said Thierry, standing up. I leaned over the banister to see four middle aged SAS bodyguards standing in front of, and behind the family group. The slim, tall, dark-haired figure of Athina stood out among the four blonde members of her family. I knew Gaby, a great beauty and former model in Paris from Switzerland, where I had interviewed her at her home in Lussy sur Morges for a television station. Standing at her side was Erik, Athina's 12 year old half-brother, dressed in a blue blazer and tie, like a British public schoolboy. He turned to whisper to Sandrine, his blonde sister. The youngest of the group was Johanna, the 6 year old charmer of the Roussel family. A very reserved Athina, dressed in a beige trouser suit, stepped forward and shook my hand. I showed them where to sit while the bodyguards went off to claim the suitcases.

Gaby was nervous, her blue eyes betraying a tension which lined her face with worry. I could see that she was making an effort to make small talk but her mind was elsewhere. Only Johanna was carefree as she eagerly opened a package her father had given her.

It was obvious from the family reaction that Thierry had put his foot down regarding the trip to Athens and that there had been some kind of an argument regarding the wisdom of this trip before the Roussels left Switzerland. I was aware too that Gaby knew that I had insisted to Thierry that if they came to Greece the trip would be worthwhile. Thierry had listened to me, taken the decision to come and firmly put the responsibility on my shoulders. Athina, sitting next to her father was now toying with Thierry's mobile phone, while looking at me with a sense of apprehension.

As the minutes passed there was an exponential increase in the conversation noise emanating from the other passengers in the now crowded arrivals lounge. Heads turned when people recognised Athina. The Greeks in the room stared incredulously, and when they were sure Athina Roussel Onassis was the girl sitting with us they smiled and pointed to us. For them the sudden appearance of Onassis granddaughter in their midst was an exciting and unforeseen event. Even more so that she and her famous family should have chosen to arrive in the public arrivals lounge and wait patiently for their luggage with everybody else rather than demanding the privacy and convenience of the independent VIP facilities at the end of the terminal building.

Those in the room were stunned at the presence of the reclusive Onassis heiress because the name Onassis and anything to do with it was almost magical, a part of the very consciousness of every Greek family. Here then, right in front of them, was Ari Onassis' only surviving descendant, Athina, the daughter of Christina Onassis. Greeks had only had a fleeting glimpse on television some years before of a smiling, shy, 9 year old girl in a party dress getting into a speedboat with her father and family before it sped off across the straights from the island of Lefkada to Scorpios Island. During that visit cheering crowds and numerous policemen had lined the quay of the village of Nydri on Lefkada to catch a glimpse of the golden heiress and her family.

Now, at the airport, I could see people abandoning their luggage wherever they had been to come closer to stare at the heiress and her family. Thierry for them was already a familiar figure.

"What do we do now?" Thierry asked me. "The suitcases are all here"

I explained that I wanted to talk to the children in order to prepare them for what was to follow. I sat next to Athina, and addressed Gaby «You should know that in Greece your family and that of Onassis is well known, and there are many people with whom you are very popular."

Gaby, caught up in the middle of the Israeli operation ordered from Greece, and uncertain about the truth of the kidnapping and murder scenario had read tens of negative articles in the Greek press directed against her husband and occasionally against herself. She looked at me with a sense of disbelief as I spoke of Greeks welcoming them. "I don't think so," she said in a very low voice, betraying, I felt, a hint of annoyance that I should have encouraged her husband's desire to bring the family to Greece at a time like this. I understood her reservations, but assured her now that many people had approached me to learn about the family and that reporters wanted stories and information about Athina and all of the Roussels. I addressed the children, but spoke primarily for the benefit of Athina.

"When we go outside those doors," I explained "we will be met by many people with cameras who will ask questions and make a lot of noise. This is because they all want to learn about you. In Greece people love you, especially in the schools where the pupils want to know all about you."

It was important for me give a simple and easily comprehensible explanation to make these four children understand the role of the reporters waiting outside. I wanted to show them that the media covering the Onassis story were friends.

"Johanna and Erik," I said, "It is not possible for thousands and thousands of Greek schoolchildren and other people who want to know about you to come to the airport and meet you. This is why the newspapers and the television companies send reporters who will take pictures and ask you a few questions. These films and your answers will be put on TV tonight so that everybody can get to know the Roussel family. That is why the reporters are there." I repeated. "They are our friends."

I was relieved to see that the simple logic of my argument was comprehensible to even the youngest of the children. One of my very important responsibilities and one I had assumed of my own initiative was to never allow Athina to fall into the inexcusable and eventually mortal pattern of relations with the media that Princess Diana developed. Diana had been badly advised and her confusion and lack of judgment had cost her her life.

There were very simple and effective ways of dealing with the media and a few basic rules to follow. I saw that imparting this knowledge to Athina and her siblings was an important part of my job as media adviser to the family. My other responsibility, a task of immense complexity owing to the damage that had been done to the family reputation by the Foundation Four was the preparation of the ground for the eventual return of the Onassis descendant to her dynastic hearth in Greece. From there Athina could then take the decision to claim her rightful position as head of the two

Onassis Foundations and fulfill a public role that Aristotle Onassis had foreseen for his descendants and family when he donated half his fortune for this purpose.

Twenty four years earlier Athina's grandfather, Aristotle Onassis had had to contend with a series of problems. Shortly after his son was killed Onassis discovered that he was terminally ill with myasthenia gravis at a time he was having problems with Jackie. She had been a prize catch when he married her. Jackie Kennedy, widow of the President of the United States, was the ultimate trophy wife. It had pleased Ari to steal her from the American establishment that had caused him so many problems in the past. First they had arrested him for buying restricted Liberty ships through intermediaries and later they had tried to ruin him by getting a syndicate of banks, led by Citibank, to call in his loans at a difficult time.

During a TV interview Robert Mayhew, a senior former CIA official admitted that the American administration with Richard Nixon as vice-president had even planned to kill Onassis. Nixon had apparently told Mayhew to ***"get rid of the son-of-a-bitch, but don't do it on American soil"***. Ari carried the scars of these old wounds and insults and a marriage to the country's First Lady would be his best revenge against those who had slighted him. This being Onassis it would also be practical. Those close to him claimed that several of the older ships of his fleet could not pass the surveys needed to enter US ports. Contacts with the American political establishment would ease these annoying restrictions.

The marriage to Kennedy's widow, apart from the press furor it stirred up in England and the US also caused a serious rift between Onassis and his two children. In spite of their earlier hostility his offspring looked upon Onassis' long-time love, Maria Callas, the famous opera singer as the lesser of two evils, since they hated Jackie. They never gave up hoping for a reunion of Aristotle with their mother, Tina Livanos.

Jackie's arrival in the Onassis family put a sudden end to those plans. Apart from the hostility of his children to his famous bride, Onassis was having other problems with Jackie. Press gossip and insiders reports reaching his relatives said that Jackie was spending money at such a phenomenal rate that even Onassis, with all his millions, had to put his foot down. More than this Jackie was nearly always away, decorating an apartment somewhere or visiting arty friends in New York. Whenever Onassis announced he was going to visit Jackie at his apartment in New York she claimed that her children had houseguests and there was no room for him! This too was not in keeping with a traditional Greek's idea of how his wife should live and behave. For a Greek the place of a wife was by her husband. Because of Jackie's reluctance to allow Onassis to stay at their New York apartment Onassis would check into a suite at the Pierre where he was more welcome.

On this day at the beach on Scorpios Onassis thought about these problems and later called a family friend to say that he could see little hope for his marriage. He turned his hopes elsewhere. Onassis desperately wanted Christina to marry well and give him grandchildren. Ari saw in this the only chance for the survival of his dynasty and the continuance of the Onassis fortune. He was also making arrangements for the other half of his fortune - Alexander's share - to be used for the establishment of a public benefit foundation in which his immediate family and their descendants would be in control. The administration, the daily work, was to be assigned to his close associates at the office, lawyer Stelios Papadimitriou and the Onassis former pilot Pavlos Ioannides who were both placed on the board of the Foundation but in positions lower down in the list in his will than the members of his family. It was a practical mix. Onassis expected his employees to take care of the details and the work while his family would give the Foundation prestige and maintain its family character. This was one of Onassis biggest mistakes.

Over the years there was a marked shift in control over the Foundation and its shipping empire. A rapid succession of untimely and in one case unexplained deaths in the family resulted in the trusted employees rising to prominence at the Foundation to the exclusion of all Onassis family members, with the exception of one cousin, Dologlou who remained on the board for several more years. This development, unforeseen by Onassis, was a decisive factor in setting into motion the most bitter and highly publicized battle when the management of the Onassis Foundation with its shipping and real estate empires passed into the hands of Stelios Papadimitriou, his three associates, and after a few years into the hands of the sons of three of the Onassis employees. Onassis world started to collapse a few months after the day at the beach at Scorpios. A new Greek government under right-winger Constantine Karamanlis turned against prominent business leaders and started a campaign to take over their businesses and assets. Onassis would have had little difficulty under normal circumstances to defend Olympic Airways, his private airline, from a government takeover. However, when the battle started he found himself more and more isolated and while his shipping business was doing well the loss of his son and the emotional isolation from his immediate family owing to his failing marriage was taking its toll. Jackie was in New York and Christina who adored her father had been traumatized by the years of emotional neglect. Her mother, Tina Livanos, now with serious problems had married Onassis' rival and worst enemy, shipping tycoon Stavros Niarchos, and Alexander, Onassis' son, was dead. To add to this Onassis was told by specialists that the lagging movement of his eyelids and the creeping impairment of his muscle motor functions were irreversible.

He asked the doctors what the cure was and was told that there wasn't one; the disease would eventually be fatal. Onassis saw once more, as he had with his son a year before that all his money, ships, banks and gold hoarded in Swiss and Canadian vaults were incapable of prolonging his life. His body was no longer his own, his marker had been called.

To add to these problems the Greek government, sensing his weakness turned up the pressure, moving in for the kill. Onassis was forced to attend negotiations with Band Aid strips attached to his eyelids to keep them open because the muscles had stopped functioning. He fought as well as he could under the circumstances - a wounded lion - but he knew that with a government which had the power to legislate he had little choice but to give up Olympic Airways. This hurt Onassis deeply. Olympic had been his pride and joy. After mastering the oceans the airline was proof that he had also conquered the skies, the only man in the world along with TWA's Howard Hughes, at that time, to own an international airline.

After he lost his favourite business "child" Onassis, depressed and isolated, knowing that he was a dying man, took several decisions in the presence of his office staff. No matter what they subsequently claimed everybody I spoke to said that they were never friends of his or more than employees, but luck was on their side. Stelios Papadimitriou, a lawyer who sold P&I insurance for several years in the port of Piraeus had recently returned to favour in the Onassis group, taking an appointment as a salaried legal advisor. He managed to convince the dying tycoon in his last days that he would be there for Christina, to help and support her with the business after Onassis was gone.

Onassis could have had no idea how his acceding to this course would in only a few years work against his family, and that before long Stelios Papadimitriou, from a position as a senior company employee would be sitting at the head of the Onassis Foundation wielding power over the heads of Onassis' granddaughter Athina and her family. His appearances on television and in the papers showed the public that Papadimitriou had now entered the privileged and powerful company of government ministers, ambassadors and heads of state to whose causes he often generously dispensed Onassis funds.

After Onassis and his children were dead there was a rapid change in the employee's lifestyle. The Greek public saw Papadimitriou, his three associates and their children entering or leaving black-windowed chauffeur-driven limousines under the protection of a coterie of armed bodyguards and a motorcycle outrider. Papadimitriou spoke to the media of his own view of being virtually another Onassis son. He claimed that Onassis on his deathbed had told him, "Look after Christina now, she is your sister."

The same man – Papadimitriou - with his three closest associates, Pavlos Ioannides, Apostolos Zambellas (an Olympic airways chief accountant and later financial director) and Theo Gavrielides (a lawyer who had worked with other Foundations and substantial clients before coming into the Onassis fold) had been present when Christina wrote her will. According to Onassis Monte Carlo office manager David Banfield one of the four Greeks had actually dictated the will to Christina (in which three of them became beneficiaries to the tune of 2 million dollars). The Greeks, in Christina's latest will were appointed majority administrators in charge of the hundreds of millions of dollars that made up Athina's inheritance.

38 days after the signing of the will in Switzerland Christina, who was in perfect health until then was found dead in Argentina. With her death the wheel came full turn and the entire Onassis fortune ended up under the control of the small group that came to be referred to as "the Four Greeks" by the international press, "Onassis' trusted associates" by the

Greek press and less charitably as "the Gang of Four" by the British tabloid columnist, Nigel Dempster.

Ari Onassis did not live to see grandchildren but in one of those strange twists of fate Christina and Thierry, after their first brief affair in Scorpios, met up again some years later, picked up where they had left off, and were soon married. Thierry for the first time, Christina for the fourth. Onassis dream of a descendant to carry on the blood line was finally realised through this marriage.

On January 24th, 1985 in the same place where Onassis died, the American Hospital in Paris, Christina gave birth to the grandchild that Onassis so craved and was never to see. The dark-haired new arrival was christened **Athena-Helene Roussel**, and soon after she was registered by her mother as a Greek citizen at the municipal registry in Athens. This incidentally is the heiress's correct registered name on her birth certificate. The spelling "Athina" that came into general use by repetition was used by the family and eventually by the heiress herself as we can see from the way she has spelled her name in the logo of the Athina Onassis International Horse Show.

The joy Athina's arrival gave to a proud Thierry and an ecstatic Christina was not perhaps felt with quite the same enthusiasm by those at the Onassis shipping conglomerate. Christina, by this time president of the Alexander S. Onassis Foundation, could not know how unwelcome her newborn daughter, tiny Athina, would later become in the empire that Aristotle had left in trust for his family and his descendants.

The baby in the maternity wing of the hospital in Paris had, unknown to the family, become a threat to anyone outside the family who would want the presidency of the Onassis Foundation for themselves. The very existence of an Onassis descendant had activated an article in her grandfather's will which resulted in a monumental financial sea-change for half the Onassis fortune. Hundreds of millions of dollars would go now to Athina instead of to the Foundation upon Christina's death.

This was the beginning of the Onassis fortune battle. Young Athena Helene Roussel was to be in the eye of the storm.

The Fortune Dispute

Christina in her last will specified that Athina's fortune would be managed by a board of five people. First on the list was the name of Athina's father, Thierry Roussel, followed by those of Stelios Papadimitriou, Pavlos Ioannides (Onassis former pilot), Apostolos Zambellas and Theodore Gavrielides, an Onassis Foundation lawyer.

Christina specified that the board should take decisions regarding the patrimony, by majority vote. This was reasonable and necessary, since the board would otherwise be paralyzed should one of the members be unavailable to attend a meeting owing to his being away, or sick. What Christina could not foresee, was that the clause regarding the majority vote would be used by the "Foundation Four" initially to override opinions of Athina's father and later to freeze him out of all board decisions. Board meetings without Roussel, subsequently ruled by the Swiss court to have been illegal, were held in Greece instead of in Switzerland. Eventually the 4 took a vote in Roussel's absence to remove him from his place on his daughter's patrimony board.

Coexistence between the four Greeks and Athina's father had been reasonably amicable until 1993 when it was decided at a board meeting that there should be a purchase of foreign currency based on a forecast of the rates moving up. The 5 member board took a unanimous vote and appointed Apostolos Zambellas to make the currency purchase. The financial forecast proved correct. When some months later Roussel called Zambellas to congratulate him on the currency transaction, Zambellas replied that he had not executed it.

Roussel told me he had been astonished and asked why not. Zambellas replied that it had been his decision not to make the purchase. When Thierry wrote a formal letter asking for his reasons for not executing the order of the board Zambellas replied that he did not feel he was accountable to Athina's father "especially when your instructions were erroneous", and would not explain further.

Athina had incurred a paper loss of 4.5 million dollars by Zambellas' refusal to carry out his mandated instruction and Athina's father was upset. From that moment there was bad blood between Roussel and the four Greek co administrators.

Some time later exchange rates swung back again, wiping out the paper loss but the initial profit could have been taken and another transaction done, claimed Thierry. The Greeks and Thierry Roussel were now at war. Christina had specified that decisions taken by a board majority would be valid, and the Greeks using their numerical advantage started taking them.

One day Athina and her father were informed by the captain of their private Falcon jet that "the Greek board members have forbidden further use of the jet by the Roussel family. The plane is for sale".

Another incident was reported in February of 1998 by Odyssey magazine which said that the Greeks had threatened to sell off Boislande, the Geneva mansion which belonged to Athina, and also to sell other real estate belonging to the little girl if Thierry did not back down in his dispute with them.

When Christina died her two Glyfada suburb houses, historic Onassis properties, went to her daughter. Pavlos Ioannides at a board meeting said that the houses should be demolished because the value of the land would go down when the nearby noisy airport relocated to out of town. Roussel was informed that he should hurry up if the administrators were to stay ahead of this disadvantageous turn of events in the real estate market.

Roussel remonstrated, claiming that it was beyond any logic that prices would go down if the noise pollution of a nearby airport were to stop. Soon after Theodore Gavrielides, the board member and lawyer wrote a letter to Thierry's lawyer Yves Repiquet in Paris saying: -

"Please ask Thierry to reconsider his refusal to agree to our decision to demolish the house".

Repiquet replied saying that Roussel specifically ordered the Greek co-administrators not to destroy the houses.

The Greeks answered saying that they, being in Greece, knew the peculiarities of the local real estate market. If Roussel insisted on not demolishing the house then he would cause harm to Athina's property. It was a strong argument. Roussel gave in and the two Onassis houses were torn down. Onassis granddaughter had lost her last base in Athens.

In July 1998 when the family was leaving Athens I was at the airport when a reporter asked Thierry what their plans were. He replied "We would very much like to build a house here on our plot so we can come more often and have somewhere of our own to stay".

On the news that evening Papadimitriou, visibly agitated stated –

"It is all a lie. They had a house here. It was he, he, Roussel, who demolished the house of Onassis".

The news channels, aware by now of the documents regarding the board decision printed a copy of the Foundation's letter asking Roussel to agree to the demolition of the properties. The Greek public was getting a taste of how far apart the two sides were.

After several incidents like this, the four Greeks voted at a board meeting to eject Thierry from the patrimony board. They also added a clause doubling their own salaries to 800,000 dollars a year. Additionally they voted to hire an accountant at 150,000 dollars a year to help out with the extra work made necessary "because of the actions of Roussel".

In Greece there was beginning to be criticism of Papadimitriou now for various things. One was that his press statements showed a lack of respect for Athina. Other stories circulated about total strangers to the family and to acquaintances of Papadimitriou being allowed to go to Scorpios.

One day, while we were sitting in Kolonaki Square having coffee at Da Capo Thierry told me that two years earlier disturbing reports had reached him about the situation at the Onassis Foundation's shipping subsidiary ASO Naveira. The financial manager of Olympic Maritime Company in Monte Carlo, David Banfield, had informed Thierry that huge loans had been taken out by Foundation companies on new tankers at a time when market prices for new building of ships were going through the roof. Offices of the Onassis Foundation in the meantime were being closed, added Banfield. There were rumours also that Olympic Tower; the Onassis flagship skyscraper building in New York was having difficulty with some of its tenants. Its ground floor offices had been rented to a series of failed restaurants it was claimed. In the shipping world there was talk of the Foundation refinancing old ships and taking out even more loans.

As a result of some of these reports Thierry decided to instruct a financial expert in Paris - Thierry St Bonnet - to look at the balance sheets of the Foundation to have a clearer idea of what was going on. Roussel wanted to know whether there was genuine cause for worry, since Athina still had a good eight years to go before she would become the Foundation's president.

The report by St Bonnet, said Thierry, was disturbing. The picture indicated by his study was of a Foundation in danger of going bankrupt if current trends continued into the future. The debt of the ships was in the hundreds of millions of dollars, the freely usable cash appeared to be minimal by comparison with a few years before. In addition the Foundation had lost its Onassis family identity. Now the four Greeks had put their own sons and relatives in positions of importance at Foundation companies. Three of their sons were on the Foundation board also. There were rumours that other relations were employed by related businesses, such as Springfield Shipping, or were on the board of Scorpios Island, which belonged to Athina.

Athina was still a minor. She would have to be represented by her father who now sought to learn about the Foundation and investigate whether there was any truth in what he had heard. Roussel wrote a letter to the Foundation Greeks asking, as the guardian of Athina, to be informed as to some business aspects of the Onassis Foundation. He told the Greeks that if the information was not supplied willingly, as it had not been up to now, he would be forced to turn to the courts for help. Athina's father received a curt letter telling him that he had no business with the Onassis Foundation. Thierry had had enough. He sent St Bonnet's report to his lawyer in Greece, Professor Nestor Courakis, with instructions to study the facts and consider if there were grounds for legal action. Professor Courakis, a specialist in penal law and correctional institutions, sent back a fax saying that in his view there was sufficient evidence in order to make a criminal complaint against certain members of the Onassis Foundation. Soon after Courakis lodged a complaint with the Athens prosecutor on behalf of Thierry Roussel, accusing Papadimitriou and his three associates of mismanagement. Most serious was a charge of embezzlement. The complaint further said that the 4 had damaged the Foundation by charging excessive office worker charges, that they had depleted the sources of cash of the Foundation, sinking it into debt, and that they had exposed it to the risky tanker market.

Roussel was summoned to make a deposition to the prosecutor together with his witness David Banfield who was still working with the Foundation at their Monte Carlo offices. Banfield told the investigating judge in the pre-trial hearing that in his view the Foundation's assets were in danger as a result of certain management decisions. Banfield later told Vanity Fair that Christina Onassis had been very distressed about paying excessive management fees for her ships to Papadimitriou. "Undue Money" is what Banfield called it. By any other name that meant money not owed. This extremely damaging accusation by Banfield was ignored by the Greeks who were more concerned with Roussel.

Papadimitriou and the other three submitted a written defense to the Athens investigator. The judges considered the case and it went to a higher level succession of decisions Papadimitriou and his associates were eventually cleared. Some of the alleged crimes described in Roussel's complaint had fallen under the statute of limitations. The four were absolved of all wrongdoing. They now sued Thierry and his lawyer for false accusation, criminal defamation and perjury.

After a new series of hearings and appeals up to the high court, the complaint reverted to a lower court which accepted the complaint of Papadimitriou and his associates. Roussel and Professor Courakis were ordered to stand trial. The Four followed up with a civil case against Thierry, this time demanding damages of 15 million dollars, an astronomical and punitive sum almost unheard of in Greek courts. The situation became even worse for Thierry. A series of extremely damaging statements by Papadimitriou was printed in the Greek and international press. Public opinion turned against Athina's father.

In the meantime the Swiss juvenile authority, the Authorite Tutelle, alarmed by what the deluge of recriminations in the press was doing to Athina who was distressed by what she was hearing at school and elsewhere, forbade all involved parties from making statements to the press. Roussel complied. Papadimitriou, as Roussel told me, knew that the law applied only to Swiss residents and ignored the ban. He continued with his press statements against Roussel.

There was more to come in the media. Papadimitriou was quoted several times as saying that Christina did not trust Thierry and that he was after her money. "Athina is a hostage," said Papadimitriou to the press going on to accuse Roussel of purposely isolating her from her Greek roots. This accusation was one that was accepted by many over the years when they saw how rarely Athina came to Greece and how little interest she and her Brazilian horseman husband Alvaro de Miranda subsequently showed for Scorpios. More was to follow. In an interview with the Greek gossip magazine "Hai" Papadimitriou said that Roussel was a "Mafioso" and that he had dealings with the underworld!

Papadimitriou was getting publicity with his attacks on Roussel. The limelight was on him after many years of receiving minimal press attention. He appeared now to be basking in the attention. Papadimitriou was seen by many at the time as the guardian of the Foundation, protector of both Athina and her assets - a sort of protective angel coming from the chamber of Christina's death vault. With both the Onassis Foundations' millions of dollars in funds and those of Athina under his control it seemed to many that Roussel and the Onassis family would be finished off by their arch-foe. Roussel's enemies had however underestimated the resilience and persistence of the aristocratic Frenchman, especially where money was concerned.

Papadimitriou did not reserve his criticism for Athina and her father only. In a magazine article in Odyssey magazine in February 1998 he told American journalist Diane Shugart that Christina Onassis was not a "real president" of the Foundation. He explained that "the real one was behind, but that even that can be a burden". He spoke against Athina and even criticized Aristotle Onassis himself, whom he accused of being an administrator without the administrative talents which he – Papadimitriou - himself had!

Around December, 1998, the president of the Onassis Foundation gave an interview to Eleftherotypia, a widely read Greek daily newspaper, saying of himself *"I have a superiority complex"*. For a man who had risen to public prominence on the back of the Onassis dispute and displayed such confidence in himself it was true that even he thought that perhaps this was going too far. He asked Georgia Linardou the Eleftherotypia journalist who was interviewing him whether she thought he would be ridiculed for this statement, and she, sensing the media mileage that this statement would bring to her interview was quick to assure him that the "superiority complex" statement was perfectly in order. Papadimitriou, a shrewd and intelligent player on the legal and shipping fields still had a lot to learn about journalists and he was, without doubt to regret his statement seeing it repeated again and again in the Roussel court cases and in media interviews. One wonders too what Onassis would have to say about his former trusted employee if he were still alive to read Papadimitriou's boast. Others on reading Papadimitriou's interviews started wondering about the man who was heading the Onassis Public Benefit Foundation and its vast shipping and real estate interests. People magazine's comment on the intramural Onassis dispute was "Poor Athina". The Sunday Times wrote of a "Girl in a Gilded Cage".

Twenty three years earlier at the funeral of Aristotle Onassis on Scorpios the images of a weeping Christina surrounded by a group of grieving women relatives dressed in black had etched itself into the memory of millions of Greeks who watched the event on Greek television. On that day in March of 1975 I and my wife Dimitra were visiting my mother at her apartment at Anagnostopoulou Street in Kolonaki. The reporter covering the Onassis funeral service read a list of names of those attending the ceremony while the camera panned slowly across the coffin before zooming in on the faces of the women sitting behind it. Ari's daughter Christina was there together with Onassis's three sisters, Kalliroi Patronikola, Artemis Garofalides, and Meropi Konialides.

"There is another sister," said my mother. Surprised by this, I asked her what she meant. "Your father who escaped from the Smyrni disaster told me that Aristotle Onassis had a younger sister living in Turkey. She stayed behind during the catastrophe in Asia Minor in 1922 and married a Turk," she explained. "Onassis sister Artemis told me about her when we were having tea together at the Grande Bretagne Hotel," she added.

I heard nothing more about the mysterious Onassis woman for several years. From time to time over the years I raised the subject with those who knew the family, but was always met with either a blank stare or a look of disbelief. No one else seemed to have heard of a fourth Onassis sister. I was finally to learn the truth during a visit by Athina and the Roussel family to Athens when they came to attend an Onassis family wedding to which I was invited.

It was July the 8th 1998. Athina and the children were in the garden by the pool at the summer villa of Aunt Kalliroi, at Lagonissi, 37 km down the coast from Athens. Thierry and Gaby had gone shopping and I was in the villa living room talking to Aunt Kalliroi who was telling me stories about her brother Ari Onassis when they were young children in Turkey. Her father had remarried and Kalliroi was Aristotle's half-sister from the second marriage. Aunt Kalliroi told me how the family had left Asia Minor in the aftermath of the collapse of the Greek military front in the Greek-Turkish war of 1922. The Onassis family had been among hundreds of thousands of refugees who had escaped during the sack of Smyrni, a city on the Aegean coast of Turkey. As Kalliroi recounted her story I suddenly remembered what my mother had said about the Onassis sister who had stayed behind in Turkey. Kalliroi made no mention of her and I thought it better not to broach the subject with her. I did make a mental note to ask one of the close family relatives when the next opportunity presented itself. A few days later the opportunity came up when I was having coffee with Kalliroi's grandson at his office in Athens. I decided the time was right to broach the subject.

"The story is partly true," he said, "She wasn't a sister, however, but the first cousin of Ari who lived with the Onassis family in Smyrni. The two of them were like brother and sister."

Up until 1922 Smyrni had been a thriving Greek city on the Mediterranean coast of Asia Minor for hundreds of years. It had been a bustling centre of eastern Mediterranean European culture with a large population of wealthy Greek merchants engaged in the trading of goods passing through the port to Europe and Asia. In the early twentieth century fashionable women in Parisian dresses walked along its corniche, past elegant hotels and busy cafes in scenes that reminded one of Vienna, Munich and Nice. These elegant women, accompanied by well dressed husbands or other family members were unaware of the impending outbreak of Greek-Turkish hostilities that would ignite old enmities and unleash violence of such magnitude that life in the city would change forever. The city's civilian inhabitants were to suffer terribly in October of 1922 when thousands of Turkish and Kurdish irregulars, backed by the Turkish army, swooped into the city, burning houses, looting, mutilating and raping. With the final collapse of the military front Greek civilians fled in panic as the first Turkish bands entered the suburbs of the town. Thousands upon thousands of men, women and children crowded the long corniche, desperately trying to get into one of the small boats available to evacuate them. Behind the waterfront the entire city seemed to have been set on fire as a wall of flame thirty metres high that began from arson in the Armenian sector and spread to the Greek neighbourhoods drove the population before it as columns of dense black smoke rose in a solid wall high into the sky.

Friends of ours who lived in Smyrni at the time recount how in the alleys one could hear the desperate screams of Greek civilians being put to the sword and the shrill cries of women and children being violated and mutilated. Roving bands of Turks and Kurds carried out their grim work while the diplomatic mission employees of Italy, the US, and Britain looked on from their houses and consulates without intervening. That was the official policy then of the Big Powers. The American consul Horton was the exception. Shocked by what he saw he pressured his government and the American war ships anchored offshore to accept the Greek refugees and as a result of his tireless action and that of a priest thousands of Greek refugee families were allowed on board and were taken away from the inferno that Smyrni had become. Years later I met Horton's daughter at a social event in Athens when she was sitting next to me, but the memories of what I had heard of the slaughter and of the heroism and dedication of her father had such an effect on me that I was unable to talk to her about Asia Minor.

My father found himself in Asia Minor at this tragic time. He was a young tobacco merchant near the town of Chesme. He had anticipated the events after a decisive battle near Ankara where the Greek army as defeated when their European allies stopped supplying them with military supplies. Manoli, my father, hired a boat to evacuate himself and as many fellow Greeks as the fishing vessel would carry. Those he spoke to insisted there was no danger. They had lived here among the Turks for centuries and they would not be harmed they claimed. Only a few listened to Manoli and boarded the boat he made available to them for their escape to Greece. Some Greek neighbours, jealous of his business success went to the Turkish authorities and said that Mantheakis was spreading false rumours about the

Turks. As a result my father was arrested and thrown into jail. One morning Turkish army officers came to the prison where my father was locked up and started hanging Greek prisoners. My father and three others were scheduled to be hanged the next day. That evening a guard came to check the names of those to be executed at dawn. When the Turkish guard, who spoke Greek, heard my father's name he asked him where he was from. My father replied from Crete, from Elia. The guard stopped and asked in surprise "You aren't Nikolaras Mathioudakis's son who went to Africa, are you?" My father confirmed that indeed he was.

The guard who was interrogating the prisoners to see which ones would be hanged had been born and had grown up in a neighbouring Cretan village and knew my grandfather well. That night he came to the cell where my father was being held and led my father outside the jail to a field where the Turk had a horse waiting for Manoli. My father thanked the guard profusely and mounted the horse. He rode through the night along the coast until he found a rowing boat with which to escape to safety and a new life after beaching it several hours later on the Greek island of Chios. Manoli Mantheakis learned later that those in the village who had stayed behind and ignored his warnings had all been killed when the first Turkish irregulars entered the village.

Against this background of general confusion the Onassis family with their cousins the Konialides made their way through the panicked and exhausted crowds milling around the Smyrni waterfront. Reaching the crowded jetty looking for a boat for Greece they were met by the sight of dozens of bodies floating in the harbour. Corpses belonging mostly to those who had been so panic-stricken that they had jumped straight into the sea without knowing how to swim.

Back on shore, Turkish soldiers, following the irregular troops, had in the meantime made their way to the waterfront of the city and were pushing their way through the terrified Greek civilians. The Onassis family, now among the lucky few who managed to secure a promise of escape to Greece had found some room in a fishing caique that was scheduled to take its passengers to safety in the Greek national waters a little distance offshore.

Onassis's relative told me the rest of the story I had wondered about for so long. Nikos Konialides, Onassis's first cousin, he said, was carrying a terrified Kalliroi, Aristotle's 6 year old sister on his shoulders as he stepped into the boat.

"Uncle Nikos Konialides sat down in the boat with Kalliroi in his lap. Each member of the family who embarked was carefully scrutinized by a Turkish officer accompanied by an armed soldier standing at the dockside. Nikos Konialides was followed by his 12 year old sister, her head covered by a scarf to hide her face. The Turkish officer leaned forward and lifted the girl out of the boat and onto the jetty. Pulling off her scarf he looked at her face. The girl was trembling with fear as the officer ran his hand over her upper body, feeling her breasts. He told the soldier accompanying him to hold the Konialides girl aside. The officer, pleased with what he saw was going to keep her for his own use."

My storyteller stopped for a moment to drink mineral water from a glass on his desk.

"Her mother desperately pleaded with the officer to let her daughter accompany the family, but he pulled out his pistol and threatened to shoot the other children of the family if she did not get back into the boat. Onassis' sister had no choice but to be quiet, to save the rest of the children. As the boat left the dock the Onassis and Konialides families could see Ari's young female cousin being led off by the officer." Kalliroi's grandson stopped for a few seconds, lost in his thoughts.

"My aunt - her mother," he continued, "The other children in the boat were hysterical by now. Fifteen minutes later the boat passed the line of British and American warships in the harbour and made its way to safety to a harbour at a Greek island nearby. That was it."

"What happened after that?" I asked.

"We never saw her again," he continued. "The tragedy weighed heavily on our family. My uncle - the girl's brother Nikos Konialides who later married Aristotle' sister Meropi, never stopped looking for her."

This tragedy was not an isolated event. Thousands of young women and girls had been abducted preceding the sacking of Smyrna. None of these girls, many from affluent middle class families, would ever see their families again.

"Uncle Nico looked for years," continued Kalliroi's grandson. "In the 1970's, after countless fruitless trips to Turkey following a series of false leads Uncle Niko went to Istanbul where he had information that his sister who had become a Turk now to all intents and purposes and had married there. When Uncle Niko came back to Greece he would not tell us if he had seen his sister. He only said that he would not be going back to Turkey again."

This is all Kalliroi's relative would say. I let it go at that, respecting the pain that the events in Smyrni and their subsequent outcome had caused the entire family.

Some time later I heard from another source that Nico Konialides had indeed found his sister in Istanbul. My informant claimed that Konialides lost sister now had children of her own, and that her current husband, a Turk, was comfortably off. She must have suffered an immense shock to see her long-lost brother Niko suddenly walking into her living room in Istanbul, so many years later, bringing back painful memories of a lost and now alien life that lay beyond the horrendous experiences she had lived through after her abduction.

Nikos Konialides, my source told me, saw that his sister had a comfortable middle class life with her children and her husband and did not want to remember the past. Her wish to be left alone hurt her brother, but it was understandable and Nikos walked out of the house and out of her life for ever. His quest of nearly half a century was finally over. Konialides was forced to face the reality that the terrified waif-like 12 year old sister he had last seen being led away by the Turkish officer into the crowd on the wharf of a burning Smyrna so many years ago had finally found peace for herself. Her new family may have spoken a different language, prayed to a different God and lived in what was now a foreign land, but she undoubtedly had the love that had been tragically denied her for years. His sister had been a victim of an incident no different from thousands of similar tragedies that had indelibly marked the lives of innocent people caught up in the tide of a now nearly forgotten war.

My genetic links with the sea go back through millennia to my maritime ancestors on the island of Crete. They were the Minoans, a bold race of seafarers whose ships brought them power and wealth and gave them the means to become the first civilized people of Europe. They were an advanced people, who 1,600 years before the birth of Christ had under-floor heating, flushing toilets and paved roads. I inherited their appreciation for creature comforts but I never felt their affinity for rocking back and forth on a flimsy seagoing vessel buffeted by the waves and the wind. With this historical maritime background, and even though I was born just fifty yards from the sea in a small colonial hospital in Tanganyika, the waves and I never got on well together. The idyllic physical surroundings of my birth in the harmoniously designed white German-era colonial building with arcaded verandas, red tiled roofs, and surrounded by lawns, frangipani bushes and palm trees in the sleepy tropical town of Tanga in Tanganyika and the sound of the lapping of the Indian ocean in the bay of Tanga were never enough to make me seek a life on the waves. I therefore made sure that many years later in 1998 when Thierry asked me to find him a yacht for a cruise to the islands of the Saronic Gulf I chose a large seaworthy schooner with working stabilizers.

The captain of the boat brought it round to the bay of Lagonissi and anchored half a mile offshore owing to the lack of depth of the sea at that particular bay. I admit that when I saw its sleek lines and dark blue shiny finish I was impressed by the beauty of the yacht. It was large enough – 43 metres – to give a promise of stability and to overcome my initial misgivings. The captain assured me that its deep draft guaranteed a calm ride in the notoriously changeable windy conditions of Greece in the summer. It was the season of the Meltemi, the strong easterly winds that churn up the Aegean in July and August, but today was a day with what passes for moderate winds in our Greek summer– Force Five.

The family and I gathered on the beach in front of Kalliroi's estate where the Roussel's were staying. The beach was a public one, as most are in Greece and the appearance of Nordic blonde heads and beefy bodyguards let everyone on the beach know that Athina was there with our party. It needed three trips in the tender to ferry us to the waiting yacht so in the meantime a few dozen holiday-makers left their towels and beach bags and made their way towards us, unselfconsciously creating a semicircle around our group while the yacht crew and bodyguards piled weekend bags and helped us into the rocking tender. Within fifteen minutes we were all on board the *Ariadne*. We shed our footwear into a basket on the rear deck and went into the chilly air-conditioned royal blue-carpeted lounge of the boat.

The Roussel children excitedly flitted from cabin to cabin, trying to decide which one was best. I took a cabin next to the stairs, which meant I could come and go without disturbing the others. Everyone settled in quickly, Thierry went for a nap in his cabin, Gaby settled down with a book and the children went out onto the deck to sunbathe and watch the changing scenery as we made our way towards Hydra island where none of the family had been before. The boat was, thankfully, stable, as the captain had assured me it would be.

I switched off my mobile phone and did not give the press our route details, only saying we would be in Hydra that evening. This was not enough for them so they scoured nearby islands to see where we would stop. The Roussel family wanted to swim and we anchored in a secluded bay opposite the island of Poros. Thierry, with a full stomach, and against the advice of all, dived in from the top of the roof of the boat and was followed by the children who went in, jumping off the ladder with a big splash as they hit the deep blue water. Soon we were all swimming. The bodyguards were strategically placed around us and our scuba diver was already three metres underwater to make sure that no one could sneak up on Athina. We spent an hour swimming in the sea and taking short breaks on board.

I was sitting on deck when I heard the chugging of a diesel engine approaching our bay. The guards immediately took up lookout positions and in a few moments a small overloaded fishing boat came round the corner about fifty yards away with three television camera crews precariously balanced on the narrow deck of the twelve foot vessel. It lurched as it came into the bay and I heard the scream of a female reporter as she and her cameraman very nearly tipped into the water with their camera and its tripod as their boat rocked when it turned to head for where we were.

"Yassou, Alexi" a voice called out. I saw it was Eftichia from Star TV. Next to her were Alexia Koulouri from Sky TV and Alexia Tassouli from Mega. The three rivals had joined forces and they now had a scoop. Their cameras were rolling and had caught Athina on the ladder as she was getting ready to board one of the jet-skis. Sandrine was already on the other one with Emilios. Athina slowly backed up the ladder and went back inside. I told the reporters that she would not come out and just wanted to swim in private. They were not so easily put off and went to a vantage point about a hundred metres away where they laid in wait. I decided to see how Athina was taking this and descended into the main lounge where I saw she was in a fit of giggles with Erik as they looked through the smoked glass windows at the reporters knowing they could not see into the yacht. I had expected Athina to be upset by the arrival of the boat, because Thierry always insisted on how disturbed she was by the presence of any media. Athina though was thoroughly enjoying the game of hide-and-seek with the press.

"It's the girl with the red hair!" she said to me.

"Alexia K," I replied, "but we have to watch her because she works for Papadimitriou!"

Athina laughed and pointed to the press boat, telling Erik something in an aside which I could not hear. Seeing that Athina was okay I went back on deck, and descended to a tender which took me to the beach where Thierry, Gaby and the others had spread their towels.

After a while the overloaded grey-painted press boat left. I knew the reporters had to get back to the Poros island phone company to transmit their news footage to their studios.

We left the bay opposite Poros after a while and just as the sun was setting we approached the small amphitheatre-like harbour of Hydra through a luminous-gold summer haze. The wind had died down completely and the sea, a metallic bronze colour was absolutely flat like the top of a burnished table. The large stone-built mansions in the port and others built on the steep semi-circular hillside behind had been constructed by 18th century shipowners, sea captains and pirates and the mansions still looked as they did a hundred and fifty years ago. The small harbour at Hydra, accessible through a narrow opening on the left was full of weekend yachts and fishing boats.

Our yacht was too big to enter the harbour, so we tied up of the seaward side of the jetty which acted also as a breakwater, blocking off the harbour entrance. The Roussel children were fascinated by the three story mansions and the picture-postcard look of the island. On the jetty now there were about 200 journalists, paparazzi, officials and onlookers. Among them I could make out the mayor of Hydra flanked by an escort of port police and island dignitaries.

Athina seeing the crowd waiting for her did not want to come out of the boat and had gone back below deck. Thierry shrugged his shoulders while Sandrine, Johanna and Erik waited excitedly, keen to disembark and explore the shops along the small waterfront.

"I will talk to Athina, Thierry" I said and went on what was a most important mission. It was time for Athina I felt to confront the media and to clear once and for all where she stood with them otherwise she would be in danger of ending up one day like Princess Diana.

Athina was sitting alone on one of the couches in the dark main lounge with her shoulders hunched. She was looking down at her feet, frightened and miserable. It was no longer the same hide and seek she had enjoyed earlier with the press from the safety of the boat. She knew that now the reporters were waiting for her outside the yacht and that they would not go away.

"Athina" I said, "I want to talk to you about something very important."

She looked at me, a distressed look on her face. She would have to understand now that we were managing the media for her own good, and not merely making appointments for journalists to upset her when all she wanted was to have a quiet holiday.

"Athina, you know now that in Greece everyone wants to know about you." I started explaining, "This is because of their admiration for your grandfather and of their love for your mother, Christina. It is more than curiosity, it is real admiration." She was looking at me now, listening intently. I continued "The Greek public demands that the media let them know about you."

Athina was following my words while fidgeting with a hairclip.

"The reporters want something to send back ever day to their papers and television stations. If they have that, then they will leave you alone for the rest of the day."

She was beginning to understand, though she was not happy.

"The next day the editors and station managers will ask for another picture and video footage, and the reporters will be obliged to get it." I could see now that she understood the logic of what I was saying. The confusing situation outside was beginning to make some sense to her.

"If you spend just two minutes a day with the press, and let them take their pictures, then you will see that you will be left alone after that. You will even become friends with some of the reporters who are assigned to you. I in turn promise that I will talk to the media and tell them that they must not bother us after they have their first pictures."

I could now hear the clamour of the reporters outside as grew impatient waiting to see the last Onassis. "Athina, Athina" they called out from the jetty by the stern of the *Ariadne*. Athina thought about what I had said for a few moments, and then I saw her straighten her shoulders, stand up and say "Alexis, let us go."

Athina had turned an important corner. She had realised what few stars of the cinema or public personas have understood about media relations. Give a little, and you get a lot – your peace.

It was only the beginning on a road that would have led her to a balanced relationship with the media and would have assured her of privacy on her own terms. It was a lesson that would have saved Diana's life when the British princess became more and more paranoid and erratic in her relationship with the press, on occasion putting paper bags over her head to try and make the press go away. It led her to that fateful and paranoid attempt to escape the media at the George V Hotel in Paris which cost her her life in the underpass a few minutes later. Athina had begun well when she took her decision in the darkened lounge of the Ariadne in Hydra but it was not long before people close to her played on her former fear of the media and fanned it to a fever pitch driving her to extremes when there was a photographer or journalist about. This developing paranoia regarding the press was encouraged by family members who stated that Athina did not want the press and tried to impress on her some time later that the media were only around because I had invited them to be there. It was to be an attempt to drive a wedge between the heiress and myself and in the end it succeeded, for how long no one knows.

No one close to her mentioned to Athina that the family chauffeur was sent at nights to the Paris Match offices in the French capital with a bulging envelope of photographs of Athina to be considered for publication. The extreme repulsion for the click of a camera shutter or a "Hello Athina" reached proportions of a psychological syndrome when waiters at a restaurant where she and Doda were dining in Sao Paolo were instructed by Doda to stand in a line in front of the restaurant entrance holding up table cloths to create a wall behind which Athina rushed to her waiting car, hidden from the cameras of the waiting paparazzi. This bizarre incident was reminiscent of Howard Hughes eccentric behaviour.

Now waiting in the yacht at Hydra young Athina waited while I went out to negotiate with the reporters. I agreed with them that they could film her as she walked off the boat and along the waterfront by the shops for a distance of a hundred metres.

"Two hundred metres" called out Polydoras, a pleasant-mannered photographer. He was discreet but determined and was always the first to arrive on the scene along with Christos Bonis wherever Athina was expected.

"Okay," I agreed. I gave the signal and the mayor of the island came on board, surrounded by photographers whose cameras were now whirring and clicking. Athina and the other Roussels stood on the deck while the mayor welcomed them to the island. He gave them the flag of Hydra to fly on their yacht.

"This is the flag we gave to your grandfather," explained the mayor. "Aristotle Onassis' favourite island after Scorpios was Hydra. He came here often, the last time with Mrs. Kennedy-Onassis."

When the brief welcoming ceremony was over the port police opened a path for us and we disembarked. Athina, Thierry, the family and I walked along the waterfront, past cafés full of curious tourists and holiday-makers from Athens. Shopkeepers came out and stood in front of their store entrances each beckoning Thierry to come inside. We stopped at one shop with interesting handmade jewelry displayed in the window. The whole family went inside and Thierry asked me to translate for him.

"No need, Mr. Roussel." said the owner, "I speak seven languages."

The girls were fascinated by some rings with intricately carved classical Greek horse head motifs on them. Thierry bought rings for his daughters and ordered a gold necklace for Gaby while the excited crowd outside pressed their faces and cameras against the store window. Our bodyguards in the meantime were trying to keep the crowd at bay. When we reached the middle of the harbourfront I turned to the press contingent.

"Okay, this is more than 200 metres, tomorrow again!"

There was some mumbling, but the paparazzi had their pictures and the television crews had plenty of footage to show on the news that night. Like a swarm of bees that suddenly changes direction and scatters, the press turned and made off through the narrow alleys to send their pictures to their offices. The television reporters went to the Flying Dolphin, the hydrofoil boat that runs from Athens to the Saronic Islands to send off their video cartridges with Onassis granddaughter to their Athens studios in time for the evening news.

We entered the narrow side streets behind the row of historic stone mansions which fronted the toy town-like harbour. Hydra is an island where cars are not allowed and as a result all its streets and alleys are full of pedestrians. The family stopped to look at artisan items, sweet shops and curio stalls. Half an hour later we found our way back through the labyrinthine alleys and backstreets to the harbourfront again. Athina and especially Thierry were surprised to see that the reporters who had been in such hot pursuit of us in the fishing boat they had hired earlier on were now sitting in the waterfront cafes. The reporters had piled their equipment next to their tables and several of them were slouched in their chairs, without even lifting their eyes for more than a second or two as we walked past.

"That is what I mean, Athina," I said, nodding towards the camera crew from Mega TV who were relaxing, drinking iced coffee and puffing contentedly on Marlboro cigarettes. Alexia Tassouli, the attractive dark-haired reporter who worked for the station smiled as I walked by, and that was it. Tomorrow I knew that the chase would be on again.

That night the family was tired and Thierry was restless. His court case was coming up soon in Athens and the decision of the Swiss prosecutor regarding the kidnapping investigation was about to be announced any day now.

I sat on the covered deck of the *Ariadne* with him drinking a beer as we watched the activity unfolding in front of us in the small port. I asked Thierry if he wanted anything else and he said no. Was I going to sleep early, he asked, as I got up to leave.

"No, Thierry" I teased him, "I unfortunately have to continue my duties even at this late hour, and have a meeting with the female press. They have demanded I have drinks with them at "Piratis Bar"."

"And not just a drink" said Thierry, a wry smile creeping across his face as he remembered his younger, wilder days.

I left him sitting in the dark on deck and made my way to *Piratis*, where most of the press had now congregated and were waiting for me. Over drinks we caught up on the current gossip. We sat under the stars outside the bar now, relaxing in the close night air. There was not a breath of wind. All the crews and visitors on the sailing boats which filled the small harbour were on deck, talking in low voices. When they lit up the occasional cigarette a suntanned face would momentarily glow out of the dark before being lost again in the shadows. On the waterfront lovers walked with arms entwined. Affluent Athenian families, headed by fathers in baggy designer Bermuda shorts ambled by.

At around three in the morning I made my way back to the boat past closed waterfront cafes. It was almost totally dark in the tiny port. My path led me along the cobbles past the bright lights of a corner café where an American girl was sitting drinking with five newly-found male compatriots who had arrived aboard a 12 metre sailing yacht anchored opposite the *Ariadne*. On the deck of our boat I saw David Weaver, the head bodyguard sitting in a bamboo chair, keeping watch. I said goodnight and climbed down the steep steps to the main lounge and from there down another level to my cabin. Within a few minutes I was blissfully settled into my bunk and drifted off into a deep and contented sleep. It had been a pleasant cruise that had gone well for everyone.

Thierry and I were chatting on the covered rear deck of the *Ariadne*, as the dark blue 42 metre motor sailer sliced its way through the transparent blue water as we travelled back from Hydra in July of 1998. Athina and the other children were sunbathing on the upper deck of the yacht.

"We are both proud of our own countries, Alexis," said Thierry, "and this is great" he continued, gesturing to the open expanse of cobalt blue sea as we made rapid progress under power, "but I want you to come to Spain, to understand what paradise is for me, to see how we live when we are alone and how peaceful our life is there. It is a place where no one outside our immediate family circle is allowed to come."

Being rather chauvinistic about the beauty of the Aegean Sea and the diversity of the Greek islands I admit I was sceptical about Thierry's Ibiza. Even so I was keen to take up the offer, my curiosity getting the better of me. The invitation came two days later from Athina when we were anchored in Hydra harbour. She had been tucking into a bowl of her favourite black Vodenon cherries; a rare variety found only in the north of Greece while next to her Erik was munching on a club sandwich. Athina asked me if I had been to Ibiza, and when I said no, both children, as if in a chorus, asked me to come back with them. Thierry who had been fiddling with a pair of binoculars sensed a good excuse to pile some more work on me and suggested a working holiday. Gaby, considerate as always, and concerned at the obvious stress I had been under in the previous months leaned over towards me and said, "Come and have a good holiday, and NO work." She looked reproachfully at Thierry, her expression chiding him for his suggestion that I should work as a condition for coming to their Spanish holiday home. I happily accepted their invitation.

Two weeks later the family had installed themselves in Ibiza and Thierry, true to his promise of a working holiday had booked a ticket for me to Ibiza with a two day stopover in Geneva first. I agreed to this arrangement because it would give me the opportunity at Boislande to select useful files from the comprehensive Onassis archive kept there. Boislande was the nerve center of the Roussel empire where secretaries, a financial controller and Pascale, Thierry's personal assistant worked in the west wing of the house, while gardeners and a permanent staff of a cooks and a chauffeur operated out of a staff wing. Thierry had invited me and my wife Dimitra to spend a week at La Jondal after I left Switzerland.

After arriving at the mansion I pored over files and documents, working primarily in Thierry's large first floor office which looks out over the rolling expanse of the front lawns, resembling those of a British public school. Fifty metres in front of the living room patio there is a 120m2 rectangular swimming pool and beyond that mature tree borders that surround the ten acre property. In the distance the grey waters of Lake Geneva stand out against a picture-postcard backdrop of blue mountains.

In Thierry's office, on the carved white marble mantelpiece, a bronze Rodin sculpture of an open hand stands next to a collection of photos and postcards. Impressionist paintings hang on the wall, slightly out of key with the glass, chrome and black leather decor of the spacious office.

After the secretaries had left that afternoon, isolating the archive wing by activating the burglar alarms, I decided to wind down in the gym by the indoor pool and then indulging myself by doing several slow laps in the outdoor pool to rid myself of the tension that had been so evident during Athina's visit, tension that had been aggravated by the security precautions and the hounding of Athina by the press in Greece. The signs of the battle between Thierry and the Greek co administrators of Athina's patrimony were apparent at the mansion. The Greek administrators, violating their duty, had excluded Thierry from their board meetings and had suspended payments of millions of dollars to him. Small but telling signs of the economic squeeze in the Roussel household could be seen in the state of the cars of the family and in details around the mansion. I noticed with some surprise that while the lawn was mowed it was full of weeds and wild flowers among the sowed grass. The wooden entrance gate to Boislande needed varnishing and Christina's Mercedes 500 SEL had problems with the driver's door sticking. Boislande was not the immaculate mansion I had seen on my first trips to the villa to meet Thierry for our legal and strategy conferences.

In the evening, after having dining alone, I sat in the high-ceilinged living-room to watch archive black-

and-white video footage of Onassis and footage of Stelios Papadimitriou's recent press conferences in which he had launched his notorious tirades of abuse against Thierry and his family.

"Roussel is a clown", Papadimitriou said, "a useless person who has never done anything in his life", "a total failure" ranted Papadimitriou to an audience of international media representatives. There was always something useful to be gained from watching Papadimitriou talk.

The drawing room, where I watched the videos, had seen much drama when Christina was alive and had played a pivotal part in the battle for the Onassis fortune. It was here that Christina had signed her will. In this same room young Athina had played in front of her doting and tragic mother, unaware that she was to lose her so soon and be tossed into a bitter conflict with a group of men she did not know. It was a conflict that would ruin her teenage years and cause her to become a cover page item for dozens, if not hundreds of magazines and newspapers in the years that were to follow.

As I watched the videos I was made aware of the ghosts of those who had lived before in this room. They could not be dispelled by the calm atmosphere created by the subtle cream and blue Afghan chintz curtains, matching fabric sofa upholstery and carpets, the bleached blond wood paneling and the soft lighting. The setting was low key, as it is in the homes of so many of the those from old money, and it was in contrast to the museum-like marble, gold and glass palaces of the newly rich one sees on the Costa del Sol, in Miami or in the

Athenian suburb of Ekali. Boislande in contrast was a home. A house built to be lived in. Everywhere I went in the mansion I saw reminders of Christina and of the emotionally charged times she and Thierry had spent together.

Framed photographs of the couple lined the bookcases and crowded the glass tops of coffee tables. On the walls hung paintings of East African scenes, of lions and other fauna, mementos of the Roussel family home near Malindi in Kenya and at Thierry's father's sprawling game farm at Nanyuki below the snows of Mount Kenya.

I left Boislande the next day at noon, a hostage once again of Stanislaus, the mad Polish driver who was delighted at the opportunity of giving me another demonstration of his inimitable driving method. His technique was simple - drive flat out, honk the horn, throw French language insults peppered with heavily accented Polish vowels out of the window. *"Eembecile'"*, *"Ahh, Alorss, putten"*, *"Couchon"*.

Stanislaus made the drive even more hair-raising by opening the sunroof at 170 kilometers per hour and waving a pudgy hand out of the roof making rude circular gestures to a startled group of Czech workers in a battered green Zastava whom we overtook on the wrong side.

"A cette route. Eel ee a beaucoop dez acceedants. Monsierre" he announced cheerfully taking both hands off the steering wheel to rummage for a cigarette lighter in his pockets. Miraculously, the car stayed on the road and we arrived at the airport in one piece.

Once we had parked Stanislaus nipped round to the back of the VW station wagon. He pulled out my suitcase with a large grunt before I could warn him that it was full of heavy files. Dumping my suitcase on the pavement with an expression of surprise he rubbed the small of his back with both hands.

"Qu'est qu'eeel y a là dedanz. Monsièrre?" (What is in there Monsieur) he asked, mystified by the unexpected weight of the case. *"Monsiere Roussel vous avait donnè de bricks d'or?"* (Has Mr. Roussel given you gold bricks to carry?)

I assured him Thierry had not given me gold to take to Spain and handed him a bottle of red wine for his trouble. He pretended he did not want to take it but happily gave in when he read the winery label, *"Ah Bon, Monsièrre, très bon!"*

An hour later I was on an Iberia plane ascending over the neat green fields behind Geneva as we left the blue strip of Lake Leman and the estate of Boislande behind us.

My long deserved holiday in Spain was about to start.

The Iberia domestic airliner flying the hop from Madrid to Ibiza banked sharply to the left levelled its wings and began a rapid descent through the late summer evening haze, leaving the sun hanging on the horizon behind us. The toasted brown shape of Ibiza came suddenly into view as we dropped bumpily down for our final descent to the airport. Our plane quickly approached a strangely shaped rock formation jutting out to sea at the end of a wooded peninsula. I was a little nervous as we passed low over the sharp perpendicular rocks – a weird formation bearing an uncanny resemblance to what looked like the dorsal fin spikes of a huge half-submerged rock dinosaur. It seemed for a moment that the rock needles would scrape the belly of the plane but we passed safely over them and three minutes later we landed at Ibiza airport. As I stepped out of the cabin door onto the platform of the passenger steps I felt a searing wind blowing from the direction of the rock needles inland and past me to the dry coastal plain that lay beyond the airport.

Ours was the only plane at the airport and the arrivals lounge was almost empty. My suitcase now was nowhere to be seen and a search of the carousels and of the large arrivals lounge was unsuccessful. Before long the airport was totally deserted except for me and a rather forlorn Ivizenka, an attractive local girl who waited with me at the small Lost and Found cubicle for the man in charge to arrive. We pointed out various shapes to him on a poster in an effort to identify our errant luggage types. Another plane was due in two hours. My case would be on it I was assured by the helpful airport attendant who however spoke nothing except Spanish and Catalan. Looking around now I saw a rather confused man beyond the glass division in the distance holding up a piece of cardboard with my name on it. I nodded, motioning for him to wait until I finished the paperwork at the lost luggage desk.

It was dark by now, and when I went outside into the waiting area I was met by the smartly dressed man in crisp whites who had held up the sign. He identified himself as Didier, a Roussel employee who had been sent to collect me.

"Monsieur Thierry has gone to New York and Madame is out with the children and her brother's family. I have been instructed to take you to the house."

It was very dark by now and we drove in silence for a while, passing small simple dwellings along a dry, dusty country road. The scene with its parched grass along the tarmac strip illuminated by our headlights reminded me of my native Crete in August. We passed over a small hill, and then descended via a dirt road to what I could barely make out to be a bay lying on our left.

"*Là! Monsieur,*" said Didier. "*C'est la maison de Monsieur Roussel.*"

Immediately opposite us was a steep hill with perhaps a hundred palm trees illuminated by concealed yellow floodlights. In addition to this a smattering of weak yellow lights like oil lanterns scattered on the hillside made the scene look like a Hollywood Arabian oasis movie set.

We followed the narrow road down and through a dry river bed, ascending on the other side for perhaps another hundred metres before stopping in front of a massive double fronted wooden gate bounded on both sides by a high white wall. Didier got out of the car and lifted my suitcase out of the boot.

"*C'est lourd Monsieur,*" (It is heavy, Sir) he said, with a slight hint of reproach, "*A ce n'est rien* (It's nothing)," I replied, wanting to make a joke. "*Je porte de bricks de l'or pour Monsieur Roussel,*" (I am carrying gold bricks for Mr. Roussel). Didier looked at me in a quizzical way. My joke had fallen flat. Of course it would not have surprised the Roussel staff if someone had been carrying gold bars for the family. I decided it was too late to explain my joke to Didier so I helped him carry the suitcase inside the compound to a beautifully designed two-storied cream Spanish villa a few metres away.

The house, partially obscured by creeping flowering shrubs and a canopy of honeysuckle was lit by small amber lights sunk into the stairwells giving it a warm luminosity. Even with my help the suitcase still had to be carried upstairs in stages to give us time to catch our breath. I held on to my end of the case, careful not to step on my own toes and took a break on the tile landing of the porch by the front door of the villa. I was startled to hear the sound of gushing water and turned round. There, in front of me was an illuminated four metre high waterfall, about seven metres wide. It was a stunning sight and I now realized what Thierry had meant when he said he wanted me to come and see how the Roussel family lived away from the public eye. A large palm tree, floodlit from its wide gnarled base stood rooted in the sand to the right of the waterfall. Didier waited indulgently for me to get over my first reaction of admiration. It was clearly a scene he had witnessed with every new visitor and I noticed he had a glint of pride in his eye. «Magnifique" I said, picking up my end of the case once more to stagger with Didier up the last few tiled steps to the guest suite landing on the first floor. The guest apartment with its Spanish terracotta floors and hand-plastered walls was large, finished in turquoise and white with light blue and cream rugs and matching curtains. It was an atmosphere somewhat reminiscent of sybaritic Las Vegas hotel suites but in good taste. An elevated Jacuzzi tub and a picture window looked out onto some distant lights which I assumed to be villas on the other side of the dark bay. The high bed itself was large enough for three. I was happy to have all this space to roll around on but I was disappointed that Demetra had refused to come.

Didier closed the curtains for me and pointing to a wall thermostat he asked «How many degrees would you like your room to be at, Monsieur?" Thierry and his family had provided well for me, and I was grateful now that after a tiring trip I would have the chance to relax my exhausted limbs in the cocoon of welcome luxury.

"I will wait for you downstairs, Monsieur, to take you to dinner. At the main house," said Didier. A few minutes later I was outside again, walking past the waterfall which I now saw was fed by a series of illuminated blue cascading shell-shaped swimming pools.

«How many pools Didier?" I asked.

"Eight monsieur!"

He was showing off now. Eight swimming pools were certainly beyond the reach of middle class living. It was probably excessive even by plutocratic standards so I had to excuse Didier's pride. I was in Thierry's wonderland now and I realised he had brought me here to knock a little bit of my Greek chauvinism off me. It was typical of the low-key foxy Frenchman not to have said anything before. He had had his own way and now he was probably sitting on the plane in mid-Atlantic, smiling wryly, knowing that he was impressing me with the summer mansion complex he had built for Athina.

"The main house is up", explained Didier, pointing to the top of the cliff which was barely visible through the mass of floodlit palm trees growing on the slope above us. "134 steps up. Sir, of course I will drive you to the villa," he said. I was not going to argue. The still night air was stifling hot. We went through the entry gate to the car parked outside and then drove round the boundary wall of the property, up a narrow winding tarred road leading to the top of a steep hill. We circled a small plateau, drove past a couple of other large estates before stopping in front of a massive pair of carved wooden doors. They had been brought here I later learned from a medieval monastery. Subdued lights lit the bushes and illuminated the long rough stone whitewashed perimeter walls of the property. Behind the doors was an octagonal tower. We entered the main house through a high-ceilinged hall passing through into a white dining and living area room with glass walls on three sides. In the room was a set of comfortable summer couches, one of which was occupied by a dozing white Labrador with a chewed slipper next to it. There were Mexican hand-carved coffee tables in the room and items of local folk art hung on the walls. Small wooden sculptures stood on a variety of glass shelves.

Didier showed me to my seat at the end of a long bare wooden table. Beyond the glass doors behind the dining area there was a terrace illuminated by a blue grotto-like glow of a rectangular swimming pool. Once again, as at Boislande, there was an almost total absence of sound. Only the gentle patter of servant's rubber-soled shoes and an occasional squeak when they swiveled to close a door quietly behind them interrupted the hush of the surroundings.

I was surprised to see that the members of the staff on-duty at this time were, apart from Didier, black. Three servants in matching white tee shirts and trousers came into the dining room to serve me. The setting brought back memories of my youth in Kenya, on a sugar and sisal plantation we owned on the Nyanza plain near Lake Victoria. After a long day I felt totally relaxed now. A wave of nostalgia engulfed me as I remembered evenings in our estate house in Kenya on a small hill looking out towards Lake Victoria on the horizon. There was the same quiet night atmosphere, the same sound of rubber soles on tiles and on highly polished cement floors. It was as if I was back again on holiday from my British boarding school in Nairobi. I looked up at the same gentle faces of the African servants in Thierry's house, the same faces with the familiar bone structure of other much loved retainers who had been with my family since the days my father was a young man exploring the savannahs and jungles of British and German East Africa. The words spoken in French by the servant brought me suddenly out of my time warp and back to the present – to Ibiza, to La Jondal - to Athina Onassis' holiday mansion.

After dinner Didier drove me back down the hill and dropped me off by the large gate outside the guest house. The ambient heat was stifling. Even though it was nearly midnight the temperature was 42 degrees Centigrade and extremely humid in the manner of the tropics though the air here was pleasantly filled with magnolia scent. I was startled when I approached the guest house to hear a voice call my name from the shadows, it was David Weaver, the head of the English bodyguard detail hired to watch over Athina day and night. I had been with David on several trips. Twice in Greece, and also in Switzerland at Lussy. I took my leave of him and went upstairs, relieved to enter the air-conditioned suite where I took a quick shower and slid into the crisp turquoise sheets of the huge bed. Taking out my pocket tape recorder I started to compose my message to the Greek media in answer to the Papadimitriou statements regarding Athina and the Foundation, but I was too exhausted and within seconds I put the recorder down next to my bed and fell into a deep sleep.

I woke up early the next morning. When I opened the chintz curtains I saw an aquamarine-coloured bay about two hundred metres in front of the house. To the left a pine-covered hill tapered down to what I now recognized as the "dinosaur" rock ridge I had seen from the plane the day before. Several white sailing boats were anchored in the gulf.

I went downstairs and out of the house past a trestle covered by a tangle of jasmine, honeysuckle and wax-flower creepers and walked in the direction of the waterfall which was now strangely silent. A hidden timer had switched off the pump late at night.

I decided to be brave and go by foot up the 134 steps to the main house. There was a landing a few metres up from where a semi-circular couch faced what was the lowest level of a series of shell-shaped swimming pools, set one below the other in the cliff-side. The water ran from one to another as each pool overflowed into the next one, and the next one down the cliff to where the last pool's ledge formed the top of the man-made waterfall.

Further up the stairs I saw a large earthenware pot, turned on its side. This proved to be the source of the water for the cascading pools. The view from this elevation, over the roof of my villa, was spectacular. Several large white mansions had been constructed on the side of the cliff opposite. Out of breath by now, after climbing more steps I passed through an arch and then up a few more steps which led to a large open terrace.

Here I saw the rectangular pool belonging to the main villa, which I recognised from the night before.

A Spanish servant was setting crockery on a round table in front of a semicircular couch covered with oversize Bedouin-style cushions. The servant appeared surprised to see a holiday guest awake so early. He explained to me that breakfast could be taken at any time and that the family would wake up later. I settled onto the cushions. There was a wide selection of cereals, cheeses, croissants and muesli. A set of silver thermos-jugs containing fruit-juices, teas, coffee and milk were filled and ready for the family and their Greek guest. Soon after I heard a shuffle of feet coming up the steps from the lower north annex of the villa where the children were housed.

"Hello, Alexis!" It was Athina followed closely by Erik and a sleepy looking stunningly beautiful Swedish au pair of around 24. "Are you going on the boat with us later?" Athina asked.

"It depends on your mother," I replied, "We haven't spoken yet."

Just then Gaby came into sight, greeted me with a kiss on the cheek and said "Of course he will." Gaby was always the consummate hostess in spite of the enormous strain her personal life had been under with the attacks of Papadimitriou on Thierry, and the accusations that regularly surfaced in the press from the same quarter accusing Thierry of cavorting with other women. Evidence never produced, but sufficiently insidious to harm his reputation. I did wonder though why Gaby would allow such a beautiful blonde au pair to be living in the house around Thierry. As they say in Greece it was enough to tempt even a saint!

The family now gathered at the breakfast table. Gaby's brother Uv and his wife joined us. A close family friend, Bo Jacobssen, an architect working in Geneva and his family arrived with a breezy hello. Last to arrive was Johann, an intense young law student engaged to Gaby's niece Maria, who had brought him with her to Ibiza.

The family spoke Swedish to each other and English to me. I later asked Thierry if he spoke Swedish. He looked at me for a second with an expression of reproach before replying, "No, I am French".

Athina like the other children had an easy command of several languages. I watched the siblings with admiration as they switched from French to English to Swedish and back to English again. In a few years time her love affair with Doda de Miranda, the Brazilian horseman she would marry, encouraged her to learn Portuguese fluently.

Johanna, 6, after diving into the pool for a quick swim wrapped a large towel around herself and joined us at the table. After breakfast we arranged to meet at noon back at the villa from where we walked down a dirt path to the beach where Manuel, the captain of the *Pickwick* was waiting to take us out in the cruiser to a quiet spot to swim. When we got back Gaby asked if I wanted to go into town with one of the drivers to do some sightseeing. I needed to get a press release ready so I had to refuse, but did ask Didier to drive me down to the guest house because 134 steep steps on a full stomach was more than I could handle.

Didier proudly led me to the car pound where I saw that Thierry had more interesting toys than the nondescript and functional VW's usually parked in the front drive at Boislande. Here two Mercedes, a Bentley, a six-wheel Range Rover and several motorcycles stood out from the fleet of staff cars and station wagons in the plot. I made a mental note to ask permission to take a particularly powerful-looking black and chrome Honda motorcycle out for a spin later.

At noon I met Gaby and the children by the main pool of the complex. We spoke about Greece and about the yacht cruise we had taken together to Hydra in July. Erik wanted to know if I had brought the video of him and his dad racing go-carts in Athens. This item had been broadcast on the eight o'clock news in Greece and Erik was dying now to prove to a disbelieving 13 year old Ibiza house guest that he had not been exaggerating when he claimed that he had appeared on Greek television driving a racing cart.

"Erik, I have the video with me!" I replied. He nudged his friend with a smug "I told you so" expression. Erik, Thierry's only son resembled his father in many ways and when I met him some years later saw that he had inherited both the good looks of his father but also his interest in good looking girls. Erik had the manners of an older person and was one of the nicest boys I had ever met. Despite being only 13 he had proved on the last family visit to Greece that he was the consummate diplomat when a television reporter working for a television station with a connection to the Onassis Foundation thought she would get something out of him to embarrass Thierry. During an impromptu interview with Erik while we were having lunch in Tourkolimano the reporter had asked him a heavily charged question on air

"Do you prefer Greece or Spain?"

Erik replied without missing a beat.

«I like *both* Greece and Spain. But Spain a little better because we have a house there. If later we build a house here in Greece I will maybe like it better here".

Thierry and I looked at each other and I winked. The reporter continued.

"Erik" she continued "do you want to learn Greek?"

A trick question. Papadimitriou had used Athina's lack of Greek as a propaganda weapon in the Greek media and in court to attack Thierry, whom he accused of isolating his daughter from her Greek roots. The matter of Athina not learning Greek had an emotional impact on the public in Greece, but also on the courts, who ignored the fact that 3 million Greek children in the US and Australia spoke not a word of their mother tongue, while young Athina, only half Greek, living with a French father and her Swedish stepmother in Switzerland was expected to know a language even her mother Christina did not learn until she was nearly 20 years old. The loaded question had now been put to Erik by the reporter. He looked at her with an expression of deceptive innocence, his blue eyes steadily holding her gaze.

"Greek is a very difficult language, more difficult than French, but I hope to be able to learn it in the future, and to speak it"

Erik had passed his first media test. When the reporter left I said to Thierry

"With Erik to talk to the media in Greece, I don't think you will need me much longer". Thierry laughed and proudly put his arm around his son.

***

"Swimming time!" Gaby announced.

We stood up as a series of crackles and beeps from bodyguards' walkie-talkies cut through the air silencing the cicadas in mid-chirp. I heard Manuel, the *Pickwick's* captain saying that the tender was being sent to the beach since the *Pickwick* was moored offshore. Christina had given the Dickensian protagonist's name to the yacht as a reference to "Mr Pickwick" and "Mrs Pickwick" that she and Thierry called each other when they were alone.

It was stiflingly hot and humid now. We walked down a steep, dusty path, the bodyguards flanking Athina who was walking a few yards in front of Gaby and I. Two more bodyguards brought up our rear. These silent former SAS commandos looked fit in spite of being over fifty. There was little doubt that they were still capable of the occasional physical stunt as one of them had demonstrated by jumping off the mast of our yacht in Greece through a lifesaver floating on the water. When he did this the Greek bodyguards guards came to complain to me that this was unprofessional. If something had gone wrong they said and the English guard had broken an arm or a leg, the whole holiday for the family would have been ruined.

The path ended at a rock and pebble beach where there was a small primitive restaurant and a shack selling pareos, goggles and other beach paraphernalia. Athina, with her teenager's curiosity, went off to the shack to look at some costume jewellery with Sandrine.

The tender was waiting to take us to the *Pickwick*, a cruiser of around forty feet. Manuel had manoeuvred the boat to about two hundred metres offshore. After climbing on board we settled on the open deck from where I could see a cook busily chopping salads in the galley as we chugged off into the open sea to seek a remote bay. After the nearly sterile seas of Greece, I was surprised to see how many fish were in the water round our yacht. The water was a clear turquoise colour, with occasional cobalt patches succeeding one another as we went over deeper stretches of water.

We anchored in about four fathoms of water and spent the next few hours diving over the side of the boat, gossiping and generally messing about, while the children put on goggles and swam underwater occasionally breaking the surface to excitedly comment to us adults on some feature of the sea bottom that looked interesting to them. Athina, tall and willow-like was an accomplished swimmer, like her father, and looked born to the sea as had been her grandfather Ari Onassis.

Gaby who was deeply affected at this time by the kidnap scenarios and the security situation wore her usual permanently worried expression. She was constantly on the lookout, telling a guard from time to time to order the children to come closer to the boat. I had learned a lot about security from the anti-terrorist police in Athens who had kept watch during Athina's trips. As a result I also found myself keeping a discreet eye on her when the rest of the family was swimming. I had received unconfirmed but disconcerting information that some of the domestic staff of Athina, and perhaps two of the bodyguards, were giving information about the family to third parties. Gaby motioned me aside and told me to be careful of what I said in front of one of the guards present because there was some doubt about his loyalty. An intolerable situation I thought when one is paying millions of dollars a year in security. It certainly must have been a strain for Athina and her family to constantly have to watch their words in their own house, on their yacht and in front of the family.

Standing on the rear deck of the *Pickwick* I was looking out to sea towards the island of Formenteira when I suddenly noticed a tattooed frogman carrying a harpoon gun swimming towards us. He had come in from a distance and was silently approaching us on the blind side of the yacht. I called for Athina and the other children to come back onto the boat which they did without asking why. Gaby saw what was happening and sent a bodyguard to tell the frogman to get away from the vicinity of the yacht. He did not hesitate when he saw a row of beefy bodyguards leaning over the rail of the deck motioning for him to move away. The incident ended there.

I was particularly sensitive concerning Athina and Thierry's security because apart from the alarming episode that had taken place recently with the arrested Israeli team there had been other disturbing incidents involving Thierry. One had taken place near the Roussel mansion at La Jondal where we were staying now. Thierry's Swedish friend Bo Jacobssen had gone to the beach one morning. After lunch he put his children, physically resembling the Roussel siblings, into his station-wagon which by further coincidence was almost identical to one of the Roussel cars. Jacobssen drove up the hill in the direction of his villa which was a little beyond that of the Roussel family. Suddenly a car roared past in a cloud of dust, gunning its engine and stopping abruptly in front of the Swede, cutting him off. Another car pulled up inches from the rear bumper of Jacobsson's car. The Swede was alarmed to see several men in black balaclava masks jumping out of the cars and running towards him. One of the masked men opened his door and pulled him out, pushing him violently against the vehicle's door. The assailant pulled off Jacobssen's baseball cap and sun glasses and after a moment of silence shouted to the others, "Merde, it's not Roussel".

The masked men then went back to their waiting cars and disappeared in a cloud of dust and spinning wheels, leaving a much shaken Bo Jacobssen and his startled family at the side of the road, wondering what it had all been about. The authorities were informed and the Roussel family's security was tightened but the people behind this sinister incident were never identified.

Another incident had occurred on Thierry's farm in Portugal when a group of armed and obviously highly-trained men in para-military uniform and masks broke into Thierry's house there, grabbed the maid and interrogated her as to where Thierry was. The terrified woman said he was at the offices on another part of the farm. The men then proceeded to the offices, entered the building and threatened the staff if they did not tell them where Thierry was. Thierry was on another part of the farm but as he approached and saw the masked men who looked like commandos he immediately went and called the police. Thierry told me that when the police arrived they took one look at the armed invaders and refused to do anything, saying that they needed reinforcements. By the time the Portuguese para-militaries arrived the armed men were gone. It was an incident that shook Thierry who did not know who the people could have been or who they may have been working for.

My nervous reaction to the frogman in Ibiza was prompted by what one of the security men I had hired in Greece had told me. "The easiest way to get rid of someone is to have a frogman with scuba gear swim up from under the victim, grab his ankle and drag him down and away. Anyone who looks for the lost swimmer will not have any indication of where to look. It will be over in less than a minute."

From that day Athina, whenever she came to Greece, had at least one scuba diver swimming under her and a couple of strong swimmers in the water for back up. It may sound like something from a James Bond film but for the young Onassis heiress it was part of her life at that time.

Thierry came back to Ibiza on the second day I was there. He drove me into town and to a dock where he was looking at some inflatable boats he had constructed in a new facility in Morocco. Thierry explained that he intended to sell inflatable boats to coast guards and port police around the world. On the way back he made a call to a restaurant and booked a table for three for nine o'clock. I presumed it was for him, Gaby and me. When we arrived back at the villa it was about five in the evening and Thierry went to his private penthouse floor with his own swimming pool at the top of the villa. Gaby was lodged in the children's wing which was one level down the hill from the ground floor of the mansion on Pogorroi bay.

"Would you like to come and play *boules* with us?" asked Athina.

"I don't know how" I replied,

"It's easy" said Erik," I'll show you how! You can be my partner"

I accompanied the children and Gaby to the shaded area at the side of the main house where there was a rolled sand pitch. Erik handed me a patterned steel ball which was surprisingly heavy for its size. I proceeded to spin a coin with the girls to see which couple would go first. There were three teams, Athina and Sandrine, Gaby and little Johanna, and Erik and I. Johanna was given a three metre handicap and rolled the first ball. The game from there proceeded in a happy atmosphere of friendly competition. Erik showed me how to play but was a clearly a little disappointed that I was not a fast learner, my first ball falling way short of the desired mark. After a few rounds little Johanna and Gaby had beaten me and Erik. Athina and Sandrine won and we all congratulated them, but it was time to go back now and get ready since the Jakobsson family was coming for dinner. Their three girls were almost the same age as Athina's siblings and were her best friends. Today one of the Jakobsson girls had a birthday and Athina was putting on a dinner party for her. As the

Roussel house guest I too was invited. We all left to get some rest, have showers and to dress. I had forgotten completely about Thierry's restaurant date.

I went to my room, attended to some messages that had been sent to me. I relaxed, showered and changed and waited until it was time to meet the others for dinner. Thierry was nowhere to be seen as was so often the case but no one seemed to miss him when we all sat down at a long table that had been set out on the north terrace next to the illuminated main swimming pool. As we sat down at the long table Gaby and the rest of us heard peals of laughter and girlish giggles coming from the staircase leading up to the main pool level where we were. Athina, two of the girls and Erik came through the arch, barefoot, holding their shoes in their hands. When the giggles stopped they breathlessly told us that they had gone to dance in the "secret discotheque" located behind the waterfall in front of the guest house and that their shoes had got stuck to the dance floor. What they did not know when they had gone there to dance to a new cassette one of the Jakobsson girls had brought for Athina was that two members of the villa maintenance staff had painted the floor with thick black paint that afternoon and the paint had not dried when Athina and her friends unsuspectingly went onto the wet dance floor of the discotheque.

Uv and Marie's fiancé had left that day for Sweden, so Erik and I were the only males among a swarm of women and girls. Present were Gaby, Athina, Sandrine, Johanna, the three blonde Jakobsson sisters, their mother, UV's fiancée Marie and the Swedish babysitter. It was a very hot summer night, completely airless and humid with the heavy scent of jasmine in the atmosphere. Above us, despite the humidity, there was a clear sky filled with thousands of stars while the candles on the table and the wavelike blue reflection of the illuminated pool danced on the villa walls near us. It was a happy evening, Athina was sitting directly opposite me at the long table and I could see she was in a cheerful mood. Presents were brought and it was a moment of delight to see the childish curiosity of Athina who turned and looked to see what each present contained as her friend sitting next to her excitedly opened the small packages. It was a moment of pure innocence and I relished it, seeing Athina, around who bitter public battles were taking place, excited like any child at the opening of each new present given to her good friend. I wondered how long this innocence would last knowing that it was only a matter of time before she would be forced to look people in the eye to see what they wanted of her. That day would come soon, and not always with the clarity of perspective that would allow the motives, good and bad, of others to be distinguished by the heiress.

Five French chefs worked for the Roussels and they were all here at La Jondal today. Thierry soon after, in order to economise, fired them all, something that made Gaby put her foot down. She would NOT become a kitchen slave for Thierry, she said and so Thierry kept on one of the chefs at Lussy for her. A cake with candles and lit sparklers was presented and the birthday girl extinguished the candles amid much puffing and laughter as we all sang "**Happy Birthday to you!**" Dinner was then served by the African staff Thierry had brought from his Kilifi seaside estate on the Kenya coast. When the waiter came round for second helpings I said to him quietly "*Nataka viazei tu*" which in Swahili means "I only want potatoes". For a moment the servant did not react but when he realised that someone at the table had spoken his native language he looked around startled at all the white faces, unable to fit the Swahili to a guest. I repeated my request, telling him I had grown up in Kenya, and he seemed more than pleased and was exceptionally attentive to me for the rest of the evening.

Looking round I noticed that Athina and I were the only two brown haired and olive skinned people amid what seemed like a sea of blonde-haired, Nordic white-skinned dinner guests. "Athina," I said, leaning forward so that the others would not hear me, 'We are the only two Greeks here!" She immediately broke out into a wide grin with a sparkle in her fawn-like light brown eyes, clearly agreeing with me. And so it was. The only surviving member of the fabled Greek Onassis dynasty and her press representative and friend were in Spain, at a dinner surrounded by family, friends, and dozens of staff, at a celebration in a magical softly illuminated hillside mansion complex. We had a bond between us that she did not share with anyone else there that evening. I thought back to the times that I had sat near her grandfather Aristotle in the Grande Bretagne Hotel bar and in nightclubs when he was at the next table and wondered how he would have reacted if he knew that the 25 year-old near him would one day become deeply involved with his granddaughter's family and would be the only person in Greece that she and her father would call their friend while the huge battle for control of her fortune and her upbringing ebbed and surged.

At around 11 Thierry cheerfully showed up wearing a slim fit black shirt, a black belt with a silver buckle and silver studs all round and black narrow trousers. The image of the tall slim blond man in black would have taken many a young woman's breath away and Thierry knew he was making a grand entrance now. Despite being 45, married twice with a brood of children and immersed to his ears in international corporate financial issues he was dressed like, and looked the playboy that he was. He had eaten he said and asked Gaby and me to sit with him at a wide semicircular couch under a thatch umbrella. We put our legs up on the canvas cushions of the couch and ordered alcoholic drinks, relaxing finally after what had been for Athina, Thierry, Gaby and me one of the most stressful years of our lives as the battle with Papadimitriou and the Onassis Foundation had gone into high gear with important court cases coming up in Greece and in Switzerland. As we wound down under the moonless starry Ibiza sky, with Pogorroi Bay with its pinpricks of lights coming from mast lights of sailing yachts anchored in the bay, Thierry said "Now you know what I meant when I said come and see how we live away from the media, Alexis."

It was indeed a magical moment. Watching Athina and her teenage friends absorbed in a cheerful conversation, gathered in a circle as they sat on the Spanish handmade terracotta tiles by a large geranium-filled urn next to the illuminated pool I had to agree that life for Athina and her family here in this mansion hideaway with its eight cascading swimming pools, secret discotheque, waterfall and African palm forest was as close to a private paradise as I had ever seen. I had yet to stay on Scorpios but that would come later, in November, when Athina, Thierry and I would go to the island for the memorial service for the tenth anniversary of Christina Onassis's death.

Onassis' surviving child, Christina, headstrong and as stubborn as her father, had strained her relationship with her millionaire parent. Ari was a traditional Greek in respect to his daughter and had fixed ideas about how she should act. He felt also that he should have a say over whom she should marry. Christina defied him on both counts, becoming something of a wild child. Her rebellious stance was explained in part as a reaction to the constant absences of her father from whichever of the Onassis homes Christina was staying at. Christina was at some stage sent to exclusive private boarding schools, something encouraged by her mother Tina Livanos, who showed an unnatural lack of parental love for her children. There were persistent reports that Tina, a well-known society beauty, could not stand to be around Christina because she considered her daughter ugly. This undoubtedly was felt by the child. During her holidays Christina was looked after by a maidservant and it was during these years that the loneliness that was to plague her throughout her life took root in her psyche.

Christina's relationship with her mother was not her only problem. She soon found that though she was born into a family of extreme wealth and privilege, she herself was secondary to her father's business and amatory pursuits. Onassis was unable to give her the time and attention that ordinary children demanded, expected, and received from their parents. Christina's behaviour as a result of this situation became erratic, often annoying both her father and her brother Alexander.

Ari was not happy with how his domestic situation was turning out. He became livid when his daughter married James Bolker, a grey-haired real estate entrepreneur from Los Angeles to spite him. Onassis managed to come to an understanding with his daughter after she divorced the American. As a result of the rapprochement she went to work in the offices of the Onassis group in Athens on Othonos Street.

Now that Alexander was dead, Ari had no choice but to look to Christina to run the empire after he was gone. He had hoped for many years that she would secure the future and the management of the Onassis fortune by marrying Peter Goulandris, the scion of an old Greek shipping family, but the desired match was not to be. Ari made other efforts at matchmaking for his daughter.

One day a friend of Onassis from Paris was visiting Scorpios on his yacht. It was Henri Roussel, the dapper and aristocratic co-owner of the Roussel pharmaceutical multinational. Roussel owned a magnificent chateau in Bonneville in France, farms in Nanyuki near Mount Kenya, properties on the Costa del Sol, Kilifi in Kenya and in Ibiza, and was a frequent visitor to Scorpios where women and yachts were a staple of his conversations with Onassis. On this particular trip he had brought with him his good looking nineteen year-old son, Thierry.

Onassis looked on approvingly as his daughter Christina and Thierry spent time together on the island. The youngsters showed more than a casual interest in each other as they wandered off in a white Mini-Moke to swim on the deserted coves of Scorpios and to take out the water-ski boats which Thierry, addicted from an early age to speed, drove at a hell-bent pace, skimming over the wave crests around the island. One afternoon, Christina, while sitting at her father's side on the terrace of the Pink House, admitted to Onassis that she was hopelessly in love with the young Frenchman.

"Thierry, I heard that you had an affair with Christina on Scorpios years before you married her. Why did you break up with her?" I asked one day when the two of us were sitting in a deserted upstairs court room in Athens during a terrorist bomb alert after the building had been evacuated.

"We were on Scorpios one afternoon when Aristotle asked me to join him for an ouzo at the Pink House," Thierry explained. "Christina was out in the garden and I thought that Onassis just wanted some male company."

"'Thierry,'" Onassis said to me, "I have known you and your father for a long time and I would like our families to be closer." I did not immediately understand, but he was a direct man and came to the point without delay. 'I like you and I think you would be a good husband for my daughter.' I was stunned by the proposal. Christina and I had just started something, but marriage was not in my plans."

"What did you do?" I asked Thierry.

"Onassis was a persuasive man but I was enjoying my freedom too much at that age, so I told him I thought that his daughter was very nice, that I respected her, and Aristotle also, but I was too young still to think of marriage and a family."

""Think about it. I shall talk to your father," Onassis said before going out of the room. Moments later my father came in looking very unhappy. I realised then that Aristotle and he had planned the whole thing from the beginning."

I knew that Thierry at that time was the toast of the young international jet set and in great demand by beautiful women and ambitious girls. He did not want to be tied down. Thierry bolted from Scorpios and the homely Greek heiress like a startled rabbit.

Ari Onassis, used to having his way, was disappointed, but there was little he could do. In young Roussel he had seen a change from the stream of hopefuls waiting to marry into the Onassis family to strike gold. For Thierry though there was just too much going on, and he would only marry for love at that stage. Onassis had stepped in too quickly.

Scorpios was a playground for the Onassis family and their friends. In Ari's time it was a jet-set stop for Rudolph Nureyev, the Kennedy family, Greta Garbo, Maria Callas and various well-known politicians and heads of state. When Christina took over the excesses of her partying were second only to her legendary hospitality when she sent her Lear jet to bring her friends and acquaintances to wherever she was. She often ordered her pilots to pick up delicacies unavailable in Greece to bring back to Scorpios. The one thing she would not tolerate was to walk in and find a maid in her bedroom or in one of the cabanas on East Beach. The servant would be promptly fired.

The island became a party haven shared by her husbands, lovers and hangers on when the heiress was there. Every whim was catered for by forty staff members and her managers. Once hearing the phrase "If Pigs could fly" from one of her guests she immediately called her pilot and demanded that he arrange for a pig to be fitted with a parachute and released from the family helicopter over Scorpios. The pilot used to Christina's notoriously erratic behaviour acquiesced. A pig was taken from the Scorpios farm enclosure, fitted with a parachute at the heliport on the top of the island behind the Forest House and hoisted on board with much squealing. Christina, beaming, watched as the helicopter lifted off and hovered above until a signal was given from the ground to let the pig "fly". An assortment of her friends and some bemused local Greek Scorpios staff not familiar with British nursery rhymes watched as a large pink bundle was pushed out of the plane. The parachute failed to open properly and the unfortunate animal sped towards the ground where it landed with a resounding *splat*. The Onassis heiress question as to whether pigs could fly had been answered.

It was a swelteringly hot day in July of 1998. Thierry, Athina, I and Athina's aunt Marilena had dodged into a café in an arcade to avoid several TV crews which had blocked off the pavement of Ermou St, the main shopping thoroughfare of Athens, just off Constitution Square.

While we sat at a small table we kept our eyes on a wall clock, counting the minutes as they dragged by. We had an important appointment coming up. Athina, dressed in a white silk dress and a grey jacket, was sitting next to me with Thierry on her other side, while Marilena sat opposite us.

The customers in the café had started turning their heads recognizing our party from our appearances on prime time news during the previous two days. The bodyguards were busy in the café now, firmly intercepting well-wishers and the curious who wanted to come to our table.

The atmosphere was tense as the minute hand of the wall clock inched towards the twelve o'clock mark. Thierry was telling Athina to relax, but to no avail. She was understandably awed and I could see that she was nervous. It was difficult for her at that moment to understand the welcome she would receive from the head of the Orthodox Church of Greece and was understandably apprehensive since this was the first time she had ever met a person like Archbishop Christodoulos. I saw her momentarily fight back tears welling up in her large, deer-like brown eyes, but she became calm again when her father stroked her shoulder to reassure her.

At exactly two minutes to twelve I nodded to Thierry and we got up. We made our way back into the bright sunshine of Ermou Street. Our guards and the policemen on duty outside cleared a path for us to walk along Ayias Filotheis alley to the neoclassical building next to the Athens Cathedral where His Beatitude Archbishop Christodoulos (translation -Servant of the Lord) of Athens and All of Greece, had his offices.

When Athina was born Thierry and Christina had decided that Athina should be christened into the Orthodox faith of her mother. The christening took place on Scorpios, and was presided over by Father Apostolis, the local priest whom Onassis had always invited to carry out family ceremonies. George Livanos, Christina's uncle was the godfather at a ceremony attended by the whole family. After Christina's sudden death Athina moved to Thierry's house to be with her half-brother Erik, her half-sister Sandrine, and Gaby. The religious situation in the Roussel household was one of tolerance and piety, with the family praying every night. When the children were at an age where they could understand scripture tales, they attended church lessons in Lausanne. The Roussel family was an interesting mix of faiths. Gaby, Erik, Sandrine and Johanna were Episcopalian Protestant, Thierry was a laid-back Catholic and Athina was Greek Orthodox. Despite this the family had no difficulty in matters of faith. Thierry had made a promise to respect Christina's wish regarding Athina's religion and so the time came in 1988 when Athina was fourteen he told me of his plans for her. He said that she was growing up now and day-by-day was enquiring about her Onassis family history. She had questions about the Greek faith also, and Thierry asked me my opinion as to whom she should see in Greece to talk to her about these matters. There was one person whom I considered ideally suited for this. The newly elected Archbishop Christodoulos of Athens and the Whole of Greece and it was the right time. Three months earlier Archbishop Seraphim, the former head of the mainland Greek Church had died, well into his eighties. He had been a man of little culture, speaking in a strong peasant vernacular, had rough manners and to many Greeks was a living relic of a divisive and troubled past. He had been accused of consorting with the colonels of the Greek junta when only a few yards away young Greek men and women were suffering physical torture and moral debasement in the dank cells of the military police. Seraphim, though controversial, had staunch supporters and was a master politician, managing to survive in his position until he died in 1998. He was replaced by a rising star of the Church, Christodoulos who was highly educated, spoke several languages and had a shrewd understanding that in the new millennium the master of the game would be he who understood and used the media.

Archbishop Christodoulos, a little over fifty at the time when we were to meet him had an expression that made one think he was bearing all the worries of the world on his shoulders. His eyes bore an uncanny resemblance to those of the late, great actor Dirk Bogarde, with that sad, knowing quality that said, "I have seen it all before". Christodoulos could light up in mirth in a second, transforming himself into a ho-ho-ho Santa

Claus-like figure. He was adored by children and the younger generation in Greece who found him "cool" and direct in his manner. He spoke also with Bogarde's polished actor's delivery when making speeches of importance.

The majority of the Greek public, with the notable exception of some leftist Greek politicians, immediately fell in love with him and churches very soon could have put up "Full House" signs wherever the Archbishop went. The young, traditionally indifferent to matters of religion, soon took to the priest with his straight talk and wise advice, sending him numerous invitations to come to their schools or even to share a drink with them at their school parties. Christodoulos did not disappoint them. Within three months of being elected he topped all the opinion polls in Greece as the country's most popular figure. He was a man who understood teenagers and so I sent him a letter asking if he would see Athina and her father. I requested that he bless her, since she belonged to a family with a long history of tragedy and pain.

Two days later I received a phone call from the Archbishop's office granting my request. We set the date for the meeting for July 7th. We further agreed that since cameras followed the Archbishop everywhere, as they did Athina, there should not be a leak to the press. We decided to allow only one TV crew and a photographer to attend the first moments of their meeting. Word inevitably leaked out and I was deluged by reporters. I denied any meeting had been arranged. A Greek newspaper "Typos tou Mitsi" wrote a strong article attacking the Archbishop, telling him not to fall in with Roussel's plans to "squander Athina's fortune". It sounded once again like Papadimitriou himself talking. I wondered whether the Archbishop would go ahead with the meeting now that he was being threatened with being dragged into a very highly charged controversy. Christodoulos ignored the paper and was at that moment waiting for us upstairs at the Church of Greece headquarters.

As we progressed down the alley towards the Metropolis cathedral I was relieved to see only a handful of journalists. I was surprised at the relative quiet as we wound our way through the noon shoppers. At the Archbishop's headquarters we were met by a priest in the Orthodox traditional black cassock and stove-pipe hat. He motioned for us to follow him up the steep marble steps into the Church headquarters building. Athina nervously hung onto her father's sleeve as we entered the gloom of a large high-ceilinged hall. Suddenly there was a blinding barrage of flashlights and a noisy rush of more than thirty paparazzi towards us. In a second or two we were engulfed. They were next to us, pushing, pulling, shouting "Athina", "Athina", as they tugged at our sleeves. I was locked into a scrum and carried forward up the steep stairs leading to the upper level where the Archbishop was waiting for us.

I was squeezed against the wall by a wedge of reporters and cut off from Thierry and a bewildered Athina who kept looking round to see where I was. Reaching the landing a large door opened and our disheveled party went inside.

Before entering the building Thierry had asked me what the correct protocol was for greeting the Archbishop. I explained that Athina should follow Orthodox tradition and kiss his hand, while Thierry as a

Catholic was not expected to do so. Thierry had not seen the Archbishop so he was not aware what he looked like. In the confusion of our entry to the upper floor, Thierry took the hand of a young priest by the door and bent to kiss it. The priest, surprised and flattered, did not react.

A bald paparazzo from Ethnos, wearing a black and white candy stripe suit forced himself ahead of me, holding me back as two young priests by the doors pushed them shut, leaving me outside in the seething mass of excited cameramen and journalists. A furious banging on the door by me caused the priests inside to open it a chink, and when they saw who it was, they allowed me through, pushing back the reporters who tried to enter with me. It was absolute pandemonium.

A smiling Archbishop Christodoulos was waiting to receive us by the door. Athina bent to kiss his hand but he withdrew it and kissed her on both cheeks in a warm welcome. Thierry likewise bent forward, but again the Archbishop withdrew his hand, not allowing Thierry to be in a position of homage that the hand-kissing symbolized. Instead he greeted Thierry warmly with a traditional kiss on both cheeks. As the massive wooden door shut behind me I looked up to see a flushed Thierry and Athina looking at me. The bodyguards were straightening their jackets and ties while along the opposite wall of the large red-carpeted reception room stood a row of black-cassocked bearded Orthodox priests. Athina was somewhat bewildered by the medieval atmosphere of the moment. One of the priests, a kindly man with jolly eyes, understanding her fears stepped forward slowly, so as not to startle her and said

"Athina, don't let our appearance worry you. We are good people!"

He turned to me and said in Greek "Dressed like this we must look somber and frightening to the little lady". It was in part true. The priests proved to be very civilized and discreet and tried to put Onassis' granddaughter at ease, asking her and her father questions in English and in French. It was obvious that they were impressed by the young teenager who carried the Onassis legend on her slim shoulders.

Thierry had asked that the meeting with the Archbishop be in private - just the Archbishop, he and Athina were to be present as there were family matters to be discussed. Marilena Patronikola, Athina's aunt and I therefore waited in the Archbishop's antechamber while Christodoulos spoke with the Roussels.

The meeting was expected to last for no more than fifteen minutes. Twenty minutes passed, then a further fifteen minutes, and another fifteen minutes. Marilena and I wondered what was being said by the Archbishop to father and daughter. Meanwhile, outside, delegations from all over Greece and one from Australia had arrived and were waiting for their own audience with the Archbishop.

The silence in the room where we were sitting under the gaze of the fifteen or so standing priests was broken every few minutes with the ringing of a mobile phone, followed by a rustling of robes as the priest in question dug into his cassock pockets to locate the ringing phone. I tried to stifle a laugh when one phone started chiming to the tune of "Auld Lang Syne".

At a quarter past one the door to the Archbishop's office opened and Marilena and I were invited to go in. The Archbishop asked us to sit opposite him at his desk next to Thierry and Athina. We talked for a few minutes, and by this time it was obvious that Athina had been surprised that the Archbishop was so friendly and that he spoke good French as Thierry later confirmed. Christodoulos told us that when he was a schoolboy he had attended the Leontios School, an exclusive educational establishment run by French Catholic priests. We sat for a few more minutes and then the personal photographer of the Archbishop, Christos Bonis, was called in to take our photos.

All this time we could hear the muffled shuffling of chairs and a lot of whispering from the ante room. The priests at the door had allowed the paparazzi to enter the room in preparation for a photo shoot of Athina with the Archbishop. Christodoulos' assistants had now wisely put up a dividing rope to keep the photographers at a secure distance in the room. A photo session lasted for five minutes with the Archbishop standing next to Thierry and Athina. For Thierry's enemies it was a clear message that the Orthodox Church had its doors open for Athina, but for Thierry too. From the Onassis Foundation there was, as expected, public criticism about the meeting. The meeting had touched on several matters related to Athina. Archbishop Christodoulos discussed Christina and Aristotle with her, and told her that whenever Athina wanted she could contact him. If she wanted to see an Orthodox priest in Lausanne he would arrange it for her, but there was no pressure of any sort and she should know this.

I did not have a chance to talk to Thierry until that afternoon when I joined him on the motor sailer, the *Ariadne*, anchored about half a mile offshore at Lagonissi opposite Aunt Kalliroi's villa which the Roussels were using as a base for their Greek holiday.

Thierry had already made himself at home sitting on the curved settee on the covered rear deck of the yacht. He was relaxing, smoking a cigarette, but I could see he was waiting to tell me of his impressions of the meeting with the Archbishop. We did not have much time for this because I had found the opportunity to arrange two important interviews in the next half an hour.

Thierry was not in the mood to talk to journalists but I had felt very strongly that this was an important opportunity to let his side of the dispute be known, so he accepted with a shrug and a sigh of feigned suffering. Roussel trusted my judgment after seeing the change in public opinion and in the media since I had started to work for him.

"The *pope* gave me his mobile phone number!" said Thierry, astonished that a high ranking cleric would have this electronic toy among his paraphernalia.

"I told you he was modern, Thierry. What about Athina?" I asked.

"She was very worried when we went there before she saw him. But he spoke well to her and besides he speaks good French. We talked about the family and other things. Athina though cried on the way back – the strain and anticipation of the meeting was too much for her. But we made a friend, I think, and that is important."

The two of us sat in silence for a while. It was obvious that the meeting had in certain ways which were not yet obvious changed Thierry and Athina. I knew it was for the best, but as so often happens, the importance of pivotal events often dawns last on those who are closest and most affected beneficially by them.

A woman's shout from the side of the boat and the purring of an outboard motor indicated that the first journalist had arrived at the yacht. In the yacht tender, hanging onto her soundman was Angeliki Kourouni, the reporter from Tribune De Geneve and young Stefanos Dianellos, a well-mannered columnist from "Ta NEA", an influential Athens paper.

Oblivious to the people around her Angeliki Kourouni was screaming as the tender pitched in the water. It took a good five minutes and much protesting by her to get her up the ladder and onto the yacht.

"I hate boats!" she announced loudly and demanded to go downstairs into the main lounge where she would not see the sea. Thierry, I, and her soundman, a silent and gaunt looking Swiss national sat down at a table where the sounds of the sea were muffled by the plate glass windows and the thick blue wall-to-wall carpeting.

Ms Kourouni had not been a particularly supportive journalist but she represented an important group of radio and television stations in Europe as well as the main Geneva paper. It was for this reason that I invited her to interview Thierry. It was a calculated risk but I hoped the benefits of the meeting would outweigh the risks.

Kourouni made it plain immediately that she was not there to write pleasant things about Roussel – she wanted a story, and she was not going to show any appreciation for the foreign press exclusive interview we had granted her. In fact the whole scene was difficult.

After the urbane and usually well-groomed girls who covered the Onassis family saga, the appearance of this journalist was a shock to us. She had short, brightly-coloured magenta hair in a wild perm, a faded outsize sweater with what appeared to be a tear in one sleeve and the rest of her outfit consisted of baggy cotton clothes of a different print. The interview was not helped by the fact that her silent and gaunt assistant kept twiddling his thumbs while she unsuccessfully played with knobs on her tape recorder, lifting her eyebrows to indicate to him that it wasn't working, while all the time firing off questions, one after another at Thierry. When I asked what was wrong she told me that she had come back from Kosovo three days before, where an Albanian Liberation Army bullet aimed at her had struck the tape recorder. She had survived, but the recorder now needed assistance since the "play" and "record" buttons would not stay down when pressed. She hissed at her silent sound man to put his thumbs on the two buttons.

For the next hour and a half he kept them there as Thierry unwound with his side of the dispute and spoke of Athina, Christina and Papadimitriou. Not once did Ms Kourouni smile. It was obvious that from the front lines of a civil war in Yugoslavia to go straight onboard a 43 metre sailing schooner and report on the problems of the rich would have been a provocation to any war correspondent's sense of social justice. Kourouni though seemed supremely professional and I told Thierry that we would have to wait and see what she would write in the Tribune de Geneve. Above all we did not want the visit to the Archbishop to be dragged into the overall dispute.

Two days later the Tribune de Geneve had a front page story on Athina Onassis-Roussel and how she had appeared in front of the head of the Orthodox Church in a provocatively short white miniskirt. Later when the pictures for the visit were published, they showed Athina, clad in a modest white dress that came way down past her calves, and a long jacket. Once again Athina had been victimized by the press in Switzerland.

Contrarily in Greece the press fawned now on Athina. Full page photographs of Onassis' granddaughter appeared in many papers and there were pages of glowing reports in most magazines. That evening the main item on all the Greek TV news stations was the meeting of the Onassis descendant with the head of the Orthodox Church of Greece. There was not one press word in discord. The Tribune de Geneve stood alone in its criticism of a 14 year-old girl who had gone to see her religious mentor.

Two weeks later, when I finally managed to trace Ms Kourouni on her crackling mobile, I understood that she was at the grisly scene of a new Balkan outrage. She explained that she had sent the article by fax to Switzerland and that it had been edited by a new reporter who added the miniskirt jibe without her knowledge. It may have been so.

My last thought was for Ms Kourouni's sullen, hollow-checked soundman who no doubt at that moment was a few feet away from her, with thumbs still glued to the "play" and "record" buttons of the tape recorder while sniper rounds from angry UCK militia combatants sorting out centuries of hatred kicked up little spurts of dust around him. It is a sad fact of life, and one that shames us all, that the readers of the

Tribune de Geneve, to whom the soundman was valiantly offering his technical services, would first read what young Athina Onassis was wearing on the motor sailer "Ariadne" and only afterwards read how many people had died that day in Pristina's outskirts.

During the internationally reported press conference given by the presidency of the Onassis Foundation in October of 1997 when the kidnapping story broke Stelios Papadimitriou launched a virulent attack on Athina's father. For these defamatory statements the Greek civil courts awarded damages to Thierry against the President of the Onassis Foundation and his three collaborators. The court also passed a restraining order on Papadimitriou forbidding him from continuing his abusive statements on pain of paying a heavy fine for each violation.

One of the things that had disturbed Papadimitriou and the others was that Thierry had requested that the 5 man managing board of Athina's patrimony be replaced by the Swiss courts by an independent administrator of the court's choosing. This served a double purpose. First, Thierry would no longer be accused of having a personal motive to govern the patrimony if he was free of the responsibility of being a manager of Athina's money. Second, it would mean that the conflicts regarding management decisions between the Four and Thierry would stop and Athina and the Roussel family would enjoy the peace which had been denied them for so long by the constant public criticism of their family life by Papadimitriou.

That evening in March of 1998 when it seemed that half the country was glued to their TV screens to watch the rare appearance in Greece of the reclusive teenage granddaughter of Aristotle Onassis the Intercontinental Hotel where we were staying was under a tight security cordon. Hotel security had roped off the press corps at the entrance of the large lobby downstairs. Greek government anti-terrorist agents were in the lifts while the former SAS commandos who were accompanying the Roussel family were stationed in the corridor outside our rooms. These measures were considered necessary because the situation with the arrested Israeli agents and the suspicions of a plan to kidnap and kill Athina was still unfolding. Things were very tense at the hotel. Athina was terrified and her parents were uneasy. Around us phones were ringing. The hotel staff, ordered to say nothing to the press or to the other guests concerning the presence of the Onassis heiress, was screening incoming calls before passing them to me. I received a telephone call in my room on the eighth floor where I and the family were staying. The call was from Alexia Koulouri, the red-haired TV journalist from Sky.

"What is it, Alexia?" I asked, ready to tell her for the tenth time that she could not come up with her TV crew and interview the family.

"There is a woman here in the lobby who lived on the yacht "Christina" and also on Scorpios. She says she has some information for you, something important."

Thierry had his defamation case coming up in two weeks so I decided to check it out. Under the present circumstances no potential lead could be ignored.

I went downstairs into the cavernous atrium lobby of the Intercontinental and met Alexia. She led me to a corner of the lounge where a pale, square-jawed woman of about sixty in a burgundy dress and a gold embroidered shawl was waiting, a heavy green file under her arm.

She introduced herself as Marianna Darousou, explaining that her husband had been a first engineer aboard the "Christina". He had worked for years for Papadimitriou and for Springfield SA, the Onassis shipping subsidiary company.

"I divorced my husband many years ago, Mr. Mantheakis, and was outraged the other day when I heard Papadimitriou call Mr. Roussel an unfit father. That is why I came here, to show you what sort of people Papadimitriou has working for him, what sort of people he has put in charge of Athina's island."

She explained that her former husband, Stefanos Darousos, who had been a trusted staff member of Onassis, was now in charge of Scorpios and was a trustee of Papadimitriou. I vaguely remembered the name of Darousos from a critical interview he had given about Athina regarding her first visit to Scorpios some years ago in the Greek magazine "Status". He had also spoken unflatteringly in an interview in "Vanity Fair". Unfortunately the four Greeks had allowed Scorpios staff and servants paid for by Athina to give disparaging interviews about both their employer Athina and her father.

"Look at these photos," the woman said. "Here is Darousos with Jackie and Onassis driving them to the chapel on Scorpios for their wedding. Here he is on the "Christina", "here he is with Lee Radziwill." The woman had a whole sheaf of photocopies of newspaper articles featuring her former husband with the Onassis and Kennedy families.

"What does this have to do with Mr. Roussel?" I asked.

She looked at me for a long moment. "Darousos behaved abominably towards me and our daughter. I presented all the evidence in our divorce case. He should never be allowed near Athina. Further, he hated Onassis and his son Alexander. "

I realised now that I had unwittingly stepped into another dispute. Here was a woman scorned looking for revenge. I sensed that the bitterness of this woman against her former husband may be more than the even the well-known enmity of Stelios Papadimitriou for Athina's father. I thanked her for her concern and started to walk away because I suddenly remembered we were due for dinner in less than an hour at Onassis' sister Kalliroi Patronikola' s apartment.

"My husband is the right hand man of Papadimitriou on Scorpios," she said, "I have been told by my relatives in Nydri that he is also in charge of the island and its finances."

There was no stopping her, but I felt that she was being completely honest.

"Darousos is an enemy of the Onassis family and yet he is there, giving interviews to the press about little Athina and her father".

I thanked her for her interest and tried once again to leave, aware of the crowd of television reporters who had focused their cameras on us across the fifty metre marble lobby of the hotel. The woman tugged at my sleeve, not letting go. I felt like the wedding guest in the "Ancient Mariner".

"Look at this here," she said, giving me a letter with official court stamps on it. "Read it and see who it was Papadimitriou sent to welcome little Athina to Scorpios, and what sort of man Onassis trusted."

She was very insistent and I gave in. I sat down on the arm of a couch to read the letter and then read another one she pushed into my hand. The dates on them were twenty and thirty years old. I shuddered to think what words had been exchanged over three decades if her passion against Darousos was still so strong.

«My Dear Marianna,
I am writing to let you know what happened here in Athens. He (Onassis) flew up in a vile temper and shouted at everyone. The man is a boor, a pig. Minutes later he calmed down and ruffled my hair in a friendly way, to show that there were no hard feelings. I despise him."

The letter had my attention and I read on –

"The young one (Alexander Onassis) asked me to take him to the airport. He drove so fast that I was furious and told him to go alone the next time. The asshole, the spoiled brat. "

I was Coleridge's captive wedding guest. I continued reading.

"I was with "auntie" (Onassis' wife Tina, mother of Christina and Alexander) I despise her, I would like to spit on her".

I was stunned. Onassis had trusted Darousos with his family and his property when he was alive.

Marianna told me Onassis had also made special mention and provided for Darousos in his will, yet Papadimitriou had kept this man on and later sent him to receive Athina and her family four years previously when the family had last come to visit Scorpios.

"There is more," Marianna Darousos said, her face taking on a gentle flush of satisfaction as she saw me reach out for the file. I wondered how many humiliations this woman had been through and how many years of bitterness had made her come to the hotel, possibly to protect Athina, and certainly to exact cold revenge on those who had spurned her.

I looked at the second letter.

"July 1964 – at Sea. Port Said

My darling Marianna,

I miss you terribly, and I want you to know how I am spending my time.

Last night I and P. waited until 2 p.m. when the captain and the others were asleep. The operation then began. I took all the necessary equipment, hoods, gloves, a torch, a crow bar and we made our way to number 4 hold. The two of us opened case after case and how lucky we were. Beautiful fabrics of silk. I took a whole roll of wonderful mauve cloth, and other items. I put them in a large bag and hid them in the cabin. Tomorrow we will go down for another raid - looking for whisky."

Marianna was looking at me with a raised eyebrow. Her I-told-you-so triumph was complete.

"Are these genuine?" I asked.

"As you can see, "she replied, "They are handwritten. I deposited them with the courts during my divorce. This is the man I was married to, and these are the people Papadimitriou uses to look after Athina and her property."

Papadimitriou often spoke of being one of the "trusted lieutenants of Onassis". It was obvious now that not everyone trusted by Onassis had respected and honoured that trust. I thanked Marianna Darousos, gave her my phone number and went back upstairs. Thierry in the meantime had been trying desperately to locate me since I was in charge of the transport and security arrangements and for getting us to dinner at Aunt Kalliroi's flat and they had lost contact with me.

Marianna Darousos proved to be a reliable, methodical, and trustworthy source of information over the next several months.

She phoned me a week later and told me that Darousos was the fifth member in charge of Athina's property that he was in fact very high up in the management hierarchy of the patrimony administrative ladder headed by Papadimitriou and the other three trustees. I found it difficult to believe that an Onassis yacht crew member was being used in such a position of responsibility by those appointed in Christina's will to manage her daughter's assets.

Over the next year Marianna Darousos' health waned and she became more withdrawn, resigned to living on the sidelines of her family's life. She told me that her daughters had turned against her after she showed her support for Athina and Thierry. Her information about Scorpios and Darousos though was right – he was later proved to be in fact a "fifth administrator" of the hundred and fifty million dollar property that was Scorpios with its five luxury villas, power generating and desalination plant, dairy farm, docks, church and servants quarters. Confirmation of Darousos' involvement with the island and its management came to light from an unexpected quarter.

When Ioannides refused the Roussel family request for me to visit the island in preparation for a visit of the family for Athina's attendance at Christina's tenth year memorial service, a big scandal broke out in the Greek media. The Foundation members attacked me personally, disputing my official role with the Roussels as well as disputing Thierry's signature on the letter of authorization I carried. I conferred with Thierry and told him I would investigate the Scorpios company records. It took no more than two days to find incredible facts in the books. First of all Darousos was on the board of directors of Scorpios and was authorized, with the signature of any other member, to take management decisions. The board of directors consisted of the following –

> Chairman - Paul Ioannides
> Vice Chairman - Captain Athanasiades
> Member - **Stefanos Darousos**

Member -Ioannis Ioannides (Paul Ioannides's son)

Another member.

Neither Athina's father, nor any Onassis relative, nor a member of the Swiss Juvenile authority had been placed on the board of the company by Stelios Papadimitriou and his three associates.

I discovered that on several recent occasions there had been unexplained changes in the published statutes of the company. Strangest of all was the fact that Ioannides and the board had passed a resolution saying that *"the shareholder (Athina) will have no right in the future to question any decisions or actions taken by the board of directors."* This was an unusual way to protect Athina's interests. It meant that neither Athina nor her father, as long as she was still a minor, could veto or question the management of her island, even if potentially damaging, but legal, decisions were taken or personal use made by the Greek administrators of the island as a place to entertain and feed their guests or the media, something that happened several times without the prior knowledge or the approval of the owners. Obviously any board resolution limiting an owner's rights over his own property must be invalid, and even more so when this is taken by the administrators of a minor's estate, administrators who later illegally voted to exclude Athina's father from the board meetings of her patrimony. It should not have surprised us then when some years later the Onassis Foundation board took a decision to change, in violation of the statutes of the Foundation, the article which referred to the Onassis descendant's right to be Foundation President without the need of election.

Even more strange was the fact that a special resolution was passed saying that the Scorpios company was no longer a real estate company but a company authorized to carry out commercial ventures. More unusual for us was the phrase "the company may open shops and commercial premises all around the world". The intention for this change in the statutes of a private island was unclear. Why had the board under Ioannides felt it necessary to make special changes to the status of the island? From the above it seemed we were missing something.

I immediately called Nuot Saratz, Thierry's lawyer in Switzerland on behalf of the family. He was the lawyer responsible contacts with the Tutelle, the Swiss authority overseeing administration of minors' patrimonies. I explained the situation to him and he was not pleased by what we were discovering in Greece. He agreed that we should look further into the matter.

I then tried to get access to the board minutes of the Scorpios company –Mykinai SA - but the Greek authorities said that beyond what was published in the company registers I would need the authorization of the company board in order to read the minutes in the copy of the board sessions deposited with the Ministry of Commerce. I could imagine the look on Ioannides or Papadimitriou's face if I called them with such a request. It was out of the question.

I sent a fax to Thierry and his lawyers. Thierry instructed Saratz to bring the matter before the Tutelle and petition them to order that all safe deposit boxes containing shares and financial instruments belonging to Athina be opened and an inventory taken.

It was certainly a risk on my part, because if the Swiss authorities, bank officers, the lawyers on both sides and the Greek administrators were involved in what was to be a major operation, and everything was in order, then I would have egg on my face. Additionally Thierry would be compromised before the Swiss authorities for having shown so little faith in the Greek administrators and forcing them to go to Switzerland on a wild goose chase. Thierry nevertheless went ahead and applied to the Tutelle to summon the Greek administrators to open the safe deposit boxes in Geneva. The administrators replied to the Tutelle that there was no reason for the effort and expense such a venture would entail. These objections were overridden by the Swiss judicial authority who ordered them to go to Switzerland and make a new inventory of Athina's shares and companies.

In January of 1998, for several hours a Greek administrator, his lawyer, the Roussel lawyer, a representative of the Tutelle, and a bank officer carefully itemized the contents of two large safe deposit boxes registered in the name of Athina Roussel. There, at the offices of Credit Suisse in Geneva, the shares of more than one hundred and twenty companies were carefully inspected, counted, and a new inventory taken. At the end of the second day the shares of all the companies were accounted for, except for those of Mykinai SA and Agamemnon SA. These were the companies that owned the twin islands of Scorpios and Sparti.

There was a silence when this fact was discovered and the Swiss confronted the Greek administrator present, asking for an explanation. This was immediately forthcoming.

The shares belonging to Athina, he said " *sont dans les mains de la justice grecque* ". The Swiss, hearing that the shares were in the hands of the Greek judiciary ordered the return of the other company stock to the safe deposit boxes. These were duly sealed and the inventory signed by all the members present.

Marc Bonnant, the Roussel lawyer present when the safe deposit boxes were opened informed me of what had happened. I was still not convinced, and told Thierry so. There was little though at that stage that we could do and the matter of Scorpios went onto the back burner now since there were more pressing matters which took priority.

Papadimitriou gave us the chance we were looking for with his court action against Thierry for defamation two months later. One morning Thierry changed the direction of the questioning and asked one of the administrators "Where are my daughter's shares of the Scorpios company?"

"They are in a safe deposit box at the Citibank Branch of Piraeus," came the reply.

They had not told the truth to the Swiss authorities in Geneva and now they gave yet another explanation as to the whereabouts of the Scorpios company shares. Previously there had been an explanation that Athina's shares were not in Switzerland because this category of shares by Greek law was not allowed to leave the country.

We waited for the case to end and then I called Nuot Saratz and Thierry in Geneva, suggesting that the time had come to appoint a specialized corporate lawyer here in Greece. Thierry agreed and asked me to find him one.

"Alexis, I have paid millions in legal fees, but I am fed up with this story with the Scorpios shares. Get your expert."

I contacted an old friend, Professor Costas Katsigeras, a respected lawyer and college professor who was the legal adviser to a string of embassies and corporations. Katsigeras in his turn introduced me to Drillerakis Associates, a specialized Greek firm of lawyers used to solving the most esoteric problems for international clients and companies doing business in Greece. Three days after New Year of 1999 when everything in Athens was shut down and those Athenians who had not escaped to the snow-covered slopes of Gstaadt and St Moritz were sleeping off the excesses of their previous nights' revels, I received a fax from the law firm of John Drillerakis. He informed me that since 1992 there were NO restrictions on the movement of shares of commercial or real estate companies from Greece and within the European Union. A photocopy of the presidential decree and its subsections were included in the fax. Once again someone among the administrators had been caught out not telling the truth, either to Athina's father, to the Swiss Authorities or to the Greek courts regarding the whereabouts of Athina's Scorpios shares.

The Swiss were not amused. They summoned the Greek administrators to come immediately and hand over the shares to them. A few days later a Greek member of the patrimony board arranged for the shares to be delivered to Switzerland. Athina's Scorpios shares were placed in her safe deposit box. Two months later the Swiss Tutelle fired the management board appointed by Christina Onassis to manage her daughter's patrimony. The 4 Greek members protested and appealed. At the end of the summer a higher Swiss court rejected their appeal and ratified their firing. The Swiss court decision stated that the "*Greek administrators had acted in ways that were unacceptable for trustees of a minor's patrimony*" and appointed KPMG, the multinational accounting corporation, to assume responsibility for the management of Athina's considerable assets. What was sure was that the family was much happier after this decision. Additionally no-one would now have access to Scorpios without the family knowing or approving of the visit.

When Marianna Darousos heard rumours in Nydri about the change in management she phoned me excitedly.

"They say that Darousos was thrown out by Papadimitriou, and that Papadimitriou was thrown out by the Swiss from Scorpios. Is it true?"

"Yes, Marianna" I said. "And despite what people in Nydri claim - that the island belongs to the Foundation - it is not true."

"I am going to hang up now as I want to phone Nydri. I am so happy!"

If revenge is a plate that is eaten cold, then this was borne out soon afterwards when I had occasion to talk to Darousos on the phone for the first and last time. He complained of his "outing" in the Greek media where his letters had been published in a gossip magazine called Ciao. I told him that his behaviour towards the family was abominable, and he should not complain. I also told him the letters where he admitted to hating Onassis and his son Alexander, and stealing from the ships he worked on came from his wife who harboured a deep bitterness for his treatment of her.

"That was 34 years ago. Mr. Mantheakis. My ex-wife is obsessed. She will not leave me alone".

If he had not been so hostile to the family, and spoken so badly about them I would truly have felt pity for the man.

"It is Athina's great responsibility to her grandfather to serve the Onassis Foundation whose money built the Foundation" Thierry Roussel

Thierry found himself in a desperate position in the beginning of 1998 when he asked me to travel to Switzerland to meet him after reading an article of mine about the Onassis Foundation. I had stigmatized what the 4 Greeks had said in a television interview where they had spoken disparagingly about Thierry Roussel but also about Athina who was still only 12 years old. The administrators had declared to the interviewer, Yannis Pretenteris that Athina would only become president of the Foundation if they elected her. She would have to know Greek and be approved of by them. The Greeks cold put her in a corner and not talks to her if they felt like it they said! Onassis' granddaughter did not have a hereditary right to the presidency of the Onassis Foundation, they insisted.

The meeting with Thierry at Boislande on January 30th 1998 was a meeting that was to bring some changes to my life. But it also, by general admission, had significant consequences for the Roussel family and the Onassis fortune. Whether it was fate, in keeping with the

Onassis tradition I will never know. Onassis himself had been a fatalist in his attitude to life believing strongly in the inexorable power of Kismet, as the Turks called Man's predestination. The far reaching consequences of my trip to Switzerland to conduct what initially was no more than a magazine interview would surely have confirmed Onassis belief in Fate if he were alive today. For Papadimitriou and his associates the results of that first meeting between Thierry and me were less pleasing.

When I packed my bags in Athens I did not know what I would find in Switzerland. I was excited by the prospect of meeting Christina's former husband and visiting the Onassis mansion at Boislande. It was a place of popular legend for us Greeks because of its association with the shipowner's family. I left on a Swissair flight for Geneva, carrying a detailed schedule faxed to me in Athens by Pascale Louscher, Thierry Roussel's personal assistant.

I was met at Geneva airport by Stanislaus. He drove me in a VW station wagon to the Hotel du Midi on the Banks of the Rhone in central Geneva. That evening Mme. Louscher arrived with several large files. We sat in a corner of the hotel lobby while she gave me a detailed rundown of the situation. The words that kept coming from her were "lies of the Foundation", "statements of Papadimitriou", "Christina's anger with Papadimitriou", "false statements to the press", and so on. It was obvious that the woman was close to the story and her impassioned speech indicated a personal dislike of the "The Four Greeks". When she had finished I took the file and my notes and went up to my room. Though I felt tired I opened the thick blue dossier she had given me and started reading.

I was astonished at what I read. **'President of the Alexander S. Onassis Foundation shall always be a descendent of Aristotle Onassis, as long as there is one... The descendent shall become President without the need of election'**

I continued reading -

> **"The Onassis descendent shall assume the presidency upon reaching the age of 21 years."**

This was an article from the deed of establishment of the Onassis Foundation.

'Upon assumption of the presidency of the Foundation by the Onassis descendent the serving President shall immediately lose his position.'

There was much more in the file which directly contradicted what Papadimitriou had been telling the public.

The next afternoon I was driven to Boislande, the Roussel mansion located among vast rolling grounds outside Geneva a few miles inland from the shores of the lake. There Thierry Roussel, dressed in a blue suit and white shirt, met me in the wood panelled living room of the house which looked out through a wall of large glass- panelled wooden doors onto rolling landscaped gardens of the mansion. Pascale in the meantime had given me another three files as soon as I entered the front door.

Thierry was taller than I expected him to be. About one metre ninety and much better looking than in his photos which usually showed him to be somewhat pudgy-cheeked. In fact he is an extraordinarily good looking man, with the slim body and athletic carriage of someone who has spent a lifetime on ski slopes, on boats and on a diet. He shook my hand firmly and led me upstairs to his office where we sat at a large round glass conference table. This then was "Boislande", I said to myself. It was the beloved and last home of Christina Onassis at Gingins, a quiet hamlet in the countryside, 30 minutes outside Geneva. The mansion had formerly belonged to Gunter Sachs, the playboy heir to the OPEL fortune.

Outside the large picture window of the first floor office I could see flat fields and hardy hedges shielding the occasional grey mansion in the bleak winter landscape. Gingins' residents are mainly businessmen or diplomats who work at various international missions in Geneva. When I had arrived at Boislande earlier that day I was surprised not to see Ferraris, Range Rovers and Rolls Royces in the forecourt and in the garage of the mansion. Only a blue Passat station wagon and a nondescript Audi were parked in the drive.

There were questions which had bothered me for a while about Christina's will - who were the beneficiaries when she died - who received what? There was a lack of information in Greece. I was also curious about the intense dislike shown by Papadimitriou towards Roussel and the contemptuous manner in which he referred to Christina Onassis and Professor Georgakis in their capacity as presidents of the Onassis Foundation. Regarding Roussel, was it envy by the former employee against the family of his former boss, envy of Roussel's stunning looks (something Papadimitriou mentioned subsequently several times, even in court) and his glamorous lifestyle, or was it the envy of an old man for a young one who had his life ahead of him? I did not know.

We, in Greece, had all seen images of Roussel on TV with his wife Gaby and with a happy Athina accompanied by her brother and sisters. Was this image we had seen one of a notorious playboy, a rake, a modern Barrabas I ask myself, trying to weigh the person sitting opposite me?

I continue reading the documents, knowing now that my trip to Geneva to hear the side of Thierry Roussel in his dispute with the current board members of the Onassis Foundation would hold considerable surprises for me. I can remember the course of the conversation that took place during the interview.

A.M - Mr. Roussel, there have been terrible statements and accusations against you in Greece by the 4 of the Foundation. You are accused of wanting to get your hands on the inheritance of your daughter for yourself, that you are holding your daughter hostage in a Swiss village, that you have isolated Athina from her Greek roots, from her family, that you are a fortune seeker. There is also the feeling that Athina is in danger. I am sorry to have to say this but there is the widespread impression in Greece - among the public - that the mysterious death of Christina personally benefited you. I would like you to answer this last question first, please.

Thierry Roussel - *Concerning Christina's death (pushing a document in front of me) you can see that this is the last will of Christina.*

The handwritten will is in a large schoolgirl script.

"I, Christina Onassis, daughter of Aristotle S. Onassis and Tina Livanou ...in the event of my death ... do hereby direct that the people listed below receive the following sums, in cash -

Stelios Papadimitriou USD 2 million
Apostolos Zambellas USD 2 million
Paul Ioannides USD 2 million –

Smaller sums follow, then -

"To my former husband Thierry Roussel I leave an annual sum of USD 1,470,000, and to my beloved daughter Athina I leave the rest of my estate to be hers upon reaching the age of 18"

> **TR** - *Please read further down.*
> I continued reading -

"...all my daughter's inheritance shall be administered by a board consisting of the following members - Thierry Roussel, Stelios Papadimitriou, Paul Ioannides, Apostolos Zambellas, Theodore Gavrielides... board decisions shall be by majority..."

> **AM** - According to the will you have no power to do anything on your own?
> TR -, *I will now spend some of your time to present to you similar documents to the one you have just read. I shall show you why Papadimitriou is negative towards me, to Athina, and to the members of the family of Aristotle Onassis. I shall not make any claims which are not backed up by documents. If Aristotle was alive today he would be furious with what has happened to me and Athina, and the way in which his former employees who are running the Foundation are acting towards the relatives- the blood - of Onassis.*
> AM - Can you clarify this - you have no control over your daughter's assets?
> TR - *None at all - I cannot withdraw one dollar if my daughter requests it while they, the 4, can send 100 million dollars to Panama in one hour.*

AM: What about the accusation that you have begun a legal battle to gain control over her money.

TR: *That too is a lie - this document - (he gives me another paper) is my request to the Swiss authorities requesting my daughters finances be put in the hands of independent professional financial managers appointed by the court. I myself have requested not to be on this new board of trustees.*

AM: And what has happened to this request? The Onassis Foundation say that you have lost every case you have brought against them.

TR. *I have won every legal action with the exception of one case we brought against Papadimitriou in Greece. This latter case would appear to have problems and has resulted in a countersuit by Papadimitriou for defamation. Papadimitriou has been summoned by the Swiss Juvenile Affairs Authority - -the Authoritè Tutelle - to explain where he has spent certain sums of Athina's' money, and why the four made certain transactions. They never appeared - instead they fought with every legal weapon available to them not to appear before the Swiss authority, constantly appealing. In the latest instance they appealed to have the judges removed, instead of just coming to Switzerland with the books. These disputes have made him attack and defame me so much - but the time will come soon when all their appeals will be exhausted...*

AM - Did you mount a media campaign against the Onassis Foundation members in the past as Papadimitriou claims.

Roussel looks across the table to Pascale who is sitting with a large briefcase in front of her.

"The media file please" he says in a low voice.

A large pile of papers in a transparent cover is given to me. It is labelled-

"Publications Contre Monsieur Roussel"

In the envelope there are 294 articles from newspapers as diverse at the Winston-Salem Journal in the USA, the Schwarzwalder-Botte (Germany), The Guardian in England, Ethnos in Athens and a paper in Finland with an unpronounceable name. 164 papers in the USA alone. In many of the translated extracts of the articles I see the words «Mr. Stelios Papadimitriou of the Onassis Benevolent Foundation accused Thierry Roussel of ..."

I read Blick of Switzerland, 7 November 1997 - *"Papadimitriou is convinced that Roussel is in the drug business, takes drugs himself, and organizes orgies...'*

TR – *294 articles, Mr. Mantheakis. And yet I am the one who is accused of running a press campaign!*

I wanted him to explain Papadimitriou's accusation that he was a playboy and a wastrel. When I first sat down opposite him I noticed his note pad was covered in neat notes in very small handwriting, the unmistakeable sign of someone who is careful with his money. I make a mental note of this. Roussel may be anything Papadimitriou says he is, I thought, but he is not one who scatters money.

I remember hearing of his father's properties in Kenya, his family chateau in France where Christina often stayed and the enormous piece of land in Marbella in Spain which Henri Roussel owned, half of which he sold to Adnan Kashoggi for 24 million dollars.

Thierry Roussel was not the chauffeur who had married the boss's daughter, neither a ski instructor servicing elderly ladies in Gstaadt or a penniless tennis player who married an heiress. Roussel came from an aristocratic family of the *haute bourgeoisie* with considerable wealth. His father had been president and half owner of the Roussel pharmaceutical multinational. I decide to ask anyway. I expected him to laugh, but instead his blue eyes seem suddenly tired as he turned to look at a family picture of him and his Swedish wife Gaby and their four children. Athina, tall and slim, leans lovingly against her father in the photo. Roussel looked interminably sad for a moment and then told Pascale *«Donnez le papier s'il vous plait a monsieur Mantheakis."*

Mme Luscher had the paper ready. It was a certified accountant's statement of the income of a 24 year-old Thierry Roussel.

It read "Income −1980. FF 5,229,835", close to 800,000 Euros and each year there are similar sums until 1984.

Thierry Roussel leaves the room for a few minutes and I get up to stretch my limbs. I have not realised that we have been talking for more than two hours. I wander across the room to look at some photos on the mantelpiece of the marble fireplace. I notice a sculpture of a human hand in the unmistakable style of Rodin. Looking at the hand more carefully I see, as I had expected, the signature of the great sculptor. Thierry comes back into the room and offers me coffee and tea. I chose mineral water instead. He drinks nothing and I ask him if I can take some photographs.

Roussel asks where I want him to sit and I point first to the leather chair behind his glass desk. After this I move over to the beige leather couch next to the fireplace and ask him to sit there. He poses patiently. Roussel, though formerly a professional standard photographer tactfully makes no suggestions while I fumble with an unfamiliar Nikon borrowed from an Athenian neighbour. I find the right buttons and shoot the pictures. I am not aware at this time that the photo I am taking will be pivotal in an important development regarding the Boislande mansion. I ask his assistant to take a photo of me and Roussel together but the picture when it is developed later in Greece comes out blurred because she was not familiar with the camera. Roussel and I return to the conference table and resume the interview.

AM - What other things have they done?

TR – *Well, Christina and my daughter would never have wanted them to spend massive legal fees - I estimate it to be around lm USD - in their fight against me and to charge this sum to Athina.*

AM - They accuse you of isolating Athina from the family.

TR - *Athina sees her Greek relatives, just a week ago her cousins were at her birthday party, and before that Athina was in London at a wedding where she was with other Onassis relatives. She regularly communicates with them. Years later Roussel confided to me that while Athina had been seated with the Livanos-Onassis relatives at the main table at one of these receptions he had been placed next to the kitchen door.*

AM - When Christina inherited her money why didn't she just keep it, because I heard you mention earlier that Papadimitriou controlled her money as well, until she died. (I had heard somewhere that Onassis in his will had given less than 50 percent to Christina and that was illegal both in Greece and in France where the only child automatically gets half of the estate. The story was that Papadimitriou had told Christina "Look, what was done was wrong, but I can arrange for you to get 50% on condition I manage the money." I asked Thierry Roussel about this.)

TR - *Christina had two choices - first to agree, thus giving control over all the assets of Onassis to Papadimitriou, and secondly she could contest the will. This would have meant she was going against her dead father - it would have been an enormous scandal - she would get no money until the long proceedings were concluded as there was a clause in Onassis will that if anyone in the will contested it they were to receive no money and the will's executors were to use the legacy to pay all legal expenses. So Christina acquiesced.*

AM - What was their relationship after this?

TR - *Christina was not in a position to manage her affairs - Papadimitriou immediately set up corporations to manage her assets.*

AM - How many?

TR - *350 - Three hundred and fifty! Unbelievable! Just to look at the balance sheets was a full time job and Christina could never follow her business affairs again - she had lost control. Papadimitriou had all the control. When Christina died I wanted to check, and I had an obligation to do so to see what my daughter had inherited. It took me 3-4 years of intensive searching and of course much aggravation and expense. This search caused bad feelings in the Four towards me - I was a nuisance. I was the father.*

AM - What will happen now?

TR - *You have heard all the reports. Papadimitriou says he will decide whether Athina will become president of the Foundation at 21. Everyone thinks there is a will saying that she must speak good Greek, that she must have knowledge of this and that, etc. and that after this she will be judged and approved or rejected for the office of Onassis Foundation President.*

AM - This was my question - what are the conditions for her to become president of the family Foundation?

TR - *Please read the articles of the Foundation –* (he pushes over a document which is open on the page with articles referring to the presidency requirements for the Onassis Foundation. It is these that I had been reading the previous evening in my hotel room.)

AM - What has Papadimitriou been saying?

TR - *He is once again not telling the truth, but so often and so convincingly that everyone believes him - please read on -*

AM - What is the problem for the Four if Athina becomes president? She will be in a minority.

TR - *She will be entitled to check the books and to see what investments have been made. She will have that power. It is her great responsibility to her grandfather to serve the Onassis Foundation whose money built the Foundation - not Papadimitriou's. Nor Zambellas nor Ioannides, nor their sons' money.*

AM - What is the kidnapping scenario?

TR - *I was approached by the police in Switzerland who warned me that I and my family were in danger since we were being watched. The police set up their own surveillance operation and waited for the six people involved to make a move to arrest them. I was terribly worried so I informed the Tutelle- the Minors' Authority - that according to a police report Athina was in danger. The six men were identified as former Israeli commandos who had been watching us all the time. From the moment I informed the Tutelle they informed the Greek co-trustees of Athina, as was their duty that her life was in danger.*

The next day most of the commandos disappeared but the Swiss police managed to arrest one. While he was being questioned to our enormous surprise the Onassis Foundation directors informed the world that they had hired the group but claimed they were just agents checking the security arrangements of Athina to satisfy a kidnap insurance clause with Lloyd's. It was the first I had heard of the insurance. Papadimitriou said I did not need to know. Athina was their responsibility, he said. Papadimitriou reacted and gave that well-known press conference.

The tape had run out again. I saw that I had plenty to think about. I thanked Thierry and shook his hand. He accompanied me to the west wing of the mansion where photocopies of his documents were being prepared for me. As he went down the stairs I saw his youthful face was tired and his shoulders slightly stooped. I saw an embattled father, a man with whom in the space of two days in Switzerland I could empathise with.

As I left Gingins in the small Ford Fiesta driven by Athina's driver Stanislaus I felt this was not the last time I would see Roussel. He was no longer a stranger. He had strong links with my country. He had after all been married to a Greek girl, had a Greek father-in-law, his daughter had a Greek name, Greek blood, Greek cousins and uncles and she owned substantial properties in Greece.

I had come to Switzerland with no idea of what I would find. I discovered now that I had been drawn into the mesh of the Onassis saga.

When I returned to Athens I phoned several papers to say I had an exclusive story with revelations both about Roussel and the Foundation. I was surprised to find I was up against a blank wall. I discovered an unofficial embargo of news against Roussel was in force. It was clear that interests that I could not identify wanted neither Roussel nor the granddaughter of Onassis to gain sympathy or a new family foothold in Greece. The same enmity became apparent some years later when despite the millions that the Onassis family had given to Greece Athina's husband, the Olympic medallist horseman Alvaro de Miranda was refused Greek citizenship to ride for the Greek Olympic team by the Minister of the Interior Prokopis Pavlopoulos.

I called a family friend, Pantelis Capsis, who was the editor of a TA NEA. When I told him about the interview given to me by Thierry in Switzerland he said he wanted to print it. I was sceptical but sent the article to his office. He would run it in three days. The next afternoon I was asked to go to the paper where the editor-in-chief of the group, Karapanayotis, informed me TA NEA would not print the story because it contained "opinions".

Two weeks later my article was accepted by Greek monthly glossy magazine "CRASH". It was advertised on television at half-hourly intervals and the issue sold very well. The embargo in the press against

Roussel had broken. We still now had to assail the television bastion.

When Thierry saw the article and the photos in Crash he invited me back to Geneva. He explained that he wanted me to undertake to help the family in their court battles. And then a strange thing happened. After the last secretary had left the Boislande mansion offices at around six in the evening a fire broke out in the archive room. The mansion was deserted and only Thierry was there in the residential east wing of the house where he had his private office. He heard the fire alarm and immediately ran down the stairs from his office, went through the dining room, then through the lounge and into the entrance hall. He rushed up the stairs on the other side and as he opened the door to the secretaries' offices a wall of flame and smoke rolled towards him. Thierry slammed the door shut just in time to save himself from serious injury and ran downstairs to inform the fire brigade. They would take 15-20 minutes to arrive they said. Thierry knew that it would be too late for the mansion which had a wooden frame and highly flammable fabrics and carpets throughout. Roussel saw that the fire extinguisher was not in its usual place and realised that the whole mansion would burn down if he did not do something quickly, but what? In a flash he remembered the Crash article and the photograph I had taken of him sitting on the leather couch in his study. He knew where to go for the fire extinguisher. He raced up the steps to his office and jumped over the leather couch, grabbing the extinguisher which was behind the piece of furniture. He then went back hurriedly to the burning west wing carrying the heavy metal cylinder before him.

Roussel opened the door to the archive room and sprayed it with chemical foam for several minutes. The searing heat and the flames started to subside. By the time the chemical agent was exhausted the fire was contained and a few minutes later the fire department officers arrived to finish off the job by spraying everything with gallons of water. The secretaries' offices were ruined and hundreds of valuable legal documents were destroyed, but the Boislande mansion had been saved by Roussel's immediate action.

I phoned him later that day to ask what had happened because the story of the fire had been all over the international news.

"Mr. Mantheakis, it was all very strange. I had been looking at the photos in Crash magazine and I could not understand what the looped object was that was sticking out from behind the couch I was sitting on. I went to look and saw it was a fire extinguisher was not on its bracket. Soon after I forgot about it completely. When I opened the office wing door today and saw the fire I remembered where I had seen the fire extinguisher and immediately ran to get it. If I had not seen your photo I would not have known where the extinguisher was. The fire officers told me that if I had delayed for five minutes the mansion would have been burned down. The photo you took was lucky!"

Aristotle Onassis believed strongly in fate and this oriental belief in the pre-ordained chain of events never left him. The incident at Boislande only seemed to confirm how fate could inexorably influence our lives. If I had not taken that photo, and if Thierry Roussel, being a person who obviously paid great attention to detail, had not wondered what the black loop sticking out over the back of the leather couch was, then Athina's historical mansion would have been burned to its foundations.

Thierry Roussel and I later discussed the matter of the battle with the Onassis Foundation members. I had studied all the documents at the hotel and at our new meeting at Boislande I told Thierry that in order for him to win what was a very difficult fight he would have to organise a two-pronged attack. Media and lawyers. We needed the additional support of a legal team with heavy media clout and we needed a concerted information campaign to let the media first of all know what was happening and secondly to let the public know the truth.

Thierry agreed. He asked me to take responsibility for the two sectors and to write a plan for him. Thierry asked me out of the blue if I would like to interview him and Gaby for television at the family home in Lussy-sur- Morges. I was delighted of course, but told him I had no camera crew.

"I shall get one for you," he said, and picked up a phone calling Gaby to be prepared. He then called Paris where he had his personal cameraman, Felix.

"He will fly here from Paris in two hours" said Thierry, smiling. Thierry and I went outside where his driver was waiting to take us to the Roussel family villa at Lussy-sur-Morges, just outside Lausanne. This was the house that Christina Onassis had bought for Gaby so that Thierry's children with their two mothers could be near one another and Athina would have her half siblings to play with.

While waiting for the cameraman to arrive from France Thierry conducted me around the villa and its grounds while we were discretely watched by members of Athina's personal bodyguard contingent. The house itself was surprisingly modest. It was a one-story bungalow of around 400 m2, with what I estimated to be a half-acre garden. The villa was not unlike a California ranch house, finished externally in pale pink stucco while inside the rooms were in light beige colours. Thierry's study had bleached-blonde wood paneling. In the kitchen there was a long rectangular dining table with a metal top − supremely practical when there were so many people to feed, while high up in the living room there was a riveting painting depicting three Moroccan warriors on camels. It was a haunting painting with exceptional use of light which emphasised their features and the movement of the riders in their white burnouses waving their rifles. Thierry took me outside to a cobbled patio forecourt for the cars. We walked in the garden and he took me across the lawn to a small house filled with children's toys, next to which was an enclosure containing two very white and woolly sheep. Thierry opened the door and the sheep came out to greet us. We now talked about his home at Kilifi Creek near Mombasa and his fishing experiences there.

A little later when we went back inside the house Roussel took me to see the children's' rooms. I was surprised to notice how "normal" they were and how modest in size. Athina' room had white furniture and next door there was a triangular room with a computer, a white desk, a photo of Christina Onassis, various teddy bears, the head of a Greek statue, I do not remember whether it was of Apollo or the Goddess Athina, the ancient Greek Goddess of wisdom. There was a bookshelf and various decorative items. What particularly impressed me was that the children shared bathrooms and how ordinary yet practical their rooms were. They were rooms for school children. It reflected the ordinariness of old money that had no reason to show off. How unlike the palatial marble palace suites of the children of the nouveau-riche in Athens with their ensuite bathrooms, Jacuzzis and room sized walk in-closets filled with rows of colour matched clothes and dozens of pairs of shoes. One thing that drew my attention was that in every child's bedroom there was a wire cage containing a live rabbit. I could not explain this, especially since there was a health risk, and wondered whether the rabbits had been imposed as a calming foil because of the kidnap scare's effect on the children or whether this was in fact some unusual way for the children to not feel alone in their individual bedrooms.

We went back into the living room where I met Gaby. The crackling of walkie talkies signalled the preparation for the departure of Athina for afternoon activities. The Roussel children came in for a brief moment to kiss their father goodbye. Erik was the most curious and immediately approached me to introduce himself before leaving. I was charmed by his good manners and his openness. He was a nice boy and I could see Thierry beaming with pride as the door closed behind his only son.

The cameraman had arrived a few minutes ago from Paris so we did a quick session of on-camera questions and answers with Gaby who had to leave for an appointment. She spoke of how much anguish the family had been through because of the media attacks by the Foundation and how the story with the arrested Israelis had shaken and terrified the children. Thierry was a wonderful father she said who never missed any of his children's birthdays and would always come back from wherever he was travelling to be with the family on these occasions. She told me off camera that the stories about Thierry and other women that were lately in the press had put a strain on the family but she said that they were united and were coping. It was not to last for ever as a few years later Thierry moved out and blog articles reported that he was living with a black girl. I never got confirmation of this and never asked as it was not my business, but I was saddened to see that a family that had been closely woven together had, when the money was finally in Athena's hands, loosened their close bonds with one another with Thierry living separately.

The interview with Thierry was conducted in a race against the setting sun. The last shots were taken as a shadow cast by the setting sun crept up on Thierry who was sitting in a chair in the garden. The final scene showed Thierry's face weakly illuminated while from the neck down his body was in almost total darkness!

The interview was shown by Mega TV in Athens soon after. Now everybody wanted photos, information and interviews with the Roussel family. Papadimitriou himself was constantly in the news after this, trying to refute what Roussel was saying about him and the Foundation. One day Papadimitriou was interviewed by Nikos Hatzinikolaou, an erudite, though somewhat distant journalist, the son of a former government minister. During a discussion of Athina Papadimitriou said "We cannot give the Foundation to just anybody."

Hatzinikolaou, incredulous, sat motionless for a moment before asking "But surely the granddaughter of Onassis is not just anybody?"

Speaking about the financial aspect of the Onassis story in the same interview Papadimitriou said that the administrators had not received one drachma personally. The newscaster took a long look at Papadimitriou. It was a moment that was witnessed by half a million Greek viewers. Hatzinikolaou who had seen the documents with Christina's will and the millions she had given to three of the four of Athina's Greek trustees did not need to say anything. Subsequent articles and interviews revealed that the Four had received around 3 million dollars from Athina in administrative fees and expense fees alone and another six million dollars from Christina's will.

Thierry at this time had been sued by the Foundation Four for defamation arising from a complaint which his lawyer, Professor Nestor Kourakis, had lodged some months before to the Greek prosecutor. The case was due to be heard in Athens on March 30th 1998 in a court where Roussel would not understand the language or the proceedings. He was to be tried in a country where the press was still hostile, primarily due to the accusations of the Onassis Foundation against him. Athina's father was portrayed as being capable of anything. As the case approached Papadimitriou appeared to hold all the aces. Most Greeks felt that the Foundation had the judiciary and the political parties on their side. Influential people were saying that the Foundation Four were the last Greek bastion against the Frenchman who would take over the Foundation. The Four were Greeks and the Foundation owned a Greek fortune claimed those supporting the attacks against Athina's father. Thierry also had to contend with a large hostile wedge of Greek society – middle-aged women who were passionately and vociferously against him for their own reasons. Roussel was a man known to have had many women in his life and had indulged in the now much-publicized concurrent love affair with two women, Gaby and Christina, impregnating both. He had also had children by "the other woman" while still married to Christina Onassis, something that was anathema to insecure middle-aged Greek housewives who saw in Thierry a dark mirror image of their wandering husbands. Perhaps he reminded some of the man who had left them in middle age for another woman. Thierry's court case would be an occasion for a general catharsis for the frustrations and humiliations of those thousands of women who had suffered at the hands of faithless husbands. Roussel had unwittingly struck a raw nerve in Greek society. In the general climate of hostility I found that eminent lawyers I approached would not undertake to represent the client when they heard that the person I came to talk to them about was Thierry Roussel.

Thierry, in an attempt to counter negative and often untrue media reports had recently opened up his home in Switzerland to journalists in the hope that they would report some of the facts and restore his family's reputation. The reporters came and went, and articles appeared about the Roussel family's clothes, their horses, Athina's hairstyle, but almost not one word was printed about the positions put forward in his defence by Roussel.

It was a difficult situation to say the least. The more I looked at it I found myself becoming involved in the Onassis saga, seeing that the truth had been twisted often and documents had been suppressed.

October 30th 1998. It was a freezing cold day at the Evelpidon law courts in Athens. The court administrator had assigned a spare courtroom for the Roussel camp. Lawyers, interpreters, bodyguards, secretaries, wives, girlfriends and daughters of our lawyers were all in the large courtroom which was now our base. Gaby found a corner for herself. As was her custom when she wanted to kill time she was reading a pocket book. In the meantime I had set up an impromptu media centre. One journalist came in after another to see Thierry. Greek, French, German, Swiss journalists each had a quarter of an hour at their disposal. Before I allowed each new one in for an interview I whispered to Thierry whether they were hostile or friendly, and what paper or magazine they worked for.

Papadimitriou had accused Roussel of being a spendthrift playboy. A man in whose arms Christina Onassis had been nothing but a helpless hostage. He was not alone in saying this. It was not a flattering portrait but the notoriety of Thierry and the sudden confrontation of this immensely polite, urbane and stunningly good-looking man melted the hearts of even the most harridan-like of the journalists as they came into the room and stood in front of him for their interview. Thierry's gentle and diabolic charm worked like a spider's web. The journalists loved it. The morning passed with us waiting for our case to be called. Towards lunchtime three intimidated and visibly impressed junior girl newspaper reporters came in together to interview Thierry. I sat them down next to each other at the lawyers' bench. Thierry, standing a full 1.90m tall immediately in front of them started telling them his story, looking down at them like a handsome Nordic schoolmaster towering over primary school children. Thierry by now had given more than ten interviews and was completely at home in his new surroundings with the Greek journalists so I went to sit next to Gaby who seemed happy to have someone to talk to.

"Look at them," she said, "they seem quite charmed by Thierry".

She was right. The girls had left their pens and open notepads on the desk top in front of them and were staring up at Thierry's blue eyes, absolutely enraptured by him. They had not written down one word of what he had said. I excused myself from Gaby and went over to stand next to Thierry. "Ladies," I said, "please note what Mr. Roussel is telling you, otherwise your readers will have nothing to read in your papers tomorrow."

The oldest of the girls smiled while the other two blushed and bent forward, quickly scribbling notes. I turned to Thierry and winked. Thierry, like the old *lobo* that he was, looked straight back at me without betraying any acknowledgement of my teasing.

Thierry had often been accused of being cold, something expressed even by some of his closest friends. I myself took a long time to come to a conclusion regarding this aspect of his character. There is no doubt that he is an intensely private person who keeps his true feelings securely locked away in an almost impenetrable vault. He has also been accused of being humourless. This is unfounded. Thierry has a sardonic sense of humour, though it is infinitely more subtle than British humour and may be missed by those who do not know him personally.

On many an occasion I observed a straight-faced Thierry making sly jokes, often in the face of the most serious situations. As to his character I could not just ask him "Thierry, are you as cold as they say?" The mystery of why he was so emotionally reclusive was explained one day when he was talking wistfully about his father, Henri Roussel, who had recently died. His dad was the well-known pharmaceutical industrialist, and a bon viveur whom Thierry had admired inordinately.

"My father,' he explained, "lived the perfect life. He had happy relationships with women, our family adored him, and his homes were always full of guests. He was very open."

This was my chance to pop the question.

"Aren't *you* open, Thierry?'

"No," he replied, "I was never like him."

"Why not?" I pressed on, "Since you admired him so much."

"All my life I had to fight. I always had to defend myself and fight, fight, fight. I was betrayed by everyone, even by my closest friends."

I had my answer. Thierry kept his emotions locked behind so many doors in his psyche that it was rare for one to see the real, emotionally fragile man inside the strong exterior. This was one side of his character, but of course there was more to him. The other side would reveal itself after he and Athina had won their court battles and taken charge of the Onassis fortune. Relatives, childhood friends and people who had been close to them when father and daughter, fearful and vulnerable in their darkest hour, saw another side of Thierry and Athina as they withdrew into private places with several hundreds of millions of dollars at their disposal. It was a development that several journalists in Greece whom I had considered extreme and hostile had correctly predicted. Thierry and Athina dumped friends, loyal associates, aged relatives, kindergarten friends and in the end each other.

Thierry now had another fight in front of him. We entered the courtroom accompanied by a swarm of waiting journalists. Papadimitriou, Ioannides, Gavrielides and Zambellas had already taken their seats on the left side of the courtroom. Among their witnesses was Eleni Arwheiler, a short, mannish looking woman with a severe haircut and a direct manner. My only previous knowledge of the woman was from appearances she had made at public functions and on television in her capacity as dean of a French university. Her position on the board of the Onassis Foundation would justify perhaps her support of Papadimitriou, but when I heard of a sworn statement she made to the Greek investigative authorities prior to Thierry's case I was not impressed. What she had stated had nothing to do with the accusation against Thierry for his claims that the Foundation had mismanaged its businesses and that its available cash had been depleted or put at risk by investing heavily and borrowing to buy super tankers. Contrarily she had launched a personal attack on Thierry in his capacity as a father. Her deposition was criticism of his alleged de-Hellenization of Athina. She had spoken of Roussel cutting off his family from Greece, when he had done the exact opposite. He had married a Greek, unlike Mrs. Arwheiler who publicly championed the Greek ethnic cause and yet in her private life had chosen to marry a foreigner if one was to judge by his name, Arwheiler. If her husband was indeed Greek I will willingly stand corrected. Interestingly, Mrs. Arwheiler stated in a television interview that she wrote her books in French, and only used Greek for minor articles!

The court case began with a series of details of procedure. That morning, as in the past, I received an anonymous phone call from a voice I now recognised. It was the man who claimed to be a Supreme Court judge. He told me that the court had already made up its mind regarding the verdict. Roussel was fighting a lost cause. I replied to the man that I took no notice of anonymous opinions and for him not to bother me unless he was prepared to give me his name. "I am too frightened to do that. They are very powerful," he said and quickly hung up. I took no notice.

My interest now was in who was on the bench. The president was a diminutive man wearing a light brown jacket and trousers of a different colour. Next to him sat two middle-aged women judges, one with dyed strawberry blonde hair with dark roots showing, and the other had short black, fluffed curls and a bored look. Not a good sign, I said to myself.

The prosecutor had typically dark Mediterranean features and a head of thick carefully-brushed hair covering part of his forehead. He had arrived at the court complex escorted by two bodyguards I was told. I learned later that he was the prosecutor charged with investigating terrorism in Greece. Why would he have been assigned to prosecute what was in essence an intercorporate battle when domestic terrorist groups were plying havoc with lives, property and the public image of Greece?

The atmosphere of the courtroom was in stark contrast to the feeling we all had in March, when Prosecutor Gerakis, known at the time to the Greek public for his campaign against public corruption, had been on the prosecutor's bench. From the outset the president showed impatience with Thierry, accepting none of his legal requests for a continuance and making it plain that he was going to judge the case himself. There would be no adjournments. On the second day Thierry was exasperated by the atmosphere in the court. It was suggested that our lawyers should declare an end to our defence in protest at the proceedings and walk out. There would be a worldwide scandal. Opposition came from an unexpected corner. Our lawyers were adamantly against the protest saying it would harm Thierry. But there was also the opinion that Thierry should pay whatever fine was imposed on him, ending the prospect of an exhausting and humiliating ordeal of weeks spent in court.

The case continued. Papadimitriou was in for a surprise the first day when he was called to give evidence. He was questioned mercilessly by Thierry's lawyer. It was important to make it clear from the outset that Roussel was not the weak foreigner who wanted to run off with the moneybags of his daughter. The message to all was that Roussel was prepared to face any risk, legal or otherwise to protect Athina's interests at the Foundation and elsewhere.

Thierry's defence team was initially happy to see that the judge was an accountant and showed great interest whenever financial matters were discussed. This was thought to be a good sign because the case was based on whether the Four had managed the Onassis Foundation well or not. The two women judges spent much of their time looking at the back wall of the courtroom or out of the window, occasionally twiddling a pen.Their faces often displayed signs of boredom. They never asked a question of the witnesses while I was present and only occasionally did they lean over to look at the judge's notes when he was questioning a witness. I was surprised that the two women on the bench never seemed to display any outward sign of interest in the proceedings in what was one of the most heavily reported and important cases in the world.

On the third day of the case Thierry stood up and asked to read a statement

"I would like to clarify for the court that the document in which such an accusation (regarding the plaintiffs receiving illegal commissions) was written in Greek by my lawyer in Athens when I myself was in Switzerland. I regret the error, but it is an error which does not reflect my opinion that the plaintiffs have put money in their own pockets."

There was an immediate and noisy outcry from the Foundation lawyer's bench. If Thierry's statement was accepted it would mean that the charge of malicious defamation would fail. I had expected the reaction and now took the opportunity to observe the reactions of Thierry's opponent's lawyers with some amusement.

Anyone else would have been happy to have a defendant retract a serious accusation. In itself it would be a reason to either terminate the case or throw out the specific charge. It would be a moral vindication for the plaintiff, and the prosecutor normally would be expected to be content that the defendant had retracted. Not so for the prosecutor and the Papadimitriou camp.

One day I was sitting with Thierry at one of the outdoor cafés of the court complex when a woman of about thirty-five approached us. She addressed Thierry in fluent French.

"Mr. Roussel, I admire what you have done for your daughter and the Greek public understands the situation. I wish you luck, but you must know that as a foreigner and because of the Foundation being what it is you have no chance at all." With this she left. Thierry looked at me quizzically.

"I don't believe that a Greek court will exercise prejudice over good legal arguments, Thierry. Ignore her."

That evening I had another anonymous phone call referring to the outcome of the trial.

"They will be merciless" said the cultured voice of the older man from the Supreme Court. "The dice are loaded against your client. Tell him to go back home, because he will spend weeks defending himself for nothing."

I could not accept his view but decided that I should mention it anyway to our lawyers the next day. Our lawyers said I should not tell Thierry. I asked why and was told that Thierry would become discouraged and would not be psychologically up to defending himself if he was informed of these pessimistic rumours, even though we considered them to be unfounded. The case continued.

I first saw him carrying a large battered suitcase outside the Evelpidon law courts in Athens. It was a bitterly cold but sunny day in March of 1998. We were waiting for Thierry's defamation case to be heard. The man who was in his mid-sixties was wearing a heavily creased beige suit. He approached me at the entrance to the court, put down his suitcase with a grunt and said -

"I want to talk to Mr. Roussel. I have something important to tell him."

"What is your name?" I asked.

"Petros."

The name meant nothing to me.

"It is very important," he said." I have the solution to the court disputes here in my suitcase. All the documents are here."

I realised now that the man standing in front of me was the obsessive former Onassis employee who had written countless letters to Athina and Thierry. Over the years he had pestered them with hundreds of phone calls.

I told him to wait and went over to where Stefanos our head of security was standing outside the room where Thierry and the lawyers were in conference. I explained to Stefanos who the man was.

"If you do have evidence which will be useful for this case you should take it to someone on the other side, they are the ones who took the initiative of bringing this case to court," I told Petros.

He looked confused for a second then he stooped to pick up his case. Nodding to me he walked off to look for Papadimitriou closely accompanied by Stefanos who from that moment made sure the man had no more contact with us that day. When I returned to the waiting room I told Thierry and Gaby about my encounter.

"Do you know that we once found him in our garden in Switzerland?" said Gaby. "He came to the house three times. He is obsessed with Athina."

"What is in his suitcase?" I asked.

"Hundreds of press clippings and letters regarding our family," Thierry answered. "He has sent us more than 700 letters! He also calls Ioannides apparently."

After that morning I forgot about the man. Ten days later I received a call on my mobile phone. A polite voice was on the other end "May I speak to Mr. Mantheakis'"

"Who is it?" I responded.

"Petros - with the suitcase." Someone had given him my mobile number. He continued, "I must explain to you that I have the whole solution to the problem of Mr. Roussel and his quarrel with the Foundation."

I decided to humour him in the hope that I could deflect his interest.

Petros continued. "I am the incarnation of Onassis. In fact I am Onassis the Second. An improved and moral version of the original, because Onassis Number One was a real bastard!"

Our conversation was going somewhere beyond the outer limits of logic now. I realized my choices of dealing with the man were limited: I could either hang up, in which case he would call again, or I could try and fend him off.

"What is it that you really want?" I asked, thinking of the options open to me to get rid of him.

"Mr. Roussel has four children, that is too many. I want to marry Athina and Sandrine. He can keep Erik and Johanna."

Athina was thirteen and Sandrine eleven.

"And how old are you?" I asked.

"Sixty two."

"You should be ashamed of yourself! They are just children!" I replied, hoping to see him off.

"I will be a father to them and later I will give them many children. I already have a house ready for them. And don't worry about my performance; I can satisfy five 20 year old women." I hung up.

Petros of course dogged me from that day on. He had read in the papers that I was the only person in Greece in close contact with the Roussel family and this convinced him that I was the solution to his problem.

"Only you. Mr. Mantheakis..." was the phrase that I heard again and again. This usually followed a telephone call that he had previously made to Katia Ioannides, the younger former Olympic Airlines employee who had married Pavlos Ioannides of the Onassis Foundation. Katia of course was not in contact with the Roussels and was unable to help Petros, so inevitably the next call was to me.

I tried to come to an accommodation with him so that he would not call me every day. We made a deal for our contact by phone to be limited to once a week, but then he would get excited by some news item he saw regarding Athina and he would call me. My postman became accustomed to delivering heavy large brown envelopes from the provincial Greek town of Agrinion. These envelopes were marked "***Strictly Private and Personal***". The envelopes contained Petros' cosmic theory as well as letters to Thierry and Athina. They came in regularly, and there were telephone calls at all times of day, on my mobile and to my office number to confirm whether I had received the latest letters. One day I opened an envelope to see the results of an examination at a fertility clinic. It was an analysis of a sperm count of Petros who included a note telling me that here was the proof that he would be a productive husband for Athina and Sandrine!

I became exasperated when I started getting five and six calls a day. I noticed after a while that I was starting to act irrationally toward him while Petros was calm and polite. Sometimes I would hang in there, and the conversation would often be about his days as a first engineer on the Onassis tankers. In the middle of the conversation he would stop and say, "Of course you remember that I am Onassis reincarnated? Onassis the Second!"

One Sunday morning Petros called to ask me if I believed in transmigration of souls and in reincarnation. Caught unawares I made the fatal mistake of saying that our Ancient Greek philosophers believed in the theory as did perhaps a quarter of the population of the world. The Buddhists too were convinced it was true. From

278

that day on Petros hung on to me like a limpet. He had found what he was sure was a fellow believer.

"Ah, Mister Mantheakis," he would say, "You are my saviour, everyone thinks I am mad, but you yourself admitted that reincarnation is possible and from now on I will only talk to you because we are kindred souls in a hostile and unbelieving world."

I talked to people who knew him from his Onassis days to try and understand where his problem lay. They told me that he had been sent home with a pension after he behaved strangely on several occasions. Petros himself recounted how he had married a Russian girl who now lived with his son in Moscow.

"I wanted to see them, but the Russians would not let me so I wrote a hundred letters to Brezhnev and later to Gorbachev. I went to Moscow and sat outside the Kremlin shouting for them to give my son back."

I was horrified at the thought. "What happened Petros?" I asked, wondering how the Russian communist regime had reacted to Onassis the Second waving his arms and shouting insults at them in the Kremlin from Red Square.

"They threw me in jail. Communists are completely materialistic in their theory. They could not understand that I was reincarnated."

He told me how he was deported from Moscow and had not been able to see his son, who was now seventeen. It was a tragic story.

"I will settle everything when I marry Athina," he said with finality and hung up.

One day in the summer of 2000 I was on a yacht of a Greek shipowner for whom Petros had worked after being fired from the Onassis group. The captain of the yacht who knew Petros from his tanker days told me that Petros had brought his Russian wife, a child bride of 16, onto the tankers which were breaking the oil blockade in the Gulf during the Iran-Iraq war.

Petros' child-bride found herself in a totally foreign and bewildering environment. She was on the tanker when it was strafed by aircraft, rocketed by shore batteries and hit by an Exocet missile. Terrified, disoriented and insecure she had found security in the bunks of Petros' fellow officers. This for her husband's fragile mind had been the final straw. After this Petros started hallucinating regularly and was soon sent home to Greece. He looked for an outlet for his frustration and before long locked onto a new target. He became obsessed by the granddaughter of Onassis and her half-sister Sandrine.

I found out later that Petros had been seriously affected by a traumatic episode in his family when he was 5 years old. He recounted to me that he had seen his father murder his mother in front of his eyes. Petros was then passed on to relatives who brought him up. On occasion when I discussed these things with him, hoping to ease the isolation he felt, he would open up but would soon get back onto his favourite subject, Athina. He was not a man to lose sight of his quarry for long. He confided to me that he was furious with the Roussel secretary working at the Roussel apartment at 88 Avenue Foch, near the Arc De Triomphe in Paris.

"Just imagine! I travelled all the way to Paris to ask Thierry for Athina's and Sandrine's hand in marriage. When I arrived at the apartment I rang the bell and a secretary opened the door. She let me in, but when I told her my name she locked me in the guest toilet. She then brought a concierge who threw me out. No sense of hospitality to travellers, Mr. Mantheakis, these French, I tell you, absolutely shocking!"

I could imagine the panic of the secretary when, standing alone with the "family friend' inside the Roussel apartment she realised that she had opened the door to the obsessive stalker-suitor Petros.

One afternoon at Lussy just before Athina was to return home from school Thierry was in his study when one of the bodyguards noticed a furtive figure in a far corner of the garden near where Athina kept her two sheep. The British guard gave out the alarm. Other guards rushed to apprehend the intruder who immediately lifted his hands in a motion of surrender. He was quickly taken to the kitchen where he was interrogated by the bodyguards. Thierry looked in to see what all the fuss was about and saw Petros in the middle of all the excitement. Thierry ordered the guards to release him after they told him not to come back again, explaining to him that he could have been shot. Petros had not only disturbed the Roussels at home that day but had another victim nearby. He had seriously annoyed a resident of the local youth hostel where he had slept the night before. Petros told me the story himself. He had run out of money by using all his resources to finance his expedition to Switzerland. On the previous evening in the youth hostel he had felt hungry. He had a plan he told me. He waited for the others in the dormitory to leave and at that propitious moment he started searching in the satchels of the absent students who were lodged in the same room. Petros was looking for food. In one bag he found two sandwiches, meticulously prepared and wrapped in cling film and aluminium foil. Petros ate the sandwiches quickly and wolfed down a bar of Nestle chocolate he found in the same bag. Pleased with himself, his hunger pangs now satisfied, he settled down on his bunk and drifted off into a contented sleep. Half an hour later he was rudely awoken by a commotion in the dormitory. Some of the students had returned.

Petros recounted what happened next. "One of the youths, a Japanese boy, was waving his arms about and protesting loudly that his sandwiches had been stolen. He looked at me accusingly. 'You were the only person here.' He said accusingly."

Petros told the complaining youth that he had indeed eaten his sandwiches, but that two thousand years ago St Paul had taught that "for the sick and for travellers there is no sin".

The protesting and hungry Japanese youth, deprived of his sandwiches, was understandably unwilling to accept this tenet of western religious philosophy and continued complaining for some time until Petros was thrown out of the dorm and found shelter in a nearby park.

This failed expedition to Switzerland made Petros even more determined. He was a man with a mission.

"I am packing my bags to go back, Mr. Mantheakis," he said to me some months later, "but I am short of money, so I will have to wait and save up my pension payments. I will call you after I marry Athina." With that he hung up.

Every Christmas a large parcel of olives of the best quality and a fine cheese was sent to me by Petros. A similar package was delivered to Athina and Sandrine in Switzerland. It was difficult for me to be angry with him even though he exasperated me at times. He only stopped calling me when Athina married Doda.

Athina's admirers were of all ages and dispositions. Some were cultured, more like opera fans, some adoring, while others were abusive and demanding. One day during Thierry's court case in Athens in 1998 a rough looking man of around 35 with a flushed red face and disheveled clothes came up to me demanding to talk to Thierry. I told him that Mr.

Roussel was busy with his court case and was not available. The man became insistent. At that moment there was a recess in the courtroom and Thierry came outside to talk to me.

"What does he want?" Thierry asked, seeing that the man had fixed him with a determined scowl.

"Tell him that I have come five hundred kilometres from my village. I want to marry Athina!"

"That is not possible," I answered," She is too young for such things and must finish her school first," giving him my standard answer whenever I was in this situation.

I translated what had been said to Thierry, thinking the situation rather funny. I saw that Thierry had a look of concern in his eyes. I turned round and saw that the suitor was now red in the face and was sputtering with fury.

"I came all the way here and will not leave without Athina. Tell Mr. Roussel to send for her right now!" he barked. I realised the man was dangerous and was likely to attack at any time.

"It's okay," said a reassuring voice just behind me. It was Costas our bodyguard and driver who made a quick move, grabbed the man in a vice-like grip by the elbow and handed him over to two policemen on guard duty at the door of the court building. The bell rang to indicate that our court was back in session and we quickly forgot the incident.

There is a permanent population of cranks who spend all day attending various trials in Athens, playing out their own fantasies and finding refuge, and possibly reassurance, in the drama of others. I had noticed in November 1998 that for a whole week there was a skinny blondish youth of around twenty sitting in the back of Thierry's courtroom, always in the same seat. He wore a beige raincoat and motorcycle boots. One day in recess he approached me and asked, without introducing himself "When is *my* situation going to be taken care of?"

"What situation?" I asked, mystified.

"My appointment as President of the Onassis Public Benefit Foundation." Here we go again, I thought.

From that day the youth pestered me regularly and eventually one evening he followed me to the hotel where Athina was staying after we returned from the Drakos wedding with the Roussel family. One of our guards called me on my mobile phone.

"Mr. Alexis," he said, "Sorry to call so late but we have caught a chap here who says he wants to see Athina. He looks a little vague."

"Does he have a blue motorbike?" I asked.

"That's him".

"Hold him at all costs, and don't let him through. He has been stalking Athina and Thierry for months.

Stefanos was on guard at the gate of the Astir Palace Hotel in Vouliagmeni, the large luxury resort hotel of several hundred acres where we were staying. It was past midnight. There were three of the Greek state VIP special branch police with Stefanos. They took the man's identification card, noted his name and told him to hop it otherwise he would find himself in jail.

That was the end of him. Or so I thought. One day the entry phone at my house in Melissia rang. I saw the face of the man on the screen of the videophone.

"I have brought some presents for Athina." I asked him for identification. He had an Arabic name. He explained that he was half-Syrian and lived in Greece. I did not let him into the house but I did send the presents to Athina, and thanked him on his inevitable reappearance a couple of months later. The last time I saw him he was in a Greek airman's uniform. Lowering his voice he confided that he had taken a leave of absence from the Syrian secret service for which he had been a specially trained agent.

He regularly popped up whenever Thierry was in Athens. My last encounter with him was when I saw him standing outside my gate. I asked what he wanted.

"Just to say hello" he beamed. I knew he was hiding something.

"What is it Abdullah?" I asked.

"I have just come back from Switzerland. I spent a month on holiday there and visited Athina's house several times, though the guards would not let me in."

He was radiant with happiness at having got so close to the object of his admiration.

Not all Athina's admirers are so ardent. One of the greatest fans I have got to know is Yanna, a 25 year old girl, short in stature and permanently dressed in black. Yanna has an inordinate affection for Athina. She arrives at the airport each time Athina comes to Greece, tracking her discreetly to her hotels, giving her flowers and sending cards at Christmas and on her birthday. She is useful in her own way as she keeps notes of everything. She watches and tapes all the news items on television and at the end of each year writes a report on Athina, rather like a train-spotter. The hand-written document, professionally bound, is given to me in triplicate, a copy is sent to Thierry, and one is for Athina.

As Athina grew older she became an attractive girl with a certain air of mystery about her. She was enshrouded by the myth of being the last survivor of the legendary Greek Onassis dynasty. She was a person beyond the reach of ordinary people. As a result she entered the Greek psyche as its national idol for a while. For a teenager it was a difficult and demanding position to be in, but she adapted well, keeping a tantalizing distance from the media. In a symbolic way she reminded me during her teens of the stories recounted by early European explorers in the Congo who described the existence of a graceful long-necked deer the natives called the Okapi. It was a slim animal which would appear for a few seconds in some small clearing in the vast Ituri forest before infuriatingly disappearing into the shadows, not allowing itself to be captured or photographed. For many years the elusive African deer was a legend. The African Okapi with its huge fawn eyes was real though, and so, of course, was Athina, but to the Greek public she remained a mysterious embodiment of the Onassis myth. As such she will always have her admirers, whether it is the obsessed Petros with his hundreds of letters or the gentle Yanna with her meticulously kept diaries of Athina sightings and her yearly homage of presents for the heiress at Christmas and birthdays. Athina's marriage to Doda and her turning her back on her relatives in Greece and all things Greek, including the family sanctuary of Scorpios Island where her mother, her uncle Alexander and her grandfather are buried has dented the myth somewhat. There are those now who regularly voice their dissatisfaction that she is never reported lighting a candle or holding a memorial service in Panagitsa Chapel at Scorpios at the silent white marble graves of her mother Christina and her grandfather Aristotle Onassis whose business acumen and vision made her and Doda's billionaire lifestyle possible. It is an accusation that Athina will have to answer herself.

People often walk up to me in the street and ask about Athina. The woman at my local newsagent brightens up when I enter her shop when she has a found a new item about Athina in one of the publications on sale. Petrol station attendants when they recognise me say "Tell Athina to come to Greece" or warn me "Tell her to be careful". The same thing happened regularly at income tax offices, in ministries, in tavernas and when I went to church when I was the Roussel family representative. Everyone, from judges and government ministers to hotel cleaning women wanted to know "What is she like?"

It seems like only yesterday when the same people would ask me "Is it true that her father keeps Athina locked up as a hostage in a village in Switzerland?" It took hard, stressful years of patiently meeting journalists, showing them documents, arguing with editors and news department heads, having meetings with embassies and with television channel reporters and their bosses to slowly change the public image of the Roussel family. The truth is that Athina, the Golden Heiress and granddaughter of Onassis was a happy teenager in a loving household until she was seventeen when discord entered the Roussel household and she left to live with Doda in Brazil. The world saw the young heiress who was hung onto her father's arm and adored him turn against Roussel and against members of her family after choosing to live with her handsome older Brazilian Olympic horseman. The question was what had Athina seen or experienced in Switzerland and in the three-story house she shared with Thierry in Brussels in the last two years leading up to her coming of age that had brought about this change in attitude? What was the incident or incidents that made her become her father's bitter opponent, not inviting him or his friends to her wedding and what indeed drove Athina to have her father investigated when she was with Doda?

The case went on day to day, week to week. Gaby in the meantime had to leave to be with Athina and the other children. Thierry spent all his days in court. Just before the Roussel case another officer, a man called Moschopoulos from Citibank Piraeus had written to Thierry, when he requested information regarding movements of funds in Citibank accounts belonging to his Athina. Moschopoulos wrote to Roussel, who was Athina's legal and only guardian, *"**We will not give you information regarding your daughter's accounts, since our legal department says you are not authorized to request this information.**'*
From Citibank 600,000 dollars had been withdrawn from Athina's funds without Thierry being able to find to whom the money finally went to.

After weeks in court following the proceedings in Greek and having to have the translation whispered to him by his interpreter Fasoulakis Thierry was showing visible signs of exhaustion. One noontime I saw that his forehead was covered with beads of sweat and he was obviously uncomfortable sitting for so long on the hard wooden chair at the front of the court. He was running a high fever. Thierry crossed his legs trying to make himself comfortable. Ioannis Diotis, the moustachioed prosecutor angrily addressed Fasoulakis. *"**Tell him to sit properly**"* he said, pointing to Thierry. "He is in a court of law here."

Thierry did not have to be in the court at all, since he was sick with a high fever. He need not even have come to Greece for the case, but he had stated before the trial, and after arriving also, that he had confidence in the Greek legal system. It was a statement that others would be more reticent to make in view of the judicial scandals that were beginning to become known and would soon result in high profile criminal cases against Greek prosecutors and judges accused of fixing cases and influencing decisions.

He had a duty to defend his daughter's interests, and those of the Foundation, he said, and he would attend. The prosecutor's sense of court propriety was ruffled because the son-in-law of Onassis, an internationally known public figure, who had honoured both the Greek court and the prosecutor by attending the court proceedings was not sitting exactly as the prosecutor wanted, upright with his legs uncrossed, for the entire duration of the six weeks' trial. Roussel sat up "properly" and uncrossed his legs as instructed. Two hours later his driver and I took him to his hotel room where we put him to bed after administering strong anti-fever medication and antibiotics. For Thierry any infection could have been fatal because he had been subjected to major surgery with removal of part of his intestine.

The next day Thierry arrived at court with a fever of 40° C. Judge Alevisos announced the start of proceedings and we all sat down. Thierry sat upright with his legs uncrossed, as ordered by Mr. Diotis. Thierry was not going to further offend the prosecutor's sense of court decorum.

I had no time to speculate about the decision because someone told us that the judges had already entered the courtroom.

Thierry stood at the front and began his statement of defence. He spoke about how he had become embroiled in the dispute with the Foundation, how Papadimitriou and his colleagues had taken it over slowly, replacing the Onassis family members with their own children whenever there was a death or a retirement. He explained the hereditary right of Athina to the presidency of the Foundation and said that the reports from both the employees of the Onassis Foundation but also the balance sheets his financial advisers had seen indicated that the Foundation was on a slippery financial course. It had been his duty, as Athina's guardian and father, to make enquiries and to demand explanations.These were not sufficiently forthcoming. The general impression was that Stelios Papadimitriou was running the Onassis Foundation like a family institution, a Papadimitriou family institution, and he had admitted as much having said the Foundation was his "fourth child".

"I have had a heavy responsibility to protect both the Foundation and the Onassis family's interest in it, even though this has brought me into direct and bitter conflict with the Onassis Foundation presidency. I have suffered intense and worldwide public denigration in the press by Papadimitriou. This though is a burden which I have borne with fortitude. I have never wavered in the defence of Athina's rights or those of the Foundation founded by my former father-in-law, Aristotle Onassis, and presided over by my wife, Christina.

What I did I did for my underage daughter, and I never flinched from this duty, however painful it was when I had as opponents the full weight of the Onassis Foundation with its enormous financial resources and the prestige of the Onassis name, which the four former employees used to full advantage against me and my daughter.

I came to Greece, to your court to let you know of my motives and to present my evidence. I did this myself, and with my expert witnesses. I did it for my daughter's future, for her future in the Foundation, and for her future in Greece.

My daughter was deprived of her mother Christina at an early age, and I had to be there for her, to give her a secure home, a family to love her, and a place where she would be safe. I knew that when she was older - as the only surviving descendant of Onassis - she would ask me many questions - and I would have to tell her what I had done to protect her interests. It is this duty that has brought me before your court, Mr. President, Lady Judges, and Mr. Prosecutor.

Thierry was visibly moved, and his voice cracked for a second. He stopped to regain his composure. Nikos Fasoulakis, the interpreter, had tears in his eyes and was having difficulty in translating. For a moment I thought I saw a glimmer of compassion in court president Alevisos eyes. What I had also noticed though, to my surprise, was that neither of the two women judges, as far as I had seen, had made a single note during Thierry's defence speech. If they had kept notes it had escaped my attention.

Thierry continued his apologia. The blonde woman judge looked out of the window.

"I ask you, with all respect," he said "to carefully consider what I have told you, and what you have heard from the other side these last few weeks. You will see there was no intention to slander the Onassis Foundation and its presidency, nor was there any personal financial, or other, motive in my accusations, since I never asked to be on the board of the Onassis Foundation. There was desperation on my side to uncover what was happening at the Foundation as reports of increasing debt and depleted cash came to my attention.

I ask you now to carefully consider the supporting evidence and to vindicate me in my struggle to protect my daughter Athina's interests and those of the Onassis Foundation. Thank you."

The court adjourned. Two court reporters who had entered the room in the last half-hour came up to Thierry to ask him questions. The case was to wind up the next day, in Building 8, in the centre of the court complex. After hearing Thierry's moving summing up I was influenced by it and had forgotten the warnings and the doomsayers. I could not envision more than a moderate fine for Thierry. This was an opinion shared by those who had come to the court that day.

*

December 12th, 1998. Day 42.

I teased Thierry that even the Nuremberg trial had not lasted this long. The wear and tear had been evident on all of us, especially on the old men in the opposition benches. We arrived shortly after 8.30 a.m. in chamber Number 9. The courtroom was one of the large ground floor halls used for important cases and it was already full of television technicians fiddling with knobs and electric cable connectors. A row of television camera tripods had been set up in the third row of the audience benches. Newspaper reporters were wandering around with small notebooks in their hands.

We were relieved to see that we would all be home for Christmas. A defamation trial had taken up the best part of two months. When the proceedings started Papadimitriou and the Onassis Foundation lawyers made their speeches. It was a grim parade as they shifted their attack from the financial issues and gave emphasis to a controversial letter Christina had supposedly written to Papadimitriou, asking him to protect her against Thierry.

This letter was repeatedly mentioned, though nobody saw fit to question the circumstances in which it was written, and why it was written. The opposition played on the fact that Thierry had had a concurrent relationship with Christina and Gaby before settling for Gaby. It was a transition of emotions experienced by millions of men and women before changing partners to start a new life. This then was the level on which the opposition lawyers chose to argue against the accusations of mismanagement that Thierry had made against the Foundation Four. Their shipping lawyer, Polis Tsiridis was the exception. He stayed close to shipping matters. His delivery though was shocking to the uninitiated and was designed no doubt to be intimidating. Repeated accusations, finger pointing, shouting at the top of his voice, wildly exaggerated gestures and histrionic expressions completed the figure of a man who had apparently lost control. Of course it was a professional act and Thierry quickly caught on to this. Gaby on the other hand who happened to be in court one day and not understanding what was going on, was visibly distressed by the shouting directed at her husband.

There was a short coffee break. I saw Polis Tsiridis coming along the courtroom corridor towards Thierry in order to go to the toilets whose entrance was a few feet behind us. As Tsiridis passed he nodded politely whereupon Thierry stretched out his hand to Tsiridis and said to me "Tell him that was a very good speech."

Tsiridis was taken aback for a moment, but immediately broke out into a beaming smile and shook Thierry's hand vigorously.

"Tell Mr. Roussel I find him very *sympathiticos*. If I was not of this side of the dispute I would very much like to stay and talk to him."

Noblesse Oblige. Thierry, the object of a violent tirade for an hour and a half by Tsiridis, had the breeding, and no doubt the cunning to shake his opponents hand immediately afterwards. Seeing this I knew that whatever happened in this case we would win in the end.

Shortly after lunch the Roussel lawyers made their winding up statements. Prof. Courakis, the head of Thierry's legal team, made an impassioned speech which touched on the issue of the court's responsibility to Athina and to the Greek nation. A sentence which would ignore these issues would be harmful not only to the defendant and to his daughter, in whose name the battle was being waged, but also to the Greek nation.

Professor Karras, a university teacher with an intimate knowledge of court procedure, pointed out the defects of the plaintiffs' arguments as relating to the law. He launched an attack on the prosecutor for the way he had handled himself in specific instances during the proceedings. This was the first time that I saw Diotis ruffled. His face became flushed and he asked to be allowed to speak in order to answer to Karras.

When the lawyers had all finished it was the turn of the prosecutor to summarize the case and to make recommendations for sentencing. He began a long drawn-out attack on Thierry, ignoring the logic of the points Thierry's defence had made, accepting absolutely nothing of the expert witnesses arguments. He allowed no leeway for even the slightest doubt regarding even a single of Thierry's points made over the last 42 days.

Diotis continued his attack on Thierry. He explained how Athina's father had acted irresponsibly by questioning the character and actions of "these four honest men". Roussel, he said, had put Athina's relationship with the Foundation presidency in jeopardy. This of course was absolute nonsense as a decision in the Swiss courts soon just days after said that it was the four who had acted in a manner unbecoming to a minor's board administrators.

The prosecutor continued his attack on Roussel seeing nothing of importance in a father demanding to know where 130,000 USD of his daughter's personal money had gone to after being sent to a Foundation company on the instructions of the Foundation Four. Samoa, a Foundation company enshrouded in secrecy had received Athina's personal money, but this was not worth examining for the prosecutor, Roussel was. Diotis began reading an old letter of Christina, written under circumstances of emotional strain, while ignoring the fact that this letter was cancelled out soon after by another letter where Christina wrote that she trusted Thierry implicitly. Nor did the prosecutor take the obvious step and say that the first letter had been supplanted by Christina's will, a public document - in fact a much more valid document - which had been signed and sealed before witnesses. In the will Christina had placed Thierry as head of the trustees managing Athina's fortune. Did this show a lack of trust? Contrarily, she showed that even though she was no longer married to Thierry when she wrote the will, she wanted him to be there, first, on the list of administrators of Athina's fortune. Not only this, but she left the guardianship and upbringing of Athina totally to Roussel.

The prosecutor, referring to the first letter, made a melodramatic reference saying that in it "we hear the desperate cry of Christina's voice from the grave". The letter, untypical of Christina, was in opposition to the undisputed fact that until the last day of her life Christina adored Thierry and she trusted him implicitly both with her daughter and to be on the board of administrators of Athina's patrimony. Diotis wound up his dramatic speech by looking directly at Thierry. He then turned to the judges and said "I recommend sentencing the accused on all counts." He had in his winding up claimed that Roussel had made up everything to harm the decent men who were running the Onassis Foundation. Thierry after hearing Diotis speech turned to me. I shrugged my shoulders. It was dark outside now and the courtroom was full. At the back of the room three rows of media people were stacked one behind the other behind the packed audience benches.

"Adjournment until 8 p.m." said the judge. "We shall return then to hand down the verdict".

Thierry and I pushed our way through the courtroom crowd and went into the dark parking lot outside where Thierry's driver was waiting for us. Around us I could see that the other neo-classical buildings had their lights on though the courtrooms were empty. Only a few people were wandering about now on the narrow asphalt paths that linked the buildings separated by expanses of lawn. Despite Diotis tirade a little while before, Thierry was feeling confident. I was too. The phone call of the day before and other warnings had been pushed aside. Driving through dark streets in the light evening winter traffic I thought little of the doomsayers.

We soon reached a restaurant, the *Academy,* in Academias Street and went up stairs to the dining room. The furnishings were plush, like a pre-war Viennese tea room and we were shown by the head waiter to a large round window table. The few other diners present turned to look at us with curiosity as we passed by them. Everyone knew Thierry from the repeated TV news coverage of him and many knew me by now because I was almost always next to him and Athina on their visits to Greece.

Thierry was in a good mood, he asked my opinion and I confirmed that I was sure that it would be a fair trial and he would not receive more than a small fine at the most. Athina, anxious as to the outcome of the case, called as we were ordering, and Gaby called during the meal. Thierry told them that everything was all right.

I had lobster tails in cream and fresh pasta accompanied by a green salad while Thierry ate fish. He told me of how grateful he was to me, and thanked me for making Greece and its visits so pleasant for him. "I have many things in my mind I want to do here, and I want to build the house in Glyfada for Athina," he added.

We chatted about his other plans, to buy a boat and moor it here permanently. He himself would learn Greek he told me. He had many things in mind and he was sure Athina would be happy to return here on many occasions and put down roots. I was glad that I had been able to organize their visits and to show them that people loved Athina in Greece. The "Four" were an exception and were not to be counted; I had said on many an occasion and the family seemed to understand it now.

We left the Academy and were back at the courts at 7.45 p.m. Nearly all the interior lights of the court buildings were off now, and only Building Number Nine was brightly lit from the inside. As we entered Thierry was wished good luck by the camera crews and by several onlookers. He took his seat at the front next to interpreter Fasoulakis, and by 8 p.m. the whole room was in a buzz. The camera crews that had tried to come forward for the decision were ordered to the back of the room and the audience benches were all full now. Journalists from all over the world were there. Among them was Angeliki Korouni, who had temporarily left the battlefields of Kosovo to report on the Roussel verdict for her listeners in France and Switzerland.

Papadimitriou and his three colleagues sauntered in, Papadimitriou nonchalantly jiggling a *komboloi*. Their aggravation after Thierry's defence speech was gone. They sat down next to their lawyers, whispering among themselves. As the president walked in I tried to discern his attitude, but could see no tell-tale signs. The two women judges' faces were totally impassive.

With the entry of the judges there was a buzz in the court and the bank of television klieg were turned on. Dozens of camera shutters started clicking and camera motors whirred as the court president told everyone to sit down. Everyone except for Thierry and Fasoulakis.

"Regarding the first charge....." Alevisos seemed to be having difficulty reading. His hand was shaking. I wondered why.

"..... Defamation with intent, one year in prison. For the second charge, eighteen months in prison, for the third charge nine months in prison........." it went on, and on, until Thierry had accumulated a total of nine years of prison sentences. There was palpable shock in the court. Papadimitriou nudged his lawyer with a smile. Zambellas for the first time in two months was beaming. Perhaps he felt that this was the end of Roussel. If that was what he felt it turned out to be a very premature assumption. Before long both Zambellas and Papadimitriou would be dead from cancer while their archrival Roussel who was incredibly resilient put the Greek court defeat behind him, set up a trust to manage Athina's money with four major respected banking institutions as co-trustees and went on to create a successful hedge fund with Rothschild Bank, Citicorp, and three other prestigious financial institutions as his fund's advisers.

The judge looked up. One of Roussel's lawyers stood up and asked to speak.

'Mr. President, it is with the utmost surprise that we here have seen that you have not in one instance recommended any mitigation of sentence or reduced them as Greek law specifically says on a first offence. We would like you to act as the law and justice allows you, and to reduce the sentences."

Alevisos went back to his scratch pad and made notes.

"Your total sentence is 60 months," he said to Thierry. This reduction was obligatory since Greek law demands that some sentences run concurrently with others. The only concession Alevisos made was to allow Thierry to pay a fine. Again this was customary, and was not a sign of clemency.

The press rushed forward to get a statement from Thierry. At the front of the group was the familiar figure of Swiss radio and television reporter Angeliki Kourouni. Thierry stopped to make a brief statement. There was a momentary hush in the courtroom.

"What I did was for my daughter Athina, who looks to me for protection. She is a wonderful girl and I will continue to fight for her, if necessary I will go to every court in the world. I will appeal the decision of this court."

As we passed journalists and the television crews, I remember only a swirl of faces of the press and the audience mumbling. Fractured sentences I heard around me at that moment stuck in my mind, sentences of shock and indignation prompted by the exceptionally harsh verdict.

Pressed forward by the crowd we were swept out in a small group across the dark gardens of the law courts and across to another building. The Greek authorities had kept the appeals office open after hours for Thierry. Fasoulakis, our interpreter, was next to me, his eyes full of tears. He had brought his sister with him and she too looked distressed. Thierry's fight had dragged in all those who were close to him, even those in a professional capacity. Our lawyers were moving around us now as Thierry and I leaned against a long wooden counter behind a clerk of the court was preparing the appeals documents. By lodging his appeal immediately Thierry was allowed to wait until a higher court made his sentence and fine final.

Twenty minutes later we walked outside, Thierry was a free man until his appeal. We walked briskly to where the taxi driver was waiting. Thierry's phone rang at that moment. It was Gaby and Athina calling from Switzerland. They had heard the news about the decision live on Swiss radio.

Costas, our driver, was at my elbow, talking to me, trying to attract my attention which was rivetted on Thierry. "Mr. Alexis go home and relax, you need it." My voice had become totally hoarse as a tide of indignation and anger swept up from my feet and engulfed me.

"We will beat them Thierry, we will beat them. I promise you," I said, determined to make a sea change in the way things had gone.

"You promised me before Alexis, You promised me everything would be okay," said Thierry getting into his taxi as he bent over his mobile phone to call someone. He was right of course. I had listened to the voices of reason and had ignored the doomsayers.

"Athina will never come here again after this, she told me," said Thierry, as he closed the window of the cab, I could see he was crying.

She did come again, but she would have been perfectly justified in not doing so to a country which had treated her father so harshly. Much smaller sentences had been given to people who had paid to have their husbands murdered and to drug dealers caught with kilos of heroin in their possession. Several months later I heard that in a grand quorum meeting of Greek judges the question of the extreme severity of the sentence against Thierry had been discussed.

"The decision was like a thunderclap in the courtroom" announced one of the TV anchors. The news of the sentence was on all the news channels now and was being broadcast live from the law courts.

"The judges took the law to its utmost bounds of severity. It was a totally unexpected decision". All the channel reports were similar. On Sky TV, Papadimitriou's son's station, the newscaster was beaming. On his programme there had been attacks on Thierry and he had not refrained from making snide remarks about Athina's father. There had even been attacks on teenage Athina herself. A few weeks before the case 12 year old Athina had been accused on the channel's prime time news of not knowing how to "administer her huge fortune" and "what sort of Greek is that that she is speaking?" When I contacted the station demanding to be heard, I was shunted off to a complaints department and then to a dead number until the news broadcast was over. A subsequent complaint to the Broadcasting Complaints

Authority by one of our lawyers was sat on for months and finally they replied that they had "lost the complaint". This was the climate for Athina and Thierry, and we would have to beat it.

As soon as Thierry left the court complex I saw a couple of shadows in the dark and saw two of our lawyers, Yannis Aletras and Miltos Papangelis.

"Let us go for a drink," Aletras said "at *Pritaneon.*"

It was a bar in a converted two-storey house in the heart of Kolonaki, the central Athens residential enclave where fashionable boutiques vied with smart cafes and restaurants for clientele. I called home saying I needed a break and would be back later.

All the time I was thinking. I had to organize our defense strategy. I had for once been caught with only a thin safety net. As we sat in the bar drinking neat whisky, among the lawyers, yuppies and long-legged blonde Athenian girls a name came to me. I blurted out to the Aletras and Papangelis, "There is a solution – Katsantonis."

I was referring to the seventy year-old dean of all law professors and lawyers in Greece. Dr Alexander Katsantonis was the unchallenged star of Greece's criminal lawyers, a man who had stayed at the top of the profession for decades. His shock of floppy gray hair, alert blue eyes and strong mouth gave one the impression that if this father figure looked after you, there would be nothing to worry about. The bar was getting crowded now and Yannis Aletras, the long-time friend of mine whom I had introduced to Thierry, Papangelis and I were wedged into the far corner of the curving bar. I took out my phone and called Katsantonis' office.

"Professor, I am the representative of Thierry Roussel," I said, "and we need your help. Can we meet?"

"Tonight's court decision was unacceptable," he replied," I am leaving tomorrow morning for the Swiss Alps for Christmas, but let's meet and talk on January 2nd when I get back, and tell Mr. Roussel not to worry, Mr. Mantheakis."

The next day I called Thierry in Geneva, and Yves Repiquet in Paris to tell them the news about Katsantonis. I suggested they make inquiries about him at the French embassy if they wanted independent corroboration as to who he was. It was not necessary, they told me. Thierry would send me a letter with instructions.

I saw that Thierry was still understandably annoyed by the verdict and I knew that Athina would have been very upset by this decision. It would be difficult for her and her schoolmates to understand that a sentence in Greece for defamation means a fine, and there is no shame attached to it.

"What do we do now?" asked Yves.

"Let us take stock for three or four days. I suggest no press releases until we see exactly where we are in this situation. Then we can make a plan," I replied. This was agreed. When the professor came back we met in his Likavitou Street offices at the base of Mount Lycabettus, the pine clad hill in central Athens.

"Professor Katsantonis," I began, "Athina distressed and is crying all the time and Thierry is indignant at the treatment he got here."

He smiled."Mr. Mantheakis," he addressed me kindly "The decision has shocked those of us in the legal profession.The sentence on Mr. Roussel is not acceptable and has been widely criticised - but remember my words, it was so severe that it has created a surge of public feeling for Mr. Roussel and it will work against his opponents. I shall be happy to take on the case."

Both the professor and I knew that once it was known he was on our side there would be enormous pressure on him, even from political circles, to back off. There was opposition to him taking the case but they had not reckoned with his stubbornness.

"A person in a very high position asked me why I was taking on this case," he said to me some days later. "I replied that my reputation would be in grave danger if I allowed Onassis son-in-law to carry a sentence like that."

Professor Katsantonis was on board, and he was the one man I felt Papadimitriou feared in the legal profession. Katsantonis was a seemingly gentle man, given to violent outbursts though when his sense of propriety was outraged. The judges knew this and the public knew it. In the courts Katsantonis was an icon. It was up to him now not to disappoint us.

The only overt reaction from the Onassis Foundation to the appointment was a comment by Papadimitriou that "Roussel is unreliable because he keeps changing his lawyers." It was the first time that Thierry had changed lawyers in Greece. Papadimitriou knew that from now on the game had changed. He was not playing on an empty pitch.

That night after the meeting with the professor in his office I drove home to where I live in Melissia, in the north of Athens, and collapsed onto a couch. All my muscles were hurting and my inner world was numb. Dimitra, my, wife came to sit next to me, rubbing my shoulders and my temples to drive away the tension that had built up over the gruelling weeks of the court case. There were selfish reasons to have a Greek wife, I once again said to myself, not ignoring the fact that they are notoriously opinionated and volatile, but they do know when to stand by their companions and I was grateful now for the soothing, strong palms that kneaded my neck and shoulders.

"We will win." I said. And we both knew we would.

My battle was not only in the courts and in the media; I had to explain some important things to the Onassis heiress and her family. Athina's father had been convicted in Greece for accusations he had made regarding the administration of the Onassis Foundation by the former family employees. I now had to give a convincing explanation to Athina, as to why her father had received a five year jail sentence from Mr. Alevisos and Mr. Diotis. How could one explain this to the Onassis heiress when a major drug dealer had been sentenced to a smaller sentence for selling thousands of doses of lethal narcotics, and two people responsible for 74 deaths in Salonica had received only a 4 year sentence, one less than Thierry's? I remembered Thierry's confession to me in his room at the Hilton one day when he had said that on two ro three occasions during the dispute with the Onassis Foundation and the problems he had faced with Greek justice he had thought of committing suicide. Prosecutor Diotis' job in the Roussel case was over, mine had only just begun.

But life plays strange tricks and Ioannis Diotis was, not many years later, faced with a very public near-tragedy in his own home that had reflections of the Onassis story in it. It inevitably brought back memories of how accusatory and personal he had been during the Roussel case when he had referred to family relationships in the Roussel household and thrown lightning bolts at Thierry in a case that was primarily one of economic and inter-corporate issues. But let me not judge others. Time will do that for all of us and, hopefully, we will all be more humble in the end. (Note – in September of 2014 prosecutor Ioannis Diotis himself was summoned by a senior prosecutor investigating a major political and financial scandal in Greece involving billions of dollars of overseas deposits by Greek citizens and politicians at HSBC, a scandal known as the Lagarde Affair, to explain his actions connected with the scandal under investigation. He was not summoned as a witness but for suspicion of criminal wrongdoing.)

The beginning of 1999 was a period of the intense legal confrontation between Thierry and the 4 Greeks. The mosaic of court actions and counter actions was so complicated, and the jurisdictions so widespread with overlapping decisions that it took me months to understand the overall picture. In the forefront were two civil court cases which had been heard in Greece. Other cases were under deliberation in the Cantonal courts of Switzerland. The Swiss Juvenile Authority - the Tutelle - an independent court authority responsible for overseeing the financial affairs of minors, had recently handed down a historic decision ejecting Papadimitriou and the entire board of the patrimony. This decision was superseded three days later by another Swiss court ruling. The new decision now suspended the Tutelle decision which had in turn given management of the fortune to KPMG, the international auditing firm. The management was now given back to the Greeks. Almost at the same time the Federal High Court of Switzerland passed down a ruling allowing the Tutelle to install another international auditing firm, Ernst and Young, to check on certain transactions carried out by the board over the previous three years. Thierry himself had an appeal coming up in Greece, against the defamation sentence passed on him in December 1998, while yet another criminal court was considering charging Papadimitriou for defamatory statements in the press against Thierry. It was a matter of note that many of the court cases initiated by the Four Greeks were defined as being "*gegen* Athina Roussel" – against Athina Roussel. The legal expenses for these cases were charged to her by her four administrators.

Fourteen legal firms located in Greece, France and Switzerland were working for the Roussel family, while a number of expensive legal firms had been employed by Papadimitriou and the Foundation in an effort to get Thierry out of their hair, allowing them to retain management of Athina's money. Against this incredibly complicated background of international suit and counter suit were the psychologically disturbing scenarios that had previously terrified Athina. 1999 was a very difficult time for the children and for Thierry as well.

Suddenly there was a welcome change of climate - an Onassis wedding in Greece. After three funerals in the family it was a most welcome change. Thierry called me to say that George Drakos, Athina's second cousin and grandson of Aunt Kalliroi, was getting married to Vicki Ioannides, the daughter of an Olympic airline pilot (no relation to Paul Ioannides of the Foundation). The wedding, Thierry explained, was to take place at the private chapel of Aunt Kalliroi's seaside estate at Lagonissi on July 3rd. Over five hundred guests were expected. The arrival of Athina at the centre of such a large family gathering would firmly place the Roussel family back in the centre of Athenian society and put the family into the proper perspective regarding their position as Onassis' rightful heirs. Papadimitriou and his associates were not invited to the wedding. It was the first public snub by the Greek members of the Onassis family against the former family employee-executives who had acted so badly against Aristotle's granddaughter and her father.

When Gaby announced to the children that they would be coming to Greece, young Johanna asked "Mum, is that the country where everybody pushes everyone else?" The rush of the paparazzi and the pressing TV crews during their previous visits had made Athina's little sister think that this is how everybody behaved in Greece!

The short walk from the VIP lounge of the East Air Terminal to our waiting cars was accomplished by our bodyguards and Greek police escort driving a wedge through the crowd of paparazzi, television reporters and well-wishers. When we settled into our cars I was pleased to see that Athina new bodyguards, two of whom were black former SAS commandos with intimidating looks and shaven heads, had an incredibly alert manner and were continuously in communication with the other members of our security team. The Greek Minister of Public Order and the head of the VIP section of the police headquarters had given us an additional escort of highly trained police officers, the same ones who looked after President Clinton and Prince Charles on their visits in the same year. Additionally I had Stefanos, our private head of security, Emilios, and a motorcycle outrider to ride next to the rear wheel of Athina's minivan as well as some other men to coordinate the team.

Our convoy made quick progress to the Astir Palace Hotel at Vouliagmeni, the exclusive seaside suburb resort of Athens. The hotel is accessed along a wide palm lined avenue that turns onto a large pine-forested peninsula. There among large villas and exclusive resort apartments lies the hotel complex in a hundred acres of lush semi-tropical grounds. Gaby had requested me to book rooms there after seeing the hotel with its three private beaches on a previous trip when we had sought refuge from the press while waiting for a delayed flight to Switzerland to be announced. The hotel staff were waiting for us and the entry bar had already been lifted at the gates as we arrived, chased by press cars and motorcycles. Getting out of our cars we swept into a large lounge overlooking the sea: heads everywhere turned to look at our party as conversation in the large hotel lobby stopped. Athina was by now used to the fuss made over her in Greece and just wanted to get up to her room to eat something as it was nearly four o'clock. The rest of us were in a hurry to change out of our jackets and ties as the temperature was over 40 degrees centigrade.

Our bookings at the hotel had been cancelled by accident from Boislande and the hotel management had at the last moment miraculously found a row of rooms for us on the top floor, no mean feat at this time of the year when the hotel was full of Greek shipowners, minor Arab princes and international businessmen and politicians. Connie Perez, the hotel's Columbian PR head undertook to escort Athina and her family and to make things smooth for their stay.

The children disappeared into their rooms in a state of excitement while Thierry, Gaby and I settled down to have a snack and a drink and to briefly catch up on what had been happening. I was surprised at the change in Thierry since I last had seen him. He looked unusually haggard, his hair was long and shaggy over his collar and the whites of his eyes were a malarial yellow.

He looked quite ill. I was worried to see that he had also lost an alarming amount of weight, a fact that could not be hidden by the padded shoulders of his blue suit. The jacket drooped on his shoulders. It was unlike Thierry to be like this and it showed me that he must have been under considerable stress for quite a while.

"What news of Papadimitriou?" he asked. It was his standard question.

"I am always optimistic about our cases, Thierry," I answered. "The Four are not the people they were two years ago."

Thierry was not to be cheered up.

"We are finished - they have the management of Athina's patrimony now, and I am very afraid they will not give Athina her inheritance easily. Athina will not be able to fight Papadimitriou alone. It is over. "

Thierry had never in the past shown this defeatism.

"Why do you say that?" I asked.

"The Swiss court gave them back the management 3 days after the Tutelle ruled it must go to KPMG."

I admit that this ruling had been a shock at the time. Later when I discussed it with lawyers in Greece they explained that it would be quite normal for a stay to be granted until the Four Greeks appeal had been heard, otherwise it would mean that the fortune would go back and forth like a ping-pong ball. All the secrets of Athina's accounts and holdings would then have to be revealed to an outside company (KPMG) before the courts had ruled definitively on who should have the management of the patrimony.

I explained this to Thierry, but he was too dejected to be persuaded by my argument.

"There is of course no guarantee that the courts will not overturn the original decision and leave the management to Papadimitriou, Thierry," I added, "but there is a logic to the way the Swiss are handling the matter."

"I don't think so," concluded Thierry. I, though, was still optimistic and told him so. He was very tired and so I left him to take a nap. He would need this break because we had to leave for the wedding in less than two hours.

At six o'clock our convoy left the Astir Palace hotel. There were once more a group of photographers inside the grounds, a situation which unfortunately was allowed by the management who otherwise were very accommodating of their famous young client.

Emilios was riding a motorcycle in front of us, shrilly blowing a whistle to warn pedestrians and other cars of our approach, while the accompanying police cars followed us, their rotating beacons warning other cars to give way. Our convoy drove rapidly along the tight curves of the coastal road, past the barren brown scenery which lies between Vouliagmeni and Lagonissi where the wedding was to take place. On the way the busy road passes in front of several typically South Mediterranean resort settlements, with their mix of apartment houses, villas, tourist shops and cafes. The presence of two parked patrol cars at the 37.5 km marker of the Athens–Cape Sounion road signalled that we had arrived at Aunt Kalliroi's lush beachfront estate. There were cameras crews and paparazzi there waiting for us. Uniformed police held them back so we could go through the gates into the property where Athina's aunt Marilena Patronikola, the mother of the groom, was waiting for us in the forecourt of the villa, next to the chapel. Marilena was with her companion, the motorcycle-riding surgeon Mihalis Gyras, a man known for his intelligent humour and his three beautiful daughters from his previous marriages. Marilena was Christina Onassis's first cousin and had been very close to her. I had met with her several times before and had been surprised the first time I saw her how like Christina she was.

Marilena, of medium height was attractive and intelligent and common Athenian folklore said that in addition to her former husbands (among whom was a well known industrialist, and the head of the largest state bank in Greece) there had been famous admirers who had kneeled at her feet – one a charismatic serving prime minister and another a famous singer whose silken voice and matinee idol good looks melted the hearts of most of the Greek female population between the ages of sixteen and eighty.

In the van behind me the Roussels were now stumbling over the folded seats of the vehicle and stepping down onto the gravel forecourt, brushing their jackets and straightening their clothes. All activity in the forecourt stopped as waiters and guests alike turned to stare at the Roussel family. Athina was wearing a long white dress, slit to above the knee, and a red jacket. Her hair had been cut short, a fact that was to be widely reported in the domestic and international media hungry for anything that had to do with the Onassis heiress.

No journalists were allowed into the wedding area because Thierry was aware that all attention would centre on Athina, something that could potentially spoil the wedding for the bride and groom. This after all was their day. The media making do of a difficult situation for them lined up outside the villa hedge. We could hear them calling out in the hope that Athina would turn round to be photographed. At the front entrance where we had parked ushers in dinner jackets were guiding the guests through the interior of the house to the lawns which bordered the beach in the front of the villa. We had arrived early and so were able to stretch our legs before the ceremony began.

Thierry was talking to Dimitra, who had come independently, and I found an opportunity to sit on a swinging garden settee from where I could observe the guests arriving. Athina and Gaby went inside the house to talk to Aunt Kalliroi, while Johanna, Sandrine and Erik wandered off to the pool, wishing they could change into swimsuits and dive in from the high board as they had done the summer before.

Smart starched linen and heavy silverware had been laid out on round tables, allowing for a total of eight hundred guests to be seated in the garden. Several attractive-looking young women in evening wear moved from table to table to make sure that everything was in place. One girl who wore a tight semi-transparent white dress caught the attention of the males who were wandering around. The girl was responsible for making sure that bowls of professionally arranged flowers were placed on every table. The image of her bending forward and tantalizingly revealing the outline of string panties through the white dress with its low cut back was broadcast by all the news channels reporting on the Onassis family wedding that day. Unknowingly, the anonymous blonde girl entered the news archives in Greece for ever; her image now part of the Onassis family heritage whenever the wedding footage is shown on television.

Looking out to the beach I saw a series of caravans parked on the sand with camera crews and their tripods precariously balanced on the vehicle roofs just beyond the perimeter fence of the Patronikola villa. Already tiny red lights indicated which cameras were rolling. Tall telescopic antennae and satellite dishes sent out the images to the television studios.

The wedding started an hour later at 8 p.m. outside the chapel near the entrance to the villa. As I stood on the lawn, among the hundreds of other guests outside the chapel, I had the opportunity to observe how at home Athina seemed here among her Greek relatives. The presence of the other guests, whose attention was on her most of the time, did not in the least bit perturb her. Athina knew who she was, and though she was just fourteen I could see that her family upbringing had given her the poise to deal with her situation.

The ceremony and reception made for an evening of unsurpassed glamour. Diamonds, emeralds and rubies from Harry Winston in New York and Cartier in Paris were in evidence throughout, together with heavy hand-beaten gold necklaces and earrings from Lalalounis and Zolotas in Athens, Geneva and Paris. Creations were displayed like the treasures of a maharani's dowry. As the bearded priest in his gold-thread embroidered robes went through the colourful Greek Orthodox ceremony, my wandering eye could not help observing the enormous expense many guests had gone to in order to make their appearance at the Onassis family estate that evening. Details stuck in my mind, especially the virgin beige soles of women's footwear indicating that much of the extraordinarily expensive apparel had been bought or budgeted for specifically for the wedding where the granddaughter of the "richest man on earth" would be in attendance.

One woman, Middle-Eastern in appearance, dripping in emeralds, wore a long gown of interwoven broad metallic azure and gold thread with matching shoes and a shimmering chiffon shoulder wrap embossed with gold stars. I could not help but think of her resemblance to an iridescent oversize blue-bottle fly.

When the chapel ceremony was over the Roussel family, I and Dimitra went and sat at table Number 2. With us was the second sister of Ari Onassis, Merope Konialides from Monte Carlo, and her Swedish daughter-in-law. Athina sat on my left, Dimitra on my right, next to Thierry, who was next to Aunt Merope. Gaby was next and the younger Roussel children were next to Gaby.

The sun had gone down now, and the whole setting was softly lit by candles and garden lights, while four long buffet tables under white awnings were receiving the attention of high-hatted chefs and meat carvers.

The guests present represented every section of Greek high society. Shipowners from Monte Carlo and London, Athenian industrialists, some with glamorous younger wives, politicians working the crowd. Internationally known film directors and some actors were also present. Onassis relatives were there and so were their relatives. A young glamorous twenty-something crowd of scions of famous families sat down next to well-exercised girlfriends with perfect tans and shiny hair. Women in thirty thousand dollar designer gowns walked by, wearing the mortgage price of an oil tanker in emeralds, rubies or diamonds on their necks and wrists, while less expensively dressed ladies hung onto the arms of expatriate banking and marine insurance executives.

When the guests were all seated the klieg lights on the roof of the TV vans were turned on, and the live band played for the entry of the bride and groom. How different indeed was the rough and contemptuous treatment of the media in Brazil when Athina and Doda wed six years later. Viki Ioannides, the bride, was ravishing in her long white embroidered gown as she swept in, accompanied by the full sound of the band, holding her wide wedding dress so as not to have it trail on the paths leading through the lawn. Viki and George went to sit at the elevated long table which was reserved for the immediate family.

From almost the moment we sat down the Swedish relative next to Athina took out a camera from her handbag and started taking pictures of the heiress, the flashbulb blinding us every few seconds. This went on all through dinner. For a moment we breathed in relief, thinking she had run out of film, but then she brought out another camera and continued shooting. I knew how Athina hated photographs and cameras because of the hounding the paparazzi had subjected her to since she was a baby, but she was concealing her feelings very well at the table. Thierry and Gaby showed no visible response to the photo intrusion by Athina's distant Swedish aunt, but I knew that they too must be annoyed, as we all were.

I had wondered when the first suitors would make their appearance at our table. I overheard the Swedish woman telling her teenaged son and daughter to make sure they sat near Athina when a chair was available. This plan was put into action sooner than I expected. When I returned from the buffet I found the woman's son firmly ensconced in my chair next to Athina. He saw me standing with my plate in my hand, and ignored me.

"Young man," I said menacingly, "That is my chair."

He looked at me with an expression of annoyance. It was clear he was not happy to have to vacate his newly occupied territory so close to a famous quarry. The same thing happened when I got up to greet a friend who came over from one of the other tables. When I turned round, the daughter of the Swedish lady had enthroned herself on my chair and was not budging. I told her once to please get up and was ignored. With the second reminder, she looked up, as did her brother, staring daggers. Their mother seeing all the time what was going on took it all quite in her stride. I was standing up with nowhere to sit, while my food was getting cold, but still the woman made no move to tell her kids to vacate my seat. It was time for action. I stepped forward, grabbed the back of my chair and tipped it forward, necessitating a quick evacuation of the chiffon-laced teenage butterball who was in dire danger of rolling on the lawn at Athina's feet. But I was not the only victim of these little predators. Thierry and I got up at some point to fetch ice-cream and fruit. This time Dimitra, to protect my rights, put her hand firmly on my chair seat, but Thierry's chair, now vacant, was plucked from the table and placed next to Athina. Thierry, when he returned and seeing he had nowhere to sit, gave up and went over to another table whose guests had left earlier. Athina, accustomed to hanger's on and persistent pests suffered this attention but was obviously relieved when Sandrine and Johanna suggested they all go over to the dance floor now that the music had begun.

In spite of the festive atmosphere around us Thierry was pre-occupied and Gaby sensed this, keeping by his side for most of the time to cheer him up. Later she went to dance with little Johanna who was having the time of her life, oblivious to the television cameras forty yards away which were filming every move the family made.

When Athina returned I noticed a small distinguished-looking man with a goatee circling round our table, his attention on us. I guessed that he was waiting for a chance to introduce himself and was not wrong. He came and spoke to Thierry. It was Nicolas Gage, the best selling Greek-American author of the book "Eleni" that had been made into a successful film. He later wrote a long article for American Vanity Fair about the heiress, an is often quoted in the media. He describes this brief meeting with the heiress in his article and he was able to speak to her twice by phone later while preparing his story. In fact he was one of the very few journalists ever to speak to the heiress, though Thierry refused to answer his questions directly and I had to ac as go-between in order to give the journalist the answers he wanted from Roussel.

For Athina the wedding at her aunt's house was to be her emergence from the Roussel family chrysalis into the heart of Athenian society. The evening was pleasant. I always had fun in those days with Athina, who was intelligent and had a mature sense of humour. Often, on other occasions, I used to make little jokes when media pressure became intense to distract her, but this evening there was to be more fun of an unspoken kind regarding the state of siege enacted by the society hopefuls circling our table, prompted on by their own ambition or those of ambitious parents who saw in the Onassis heiress the answer to so many of their prayers. An additional spur to their interest was that Athina was now a young woman with exceptionally good looks. She sensed this power, and though we did not discuss it directly, a casual glance between us and the twinkle of mirth in her eyes indicated that even at fourteen she knew the attraction that both her name but also her good looks were having on the young men who wandered deliberately close to our table.

I found Athina interesting because beneath her poise and air of nonchalance in public their was a very normal and curious teenager who would often show great surprise at some story I would have to tell, or laugh at some titbit of innocent gossip.

Having brought up a teenage daughter to whom I had always been close I had a feeling for what little girls and teenagers found interesting and what annoyed them in adults. I enjoyed seeing the amusement of Athina at some little thing I said, or her curiosity for an unknown fact. Journalists always asked me the standard question "What impresses a girl with a billion dollars and the whole world at her feet?"

"Little things," I said, "and a sense of humour."

Athina, tall and poised – 1.78m - moved among the crowd that evening with the confidence of someone who knows that all eyes are on her. The next day two television directors confronted me, accusing me of coaching Athina how to act that evening in front of the cameras.

"Why do you say that?" I asked.

"Every time she got up to get something from the buffet, she would walk for a few steps looking at the various dishes on the table, as if reviewing a guard of honour, than she would stop, pause, and turn 3/4 profile to the cameras. After this she continued walking without once showing she was aware of our six cameras filming her. Her pacing and her pauses were too professional a performance to have been accidental."

"I am innocent!" I replied laughing, though I knew they were not convinced. But it was the truth. Athina was the perfect media girl that evening. She had both the Roussel poise and the Onassis flair in handling the press. Sadly this was to change when things went terribly wrong three years later in the Roussel household.

We left the wedding reception at 2 a.m. Athina had stolen the show all evening. Normally blasé multi-millionaires and granddames of legendary shipping dynasties had been reduced to eating out of her hand. It was clear that on July 3rd 1999 the granddaughter of Onassis had stepped into her famous grandfather's shoes for all to see, and I could see how proud Thierry and Gaby were of the way she had carried herself that evening in front of eight hundred critical pairs of eyes present and the adoring eyes of millions of television viewers watching the live television broadcast of the heiress with the Mona Lisa smile.

The next morning I picked up my newspapers from Mrs. Meli, who owned the newsagents shop near my apartment in Melissia.

"Athina was a princess. Onassis would have been proud and so would her mother if she were alive," she said, handing me a pile of morning papers with full page articles on Athina. There were large photos of her with admiring headlines   *"A Beautiful Athina returns"*, *"An Onassis wedding – glamour again"*, *"Athina stuns with her new look"*.

Of all the headlines the truest one was *"A Star is Born"*. The television footage of the wedding that evening showed Athina walking on the lawns by the sea among the hundreds of glamorous guests. Tens of black-tied waiters, the illuminated pool, the live orchestra playing Latin, Greek and pop music and the flickering candlelight under the star-filled sky brought back memories of a distant past to another member of the Onassis family. Most of those at our table were on the dance floor moving to the rhythms of classics like "Day by Day" and "Vamos A La Playa". I was sitting now next to Merope Konialides, Aristotle's sister. She told me what life was like in Argentina when she and Aristotle had lived there.

"It was like this every night," she explained, "until Peron's regime stepped in."

Despite the romanticized Argentina we had all seen in "Evita" I knew the reality was very different and that a way of life that had been the envy of the world and the inspiration for movies such as "Gilda" had been destroyed by the violent social changes which the populist dictatorial regime Peron had brought in.

"This reminds me so much of Buenos Aires in the Thirties and Forties," Merope repeated, her eyes misting as memories of her youth flooded back. Then she looked up and seeing that Athina had returned and was sitting next to me, on my left once again, chatting with some friends, said quietly, "If only Aristotle had been alive tonight to see Athina."

There was a strange closeness, like a presence at the table at that moment. I think we all felt it. Perhaps Onassis *was* there, sitting with us and watching his granddaughter. Or perhaps it was just the scented moist sea air which hugged each of us as the atmosphere cooled with the approach of dawn of a new summer day.

The Maidservant in Black

Anyone who reads about Christina's life and her death will sooner or later hear the name of her maidservant, Eleni Syrou. This austere-looking woman in black, resembling a member of the chorus of an ancient Greek play was the unsmiling shadow of Christina for many years. Syrou travelled with Christina, stayed near her, always keeping a close watch on her mistress. The question - *for who* - has not been answered yet. That she constantly spied on Christina Onassis, even when the latter was married to Thierry, is claimed in the book by Onassis former secretary, Kiki Feroudi "The Onassis Women". Mrs. Feroudi, in whose office at Olympic Airways Christina spent a short internship, writes that Eleni Syrou, whom she knew well, would stand outside Christina's bedroom or outside phone booth doors to listen to what her mistress was saying and to whom. Who gave her the authority and why this maid spied on her employer is a question that has never been answered.

There are other questions concerning Eleni Syrou. Dimitris Liberopoulos, a Greek reporter who obsessively chased after Onassis has repeatedly spoken on Greek television asking why Eleni Syrou on the night Christina died went to sleep at a hotel in Buenos Aires, leaving Christina alone. It was the first time Syrou had not slept near Christina's room in 17 years, he claimed. Syrou's explanation, as given by Liberopoulos, was that she was told to go elsewhere that night. By whom and why?

The first time I saw her was in the business lounge of the Intercontinental hotel in Athens where Athina, I, and the Roussel family were serving ourselves breakfast. Someone told me that the woman in black sitting in the corner was Eleni Syrou. I myself found that the middle-aged woman had something about her, something indefinable that made me feel uncomfortable in her presence.

Much has been written about Eleni Syrou, and through the years the mention of her name in the will of Onassis and Christina and her connection with the Onassis family makes one forget that she was a maid who later became a sort of travelling housekeeper for Christina. I was to learn more about her one day when Thierry and I were in his office at Boislande at Gingins where Athina lived until her mother died.

It was a particularly hot and airless day. We had taken off our jackets, opened the windows of the first floor office and were taking a break from a long session with the assembled lawyers of Thierry who were preparing his defence for the upcoming defamation case brought by Papadimitriou and the other three of the Onassis Foundation.

Immediately before our break from work we had been reading the will of Christina in which she had named Eleni Syrou and her husband George, among others, as beneficiaries in the event of her death.

"Thierry" I said, "I have never understood your refusal to father another child with Christina, and I must admit this."

"Alexis, there was a reason," he replied, "and it had to do with when I first married Christina."

We were now standing on the small covered wooden balcony facing out over the rolling Boislande lawns. The shining silver strip of water which was Lake Leman lay in the distance. As Thierry spoke I could not but help see why Christina should have had such a desire to have another child by this stunningly good-looking man with his intense deep-blue eyes, and thick blond-accented hair.

"The problem existed even when I married Christina. She was taking drugs all the time. Amphetamines to wake her up, other pills to boost her in the day, barbiturates to make her sleep. It was awful. I told her that she would have to stop the drugs. Especially if we were to have a child. Finally I gave Christina an ultimatum and to her credit she broke her habit."

I myself had heard of Christina's reliance on drugs and her binges in the past. There have been numerous passages in the international press about this. The drug problem was never denied by those who were close to her.

"The worst thing was that Christina would go through sudden changes in mood," explained Thierry, "I did not want the future mother of my children to take drugs. Anyway, Christina who was a very strong person understood this and stayed clean for months. She eventually became pregnant with Athina. We were in Eleuthera in the Bahamas when we found out and it was one of the happiest times of our life together."

Thierry looked down for a moment, his face clouding.

"One day I came back and saw that Christina was completely confused. It was obvious she had taken a large dose of pills again. The sight of her swollen belly made me angry and I worried that she could have done such a thing. I wondered where she had got the drugs from, and we had a big fight with Christina. Eleni, who had just come from New York, was a witness to the scene."

As he told the story I could see Thierry was in a state of distress at the painful memory of those days.

"One day I walked into the house and Christina was not there. Eleni had not seen her either, so I went into the garden to look for her. Christina was lying on her back on the lawn, unconscious. I rushed her to the clinic and the doctor confirmed that she had again taken a large dose of drugs. She regained consciousness later and we returned home. I was worried sick as to whether our baby would be affected by what Christina was doing and so we flew to Paris where I sent Christina to our obstetrician for a check, and also to prepare for when she would have the baby. The obstetrician, when we went to see him, called me outside the room, looking very concerned.

"Mr. Roussel," he said to me, "with the amount of drugs your wife is taking I am worried for the baby unless something is done quickly""

Thierry's mobile phone rang at that moment; it was the driver saying that he was waiting downstairs to take him back to Lussy. Thierry rang off and returned to our conversation.

"The doctor said that in order to save the child Christina would have to have a Caesarean operation.

The baby would be premature but if we waited then there was no guarantee what could happen".

"I explained the situation to Christina and a Caesarean was performed the next day. Athina was born, healthy and safe. After that experience, I could not risk Christina becoming pregnant again and giving birth to a child which might be born mentally retarded or physically disabled. The risk was particularly great after we divorced and there was no one by Christina's side, except Eleni Syrou, to see that she would keep away from the masses of pills she took whenever she was depressed or alone."

The last time I saw Eleni Syrou was at the wedding of Kalliroi's nephew George Drakos at their summer beach house in Lagonissi. After the ceremony I was talking to Dimitra in the lounge of the villa waiting to be called for dinner which was to be served in the garden. Athina was standing immediately on my left and was engaged in polite conversation with a guest and had her back to us.

"Who is that woman?" my wife asked, a look of unease on her face. I turned my head and saw a woman wearing black reaching forward with her palm outstretched to stroke Athina on her back.

"Eleni Syrou," I answered.

Dimitra stepped forward telling Athina that she should go to her father who was out on the terrace. Syrou apologised to us, saying she had to leave to go somewhere else, and she left. It was the last time I saw the woman whom fate had so inextricably woven into the short life of Athina's tragic mother.

Costas Gratsos - "You were the best, Ari, and you were the worst".

Ari Onassis drank. He enjoyed alcohol just as he enjoyed chasing women and making money. I remember Onassis on several occasions as he sat at an adjacent table in the gloomy Grande Bretagne Hotel bar, drinking with his business colleague and friend Professor Georgakis. Late at night when Ari had things on his mind he would go to Tourkolimano, the C- shaped picturesque yacht harbour in Piraeus. There in one of the hole-in-the-wall eateries with rough stucco whitewashed walls decorated haphazardly with bits of fishing nets, fading posters of Fix beer, bits of mirror and dog-eared calendars Onassis would sit on one of the Spartan wood and raffia *kafeneio* chairs knocking back one glass after another of Tsantali ouzo or Johnny Walker whisky. He did this, eating *mezedes* as he took the pulse of street life, chatting with a hodge-podge of out-of-work sailors, labourers, lottery ticket sellers and prostitutes who came in to have a bite to eat and something to drink. Bars and alcohol were a way of life for Onassis. It was a chance meeting in a bar in Buenos Aires when he was in his twenties that was to change his life and connect him to shipping.

Costas Gratsos was the son of an established Greek shipowner. It was customary in those days before the invention of training simulators for the scions of shipping families to travel on the family vessels to get first hand knowledge of how the ships were run, how the crew functioned, where to get supplies and to meet their agents and Greek Consuls in far away harbours where the family-owed fleet plied its trade. Costas Gratsos was an urbane young man and accepted this apprenticeship as a necessary part of his training as a rite-of-passage to becoming a full-fledged shipowner. This was not to say that he did not miss the night life and the girls when he sat with the captain on the bridge of a boat looking out across dark seas on a stormy night. But each trip ended with a harbour and Gratsos looked forward to the next landfall and its welcoming fleshpots.

The boat he was travelling on during one particular trip docked in Buenos Aires. That evening after showering and changing into his smart hand-tailored land clothes Costas Gratsos made his way to a bar in the city. As he sat in the gloomy interior he noticed a short young man of Mediterranean complexion sitting a couple of stools away. Gratsos cosmopolitan eye observed the expensive cut of the young man's clothes and discerned an unusual confidence for a man who was barely into his twenties. The two of them soon struck up a conversation and Gratsos was happy to find that his new found drinking companion in this exotic setting was a fellow Greek. The man told Gratsos that his name was Ari Onassis. He was a refugee from Asia Minor and was now in the cigarette trade in Argentina. Gratsos was immediately impressed by the young and brash Onassis. There was something compelling in his confidence and in the way he spoke. Onassis it was obvious was fiercely determined to make money, something Gratsos already had. As the two Greeks sat drinking their talk turned to women, something for which they both shared a passion. From that day on their friendship was sealed. Gratsos was constantly with Onassis, acting as a mentor. Onassis in the meantime, with Gratsos at his side, made money and more money. He also admired Gratsos cosmopolitan ways. Gratsos was a bachelor who spent a fortune on expensive hotels, glamorous women and a high profile lifestyle. Onassis soon followed suit, mimicking and soon surpassing his friend's penchant for the good things in life.

When the two met Onassis was having a problem with his cigarette business. Rents were high in Buenos Aires and Onassis did not know where to store his stock of cigarettes. Gratsos suggested that Ari should look at one or two of the small ships which were tied up in port. There was a recession at the time and there were many boats off-charter going for a song. Onassis went down to the harbour with Gratsos the next day and bought a small vessel to use as a floating storage warehouse. The first step had been taken, Onassis had become a shipowner and it was Costas Gratsos who had set him on his way to becoming the world's best known shipping tycoon

Gratsos stayed with Onassis for the rest of his life. There was a bond between them which was stronger than that among many brothers. After Onassis died in 1975 Christina slowly pushed Gratsos out of her life. It was said that she was influenced in this by Papadimitriou. What is known is that a member of the

Onassis Foundation, Vlassopoulos, a shipowner's son himself and a childhood friend who went to work for Onassis wrote in his book "Memories of a Life" that he had an argument with Papadimitriou because the latter kept speaking badly about Gratsos to other members of the Onassis Foundation after Gratsos death.

In October of 2001 during a television interview I casually mentioned Gratsos and his lifelong friendship with Onassis. I explained that Papadimitriou had been an employee of Onassis and one of his in-house lawyers but that he was never a bosom friend as he had been presented in some Greek newspapers. I supported this with the fact that few knew Papadimitriou before the conflict with Thierry Roussel. Those who did know him knew him primarily as one of Onassis legal staff. It had always been Onassis and Gratsos as long as I could remember. Gratsos was the only lifetime friend of Onassis.

The next morning I received a call from the Gratsos shipping offices in central Athens. It was Constantine Gratsos, the nephew of Costas on the phone, telling me he had seen the programme the previous evening and was pleased that I had finally put the record right regarding his uncle. We chatted for a while and agreed to meet. A few weeks later I went to the glass and marble Gratsos Shipping Building on Panepistimiou St where Constantine and his brother have their Standard Bulk Shipping fleet offices on the 6th and 7th floors.

On entering the reception area I saw the usual metal ship scale models in glass display cases but here the woodwork of the offices, the expensive blue and grey carpets, bleached wood paneling and white marble radiated opulent good taste. The Gratsos offices smelled of "Old Money", something that Onassis had respected.

I met Constantine Gratsos upstairs in his large office and we chatted about Onassis and about Costas Gratsos who had been the *bon viveur* of the family. Constantine Gratsos the younger had many tales to tell me about Ari Onassis. He recounted how one night before the war Ari and uncle Costas Gratsos were at Claridge's Hotel in London. As usual the two men were drinking in the bar. One drink followed another, and then another, and then another. Onassis mentioned to Gratsos that he had booked a flight to Oslo the next morning to meet some Norwegian shipowners about a deal he was setting up. As the evening progressed the two friends became more and more intoxicated. When the night wore on even further Gratsos finally decided it was time for him to return to his suite. Onassis stayed behind to finish his drink.

In the morning when Gratsos came down for breakfast he noticed that there was some agitated discussion in the reception area. He asked what was happening and was informed that there had been an aviation disaster that morning. The flight from London to Oslo had crashed, killing all aboard. Gratsos was stunned. It was Onassis' flight. Not knowing what to do he headed directly for the bar to mourn his friend.

After the second or third drink he heard a rasping sound by his feet. Looking down he saw Onassis happily snoring on the floor. He had passed out at the bar and spent all night hugging the foot rail. Onassis had missed his flight and saved his life. As I sat listening to these stories the door to Constantine Gratsos office opened and a man came in who introduced himself as the other Gratsos brother. He sat down and joined in the conversation with his own reminiscences. The Gratsos nephews have many memories of Ari, something attested to by several photos in the office showing their father with Onassis at their villa and on the "Christina".

Whenever one hears of Onassis and Gratsos one will inevitably hear in the same breath some anecdote concerning ships, a drinking episode, or glamorous women. One of these episodes had to do with the time when the two young friends were walking in Manhattan on their way to P.J.Clarke's, the famous New York bar and watering hole of the rich and famous. Onassis and Gratsos were regular clients at P.J.'s, whose proprietor had a soft spot for his sybaritic Greek clients. Onassis however had a problem with P.J.'s. He did not like the food there so he made an arrangement which allowed him to bring his own sausages to be grilled and served to him at the bar.

On this particular occasion Ari and Gratsos were on the way to the bar when they were stopped in the street by a man called Moore, the then President of Citibank. It was a time when everyone in New York knew everyone. Moore was curious to know what was in the limp package Onassis was carrying under his arm. Ari obliged him by taking out a string of sausages and explaining to the startled banker that this was the fare that he had arranged for the owner of P.J.'s to cook for him and Gratsos. The banker looked in wonder as the two young Greek millionaires disappeared inside the bar carrying their sausages with them.

It was at this time that anyone who was anyone would dine at the El Morocco. In the famous club there were three zones with strict social delineation. First there was a seating area for celebrity clients, and then there was the dance floor. Directly beyond this was a third section, a seating area known as Siberia because only the tourists and unknowns would be seated there.

Onassis and Gratsos arrived at El Morocco one evening without a reservation. The celebrity seating area was full and there was no question of the proprietor seating them in Siberia, so he put a table for the two Greeks on the raised dance floor. This was the Holy of Holies for diners. Only one other table was allowed on the dance floor that night. When Onassis looked over he nodded almost imperceptibly to its sole occupant, so as not to be noticed. The table was occupied by a much feared Sicilian mafia boss who controlled the New York waterfront. Onassis of course knew him. Without the don's blessing and cooperation no ship could load and unload if the owner wanted to avoid problems and Onassis was not a man to have his ships delayed by striking dockworkers.

Years later the services of Gratsos were called for by the Onassis family in a particularly delicate matter. Christina, against the wishes of her family, had married Serge Kausov, a Russian shipping manager who was reputed to be a KGB agent. Gratsos, acting for the family undertook to go to Moscow where Christina was living in a two room flat. Larger dwellings were just not available nor were they of course for sale under the Soviet Communist regime.

Instead of returning with Christina Gratsos ended up staying months in Moscow after succumbing to Christina's pleading for him to help her get a better apartment. Gratsos called upon the services of an old student-days friend to do the impossible. The Russian friend in question had been with Gratsos in Paris and in Zurich in the Twenties. The Russian was an exiled prince who had escaped the Bolsheviks with his life and little else. With Gratsos they had shared in high jinks as students. One notorious incident involved the hoisting of a Communist flag in conservative Zurich shortly after the Russian revolution. The effect on the conservative burghers of Zurich on seeing the Red flag waving in the central square can only be imagined. The prince being a man of supreme practicality and exhibiting acute judgement for new opportunities later decided to go home to Russia where he buried his royal past and became an active member of the Revolutionary Communist party. His rise to the top of the Union of Soviet Socialist People's Republics' power structure was rapid. By the seventies when Christina was in Moscow without a decent home, Gratsos found that his old friend was now a member of the Supreme Soviet Politburo, the governing body of the Soviet Union.

After some marathon drinking bouts and tearfully nostalgic reminiscences with his princely friend, interspersed no doubt with eyeing and discussing the potential for bedding several blonde *Krassny Narodny* Volunteers Gratsos' friend pulled the right strings and like magic a seven-room apartment materialised for Christina. After this Gratsos took his leave of the Kaousov's and returned to the Free World to resume his capitalist preoccupation with making money and living the good life.

What wounded Gratsos soon after this episode was that people close to Christina managed to turn her against this most loyal of her father's friends. When Costas Gratsos died Christina sent a large wreath of flowers to the funeral but she herself did not to attend the burial ceremony because she had checked herself into a hospital that morning. It was a betrayal of the sort that the Onassis have sprung on close friends with each new generation.

After Costas Gratsos, perhaps the best known of Onassis' associates was Professor Georgakis, a brilliant man described by his enemies as being a man with many weaknesses. In the years immediately before Onassis death Georgakis was constantly by his side though few knew that this friendship also had a Gratsos connection.

During the Second World War the brother of Costas Gratsos had been active in the Greek resistance as part of the underground network which hid Allied pilots and helped them escape Nazi-occupied Greece. The penalty for harbouring Allied airmen was death, and Greeks hosts were being sent daily to the firing squads. Gratsos brother's underground cell was betrayed ironically by a Cypriot whom Gratsos' brother's group had helped. The Germans arrested Gratsos' brother and threw him into Averoff prison on Alexandras Avenue. Soon after his arrest he was brought before a German occupation military court. His wife desperately sought help to save his life and found this in two Greek lawyers who were prepared to defend him. The first lawyer (who later became the head of a Greek ministry) demanded payment of a substantial amount which he insisted be in British gold sovereigns. The money was paid in advance. The second lawyer, a young man in his twenties, did not mention his fee.

It was an open and shut case. There was a prosecution witness, the Cypriot, and the penalty would be the death sentence. When the prisoner was asked by the German military judge if he had anything to say, Gratsos brother answered in his own defence in German. He spoke fluent German having received a PhD in Zurich prior to the outbreak of the war. The German judge was impressed and said in his verdict "The prisoner is found not guilty since it is inconceivable that anyone who has been exposed to German culture will do anything to harm the interests of the Third Reich."

Gratsos brother was free. When he left the prison he asked the younger lawyer who had not been paid what his fee was.

"I do not charge money to patriots," came the answer.

The young lawyer's name was Yannis Georgakis and Gratsos brother did not forget him. When Onassis asked Gratsos some years later if he had any suggestion for a good lawyer, Gratsos immediately mentioned Georgakis who by now was a well known professor. Onassis asked to meet Georgakis, took a liking to him and immediately hired him. They became good friends and would often be seen in the late hours staggering out of a bar. I saw them on several occasions in the Plaka, the old part of Athens whose narrow streets with whitewashed houses, tourist tavernas and noisy discotheques had become a Mecca for wealthy Athenian youth and foreign hippies in the Seventies.

In Plaka there was a youth dive called The Trip where I saw Onassis and Georgakis on more than one occasion wander in after two in the morning to sit at the bar. Onassis was just at home rubbing shoulders with 18 year old girls and boys there as he was at a society gala in Monte Carlo. This ability to mix with everybody was one of the reasons that the Greeks loved him.

Gratsos always liked to tease Ari about the time he had interceded for Onassis to go to visit one of the world's biggest shipowners. Ari desperately wanted to do a deal with the Norwegians and had begged Gratsos to help make the contact for him. After a couple of weeks Gratsos called the Norwegian shipping tycoon to find out how Onassis was getting on.

"I really don't know what to say about your friend," said the puzzled Norwegian to Gratsos. "Onassis is the laziest person I have ever met: he is also the most brilliant."

The Norwegian had been amazed by the acuteness of young Onassis and his original ideas but had been thoroughly shocked by Ari's penchant for waking up at two and three in the afternoon after revelling all night in Oslo's red-light district.

When Onassis died Gratsos stood over the coffin and pronounced the last judgement on his gifted and flawed friend.

"You were the best, Ari, and you were the worst!".

After the four Greeks lost the administration of Athina's billion dollar fortune in 1999 and the perks that went with it they lay low for a few months. Thierry and the family took a well deserved rest, far from the media, only answering phone calls from those closest to them. They enjoyed their first carefree holidays in ten years. Athina though had lost her best years of innocence. She had prematurely matured in character though she was not yet sixteen a direct result of the battle that had raged around her since she was a toddler.

The summer of 1999 was spent in Ibiza, and in the winter the family went to their chalet in St. Moritz and to the sprawling Roussel chateau at Sologne with its ten thousand acres of grounds. In the white neo-classic building opposite Hadrian's Arch that is the headquarters of the Onassis Foundation the four Greeks were secretively hatching plans. The humiliation of being publicly booted out of the patrimony administration must have weighed heavily on them. As with all defeats the seeds of serious dissent appear to have been sown at this time among the Four.

Their carefully hatched plans were to surface by accident some months later when the heavy scent of roses, honeysuckle and bitter-orange blossom was wafting over hedges surrounding the sprawl of new villas in the suburbs and in the narrow historic streets of the Plaka district in central Athens. In Mid-May of 2000 a plain brown envelope was placed anonymously on the desk of a journalist at the Athens daily "Eleftherotypia".

The journalist phoned to ask me what I knew of a criminal complaint for perjury.

"Against you?" I asked, surprised

"No, against you," came the reply.

It was a complaint that had mysteriously lain hidden in the legal system computers, unseen by the court journalists who check the new court filings every day. I certainly knew nothing of it. The complaint quoted me as saying "I saw Papadimitriou making statements regarding Roussel taking part in orgies and using drugs". The complaint also mentioned that Papadimitriou and his co-plaintiffs had lost a fifteen million dollar civil court action against Thierry because of my deposition which the plaintiff said had swayed the judge's verdict.

I had heard of several references to gross allegations about Thierry made by Papadimitriou and had of course had read the articles. It was this that I said in court. The articles are on record. The Daily Telegraph is an example that comes to mind. Jonathan Rendall wrote that Papadimitriou had described Roussel as "a regular orgy participant". Papadimitriou now claimed that Thierry had forced and pressured me to make the "false statements" in court. Thierry had not even been in direct contact with his lawyers before the civil case, which took place in Greece, beyond perhaps a two-minute telephone call, if that. He was at the time nowhere near Greece as he was travelling on business constantly between Switzerland and Morocco. Interestingly the criminal complaint was signed by only three of the "Four", the journalist from *Eleftherotypia* informed me.

Noticing this she had called Gavrielides, the one who had not signed. He confirmed that he had left the Onassis Foundation, taking his Harvard-educated son with him. It was a bombshell. The Papadimitriou group, or the "Gang of Four" as the British press had unkindly called them, had broken up.

Papadimitriou must have been annoyed when the paper called about the documents for confirmation as to their authenticity. He had not revealed the resignation of Gavrielides for months and asked how the documents had arrived at the newspaper offices. It was obvious to all that only someone with access to the Foundation's files could have sent the information to the newspaper. There was at least one enemy of Papadimitriou in the Onassis Foundation.

This revelation was followed a week later by another. It was learned that the Papadimitriou "3" had recently sued Athina in an Athens civil court for nearly 2 million dollars for overtime pay for 11 years managing her patrimony. Interestingly they had, until they were fired, been paid 100,000 USD each per annum, plus expenses and perks such as accommodation in suites at 5 star hotels in Switzerland where they held board meetings.

Full page articles appeared the next day in the Greek press. A headline, typical of the mood in the press, appeared in a paper formerly friendly to Papadimitriou. *"Athina, you owe us 700 million drachmas in overtime!"* Public opinion in Greece was shocked that the administrators would sue Athina. Though the press and television bit into the story and made it a major item of discussion in Greece there was total silence from fellow Alexander S. Onassis Public Benefit Foundation board members such as Senator Brademas, Mrs. Arweilher, Ambassador Sotirhos or Archbishop Anastassios. How did these prominent board members view the attacks of Papadimitriou on the granddaughter of Onassis, their future president? We asked the question in public. There was no answer.

All four major TV channels now asked for a statement for the evening news for this latest scandal involving the former administrators. I announced that the public finally had incontrovertible proof of what Roussel had said all along - that Papadimitriou and his group were interested in managing Athina's money. Papadimitriou replied saying that the money he had received in total from the Onassis estate in 11 years (approx. 11 million USD with his colleagues) was "*a ridiculously low amount. We even put money into Athina's management out of our own pockets*!" Papadimitriou wanted to make his position clear. "I am not interested in money, Honest Injun!"

If this was the case I asked Papadimitriou via the press why then he had sued   Roussel for millions of dollars and had not confined himself to striving for a legal decision that would give him one drachma in damages and moral vindication? There was no reply.

To add to these attacks against Thierry and Athina there was a new development. Athina received a court summons two days later from Papadimitriou's lawyer in Switzerland, a Maitre Augustin, who was demanding 20 million dollars from the teenager for legal services rendered to the Four when they had gone to court to fight to stay on the board of Athina's patrimony. Papadimitriou, who had not revealed the existence of the claim, was now forced into a corner by the journalists.

"We hired Augustin when we had the responsibility for the patrimony and paid him off, in full, when we gave up the management," he explained to Ta NEA, disclaiming all responsibility for this latest attack against the teenage heiress. Shortly before her sixteenth birthday Onassis granddaughter had received another taste of the Byzantine world that she would have to inhabit as the price of inheriting the Onassis fortune. For the general public the overall situation seemed at times to have an element of farce, something not apparent to the young girl preparing for her exams at her high school in the Swiss hamlet of Lussy-sur Morges near Lausanne.

Almost a year later there was a high court decision in Switzerland instructing the four Greeks to pay their own legal fees to Augustin. The amount was not specified but in the First Instance Augustin had made the astronomic demand of 20 million dollars in legal fees against Athina for three court cases where he had been involved. A Greek paper wrote "A 20 million dollar birthday present for Athina". I was invited the next day to speak about what had happened to the state television channel NET. Other television channels picked up the story and ran it on prime time news.

This development was followed by a very abusive press release signed by "The Former Administrators". In this press release Papadimitriou denied the claim by Augustin. The lawyer had asked for a "symbolic sum" only, he said. Papadimitriou proceeded to attack me personally, and reserved the same treatment for three top Greek journalists, claiming they had broadcast or written false stories. It was not a clever move. The journalists, all seasoned in their profession, knew that I had the Augustin documents.

I now faxed a press release in which I included pages from Augustin's Swiss court claim against Athina. Clearly written was the sum he had demanded - 36,505,000 Swiss Francs – it was more than twenty million dollars!

No matter what I felt regarding the battle between Papadimitriou and the Roussels it was not pleasant for me to see the Alexander Onassis Public Benefit Foundation identified in the mind of the public with this situation. It *was difficult I knew for the public to differentiate between Papadimitriou as the co-administrator of Athina's patrimony and as the president of the Onassis Foundation. As if this was not enough a new announcement was sent by the former administrators from the offices of the Onassis Foundation. This time Papadimitriou admitted that his lawyer <u>had</u> demanded the 20 million dollars, but claimed that Thierry's lawyer Nuot Saratz had claimed this size of fee first (a lie) and that "our lawyer, (Vincent Augustin) being unable to do otherwise had followed suit." It was pointless for me to make any further comment on this press release. The truth was out.*

In the summer of 2000 I received a very welcome invitation from a friend. It was from Polis Xatzioannou, who with his brother Sir Stelios and his sister Clelia owned the Easyjet airline. Thierry and his family were off to Ibiza so it was a chance for me and my family to be with other friends and to "recharge my batteries" on board the Clelia II, the largest of the Xatzioannou yachts - a stunning 290 foot yacht with a crew of sixty five and all-suite accommodation.

We spent ten days on the Clelia II in good company with our great host. Dimitra and I were given a large suite with a private dining room and two bathrooms while my daughter Marina, to her delight, had her own double suite. The boat had a Turkish bath, a gym, several tastefully decorated lounges, a pool, a hot tub and Jacuzzi and a book and video library as well as a permanently open bar, something that especially delighted the English and Norwegian guests on board. I was particularly glad that Marina was kept busy by the small crowd of her own age and she thanked me for insisting she come along.

The first leg of our cruise was to the pristine and little known (outside Greece) idyllic island of Kastelorizzo with its beautiful harbour and spotless white beaches. We then went on to Limassol in Cyprus, stayed for a few days and returned via the fortress island of Kos, to little known Simi, a former pirate's hideout with its picturesque port houses built up the sides of the hill in a gash in the wild barren island. Our final destination was Myconos with its well-known Aegean architecture, narrow white streets and its frenetic night and day life. There we saw many of our Athenian friends from the capital. Soon after we returned to the calm of Athens in August. We had spent ten days in paradise aboard the Clelia II. I was relaxed, sunburned and exercised though I had put on a few pounds from the open dining rooms and barbecues on the Xatzioannou boat.

This peace did not last.

Two days after our return a reporter asked me when Athina would be coming to Scorpios, since we had left that option open. I called Thierry in Italy where Athina was at a riding competition and he confirmed that for this summer there would not be a visit by the heiress to the island. I gave this information to the reporter. That same day Papadimitriou went on television to make an unpleasant comment about Athina and her family. "She is growing up in a family with no dynamism and no culture" he said. And this because Athina had not visited her own property that summer!

When I informed Thierry he decided that enough was enough. Papadimitriou had no connection with the family, he said, and had no rights over it. He also had no more connection with the patrimony. The string of intrusions into Athina's affairs was disturbing Athina and the Roussels. We decided with Thierry that the board members of the Foundation must take a public position on these attacks on the Onassis heiress. I wrote them a letter of some fifteen pages on behalf of Thierry, pointing out in detail the abuse and the distress that Papadimitriou had caused to the family of Athina and especially to the Onassis descendant herself. The letter was sent by fax and was given to the press too. Private letters were then sent to some of the more important members of the Onassis board such as Andrew Athens and Senator John Brademas in America. The letters asked them to intervene on behalf of, and for the protection of Athina. We invited the recipients to state publicly whether they supported this continuing state of affairs regarding Athina and the personal attacks by the president of the Foundation. A letter was also sent to the Archbishop Anastassios of Albania, a member of the Onassis Foundation. He was an Athenian Greek known to have a particularly high standard of education and was known for his charity work. It was thought that this man who had received millions of dollars from the Onassis fortune for his projects and for destitute people in Albania would be particularly sensitive to the distress of the granddaughter of his benefactor.

The letter to the board caused a sensation and brought the question of the Foundation president's behaviour to the surface. There was of course an angry reaction from him. A few days later I learned that Athina was very happy that I had sent the letter on behalf of her father to the Onassis Foundation board and that she herself was sending me a letter of thanks.

It was the first time the heiress was going to take a public stand regarding the Foundation. Needless to say the news of a letter from Onassis's granddaughter was a major news item in Greece and was quickly taken up by the international press. The letter, written on pale yellow paper arrived by courier from Sweden the next day. I had prepared the press by calling a conference at the Astir Palace Hotel by the sea in the Athens resort suburb of Vouliagmeni. About thirty journalists came and six television crews set up their cameras in the conference room. The briefing was reported by live television links set up by the studio in the hotel.

"Athina speaks" was the title of most of the broadcasts. The brief contents of Athina's letter were seen by viewers in Greece, Australia, Africa, the Orient and the Americas.

At 2 o'clock there was an announcement that the Onassis Foundation presidency would be giving their own reply in a press conference the next day at the Amalias Avenue headquarters. At the press conference there was only Papadimitriou, Ioannides and Zambellas. No one else from the board was present. The 3 explained that they were there only in their capacity as the executive committee, and were not speaking for the other board members.

Stelios Papadimitriou started his briefing by coughing repeatedly into a large handkerchief, clearing his throat, making asides, wiping his brow and finally settling down to make a speech in which he said he "welcomed" Athina's letter, but that went on to say that she should "retract". Papadimitriou made a point of attacking me in person. Much to the amusement of several of the journalists present he said that I could not be trusted because I had once been an actor and that people of the theatre weren't trustworthy! Forgetting me momentarily Papadimitriou went on to say how much good work the Four had done at the Onassis Foundation and how fair the system of electing new members was, virtually ignoring the question of Athina and the attacks on her, which he denied ever having made. At the end of the briefing one of the journalists, Eleni Bistika, asked how many other candidates there had been when the sons of the Papadimitriou group had been proposed for election to the Onassis Foundation board. Papadimitriou, particularly annoyed by this question from a journalist whose son had received an Onassis Foundation grant, replied "Two, the first time."

"And how many the other times Mr. President?" Bistika insisted. Papadimitriou answered curtly, "One."

Eleni Bistika had not finished. "A few handwritten lines in a letter by a young girl have precipitated two major press conferences and a flurry among members of the press who have filled up this and another room, Mr. President."

She was right. Just a few lines from Athina, just 15 years old at the time had caused a major upheaval at the Onassis Foundation and in newspaper and television offices across the country. The two press conferences had proved to everyone the enormous power wielded by Athina. It was this ability to captivate the attention of the media and rivet the public that Athina could have brought to the Foundation if she was to decide to assume its presidency. There was no doubt that on that hot August day of 2000 there must have been a lot of soul-searching by other directors of the Onassis Foundations who were not present at that press briefing.

Archbishop Christodoulos, the leader of the Greek Church had shown his empathy for the tragic Onassis family and had kept in close touch with Athina, visiting Scorpios, despite a punishing schedule to hold a memorial service for her dead relatives. He had a way with young people and within three years of becoming Archbishop had filled the churches with youthful congregations in jeans. Youths with spiky hair and earrings were welcomed to church and the young fawned over him. He had impressed Athina when she visited him at his offices in July of 1998 with his compassionate and direct manner. We had expected the same from the Archbishop Anastassios of Albania, only more so since he, as the beneficiary and office holder of the Foundation had two extra reasons to want to be close to the granddaughter of Onassis. After writing the letter to him I was sure that this respected cleric would communicate privately with the family and ask to speak to Athina.

I was wrong.

Anastassios ignored the teenager's cry for help. His position as a cleric made this all the more surprising. Since then I have often wondered about the man, why he did not respond to Onassis only surviving descendant, a member of the family fraught with tragedy and early deaths. I still sought some clue as to his attitude and therefore watched carefully some months later when he appeared in a long television interview. I wondered what made him act in the way he had. Anastassios Pagoulatos had been in Kenya, where I and Thierry had grown up, and he spoke of his good works there. During the interview a certain self-satisfaction which was unusual for a man of the cloth came through. When asked how well he did at school he said "I did badly in composition. I only got a mark of 19 (out of 20)."

The Archbishop of Albania told the reporter that he did not play football like the other Greek boys and claimed to have only indulged in the more refined sports of ping pong and basketball. Anastassios had been a top student at his school and had gone on to higher studies in Germany, "Without any bank or similar organisation to back me up." What did he mean, I thought? Why would a Christian cleric who has taken vows of poverty talk about having a financial institution to back him up? The answer came soon after in the same interview. Asked why he had become a university professor in

Athens and why he had kept that post when he had gone to Africa he replied, "The university gave me the financial freedom I wanted. I could go wherever I chose."

He described how he went on to collect millions of dollars from the Greek Orthodox faithful for the church. Poor Athina, I thought. You wanted someone to listen and find sympathy for your problems with the Foundation presidency and whisper a word of encouragement in your ear. Anastassios for one knew of the terrible time you had been through, knew of the incredibly humiliating defamatory allegations against you in the depositions of the Israelis where there were even allegations of suspicions by a member of the Onassis Foundation that your father was having incestuous sexual relations with you, knew of the hair-raising depositions of other witnesses in the kidnap story investigation in 1997 before the protagonists were exonerated and the matter put to rest.

Archbishop Anastassios had been a pillar of support for his flock, but for one young girl in need – Aristotle Onassis granddaughter, the future president of the Foundation that had given him millions to distribute to his flock- sadly he was not there.

I wondered about the stance of the Archbishop later regarding another matter. In 2001 the Onassis Foundation officially invested a large amount of its money and became a part owner of a new television company Alfa Digital which was subsequently to fail miserably and collapse. Papadimitriou and his associates were very prominently photographed at a public ceremony next to the other owner of the Alfa TV group and manager of the station, Stathis Tsotsoros. This station daily broadcast three sex programmes with at least one - "Private Blue" - sending images of extreme and graphic pornography into thousands of Greek homes. Why was the Greek Orthodox Archbishop Anastasios of Albania still with a Foundation that was connected, via its sister Onassis Business Foundation and a partly owned company, with the electronic distribution of pornography? If this is what Onassis had in mind when he spoke of creating a Foundation to disseminate culture Ari might have stopped to take a look, but it would certainly surprise his granddaughter.

A Snowstorm in Athens

In February of 2004 it was agreed with Thierry that the whole family would come to Athens in a show of unity and also because a court case was coming up in which Papadimitriou had brought charges of perjury against me personally and against Thierry for allegedly telling me to lie in a very important court case where the Foundation had sued Athina's father for 15 million dollars. The Foundation had in effect lost the civil case and Papadimitriou considered me to have been responsible for this result since the award was around 180,000 USD, a similar amount being awarded to Thierry in a counter case brought by him. I had been the family witness, the only one in both cases as in so many others and for my trouble I had been dragged through the criminal courts by Athina and Thierry's enemies on unfounded charges. In 2004 the visit was considered necessary and the appearance of Athina would help remind public opinion of who was who. Athina was a mature young woman now, 19 years old and her appearance would make the point that the dynasty was back and would have a role to play in the future.

Thierry was on a plane from Paris and an hour later Gaby would come in from Geneva with Athina and they would stay in the Grande Bretagne Hotel on Constitution Square in the centre of Athens. I had made all the security arrangements for Athina. Police general Stelios Syros, a friend of mine who was in charge of the anti-terrorist division of the Greek police had given us two 4x4's with several specially trained armed anti-terrorist officers to accompany and protect Athina during her two day stay in the capital. There were several other levels of security also. Athina would be traveling with her own head of security, a Swiss called Guy. I had arranged for Stefanos and four other experienced Greek security guards to accompany the heiress with two cars, something which they agreed as a personal favour to me to do without charging any fee for the vehicles or for their own time. Thierry at this time was extremely careful with money and I knew it would please him to not have to pay for security services, except for the tip he customarily gave the Greek bodyguards at the end of each Roussel family visit to Athens. Everything then was in place when news came of a rapid worsening of the weather in Athens. The driver and car I had booked picked me up and as we started to make our way to the airport when a sudden snow storm hit the Greek capital. The driver of the Mercedes 500 was having difficulty now driving along the new state-of-the-art motorway to the airport. Snow piled up everywhere within minutes. A dark gray cloud enveloped us, almost totally blocking visibility while other less powerful cars around us were being forced off the road.

When we reached the airport the bodyguards who were waiting for me announced that the airport was about to close and that Thierry's flight had still not landed. I had booked the VIP lounge for Athina, Thierry and Gaby and when I went in I was met by the Greek duty officer who informed me that Thierry's plane had just landed but it was the last one allowed in to Athens' Venizelos airport which was now closed because of the snow storm. Soon after Thierry came through the gate wearing his customary blue suit, carrying his heavy black leather briefcase and wearing his favourite Tod's driving shoes. He wanted to know what was going on as he had seen the snow that was piling up at the airport.

"All flights are cancelled, Thierry," I replied.

"I must phone Gaby to see where she is with Athina. They can come tomorrow."

Thierry called Gaby on her mobile phone explaining the situation and asked her to take the first flight in to Athens the next morning with Athina. I could hear them making arrangements as alternate flights were sought, but then there was a delay and it was clear that something had suddenly changed. I heard Thierry say, "Let me speak to Athina."

The conversation went on for a while with Thierry explaining to his daughter that there were morning flights and that he would be waiting for them to come the next day. It was clear that Athina was not cooperating. She had by this time already been with Doda for a few weeks and the fact that she had agreed to come at all was in itself an accomplishment for Thierry and Gaby. I saw Thierry resignedly fold his mobile phone and shrug his shoulders.

"They have been at the airport in Geneva for three hours already and Athina does not want to go back again tomorrow to the airport. She is returning to Brussels." He looked crestfallen. Then he looked up, smiled, patted me on the shoulder and said, "Let's go to the hotel, Alexis."

When we arrived at the Grande Bretagne I saw Thierry was uneasy. It was his first visit and though there were no media at the airport or the hotel, as he had requested, he still clearly had anxiety from his last visit and from the prospect of another criminal case coming up. If the case went badly, despite the false charges, it could mean Thierry being considered a repeat offender for perjury which would in all probability have meant that this time he would go to jail as a recidivist. Greek justice, like its politics, was subject to influences, and few people, including judges themselves could vow that all trials would be fair. Of course the burden was on me as the prime defendant and on our lawyers to win the case but everything was possible, especially since I had offered proof in the form of a video recording made in public which answered the main part of the accusation against us, and the investigating prosecutor, a Mr. Dassoulas had indicted us all the same, referring to the cassette but not to its contents that proved our innocence. Worse for Thierry was that Dassoulas had indicted him too, stating in the arraignment document that though he appeared to be innocent since he was not in Greece when I was making my deposition in court Thierry Roussel should have the opportunity "to prove this in a court of law". It was Greek justice at its worst and Thierry was understandably apprehensive. I could see when I left him at the Grande Bretagne that he did not want to be alone. He looked like he would be in for another sleepless night as had happened on so many occasions during his forced stay in Greece in 1998 when he was in the dock of the accused for the action that Papadimitriou and the Foundation had brought against him for perjury and defamation.

When I phoned him an hour later he asked me where I was. He was unsure of himself and asked me what would happen if he had a problem with his health that night. "Don't worry, Thierry, I have booked myself into a room in the NJV Meridien Hotel, next door to the

Grande Bretagne where you are. Anything you need call me on my mobile and I will come round immediately."

After breakfast I went to his suite at the GB and saw that he was sitting in a chaise longue on the balcony. The weather, in its typically Greek changeable fashion has turned into a glorious day. Bright sunshine was made even brighter by the dazzling reflection of the sun off the snow that had blanketed the mountains around the city the previous evening. As we sat on the balcony looking out across the square to the Houses of Parliament and to the Acropolis Thierry looked happy and relaxed, his stockinged feet up on a stool.

"Alexis, last night I had the best sleep I have ever had!"

I was sorry that Athina had not come because it would have been like old days with me and the whole family together where I would have had the opportunity to speak to Athina about several things and about Doda. It would have helped ease some of the tensions that I felt were building up recently when a wedge of rumour was being driven between me and the heiress and it was surely for the money. Perhaps my stance for the family and friendship with the heiress as it had developed when we had been together in Switzerland, Spain and on several occasions in Greece and on family yacht cruises could be seen to have an influence over other matters. It was the beginning of the undermining of a cheerful relationship where we exchanged little jokes, chatted together and travelled happily with the rest of the family in various parts of Europe. But this being an Onassis heiress there were always those close to the Onassis heiresses who did not want competition or an independent voice that could influence the heiress, who after all was the one who had the money that everyone, or almost everyone, was interested in, no matter how close or distant their blood bond to the Onassis heiress was.

This alienating process had already been set into motion that February 2004 morning as Thierry and I sat enjoying the view of Athens from the sunny balcony of the Grande Bretagne hotel.

Athina from a very young age has displayed a competitive streak in her which the Greeks attribute to her grandfather Aristotle Onassis. The French probably like to claim that it is the combative streak that her father Thierry has shown in his long standing fight with Papadimitriou and his colleagues at the Onassis Foundation. Whatever is the truth Athina chose one of the most difficult and competitive sports in which to compete. Show jumping. Not a team sport with supporting fellow players, just her and her horse against obstacles which she keeps raising higher. It is a sport which demands determination and courage. It demands precision but has a permanent element of danger unlike the elegant dressage with its finely choreographed steps.Seeing photos and videos of Athina riding many Greeks felt a vicarious pride at her achievements. Greeks no doubt are pleased to see in her that she is Onassis' fiercely competitive granddaughter. The French of course will feel a similar pride that the great-granddaughter of Gaston Roussel the man who offered so much to mankind through his medical discoveries is ahead of the pack. The Swiss, I suspect, will say that it is their facilities and horses that gave her the ability to reach a high standard among the world's best riders.

In February of 2001 I had a call from a distant relative who is vice-chairman of a prestigious riding club located outside Athens.

"I would like you to please pass on a proposal we have for Miss Athina Roussel. Our riding club belongs to the Greek Equestrian Federation and have very good facilities in Koropi where we are currently training two girl riders to take part in the Athens Olympics in 2004. We would like to make a proposal to Athina to join us and to take part in the Olympics too.I knew very little of horses and even less about competitive jumping, so I asked for more details.

"Athina will have particular advantages and an increased chance to ride if she joins the Greek national team. As the host country we are allotted extra places for competitors. Athina will only need to come to Greece once or twice a year. The sole requirement regarding her registration is that she signs with us. That is no problem since she is a Greek citizen and we will send a trainer to inspect her at regular intervals wherever she is."

The proposal sounded interesting. I wondered though what would happen if Athina, who in her own right attracts the media in droves, rode in the Olympics before a billion television spectators. There is no question that she would be propelled from the status of a star, which she already had, to that of a national and international idol. It would also mean phenomenal coverage for the Onassis Foundation to have its future president idolized by tens if not hundreds of millions of viewers.

That Sunday I went out to Koropi. The person who had made the proposal to me owned an attractive rural property of around ten acres on a hilltop near the riding club. On his property there were three sand coloured Spanish-style villas with tiled roofs, a pristine sparkling swimming pool with views over the Mesoghia plain below, and extensive gardens and orchards around the main house. Inside there were armchairs covered in English chintz fabrics, there were riding scene oil paintings on the walls while upstairs there was a panelled study full of brass items, silver competition cups and other prizes. The feeling was very much that of an English country house. Next to the guest house there was a paddock in which five or six well-groomed horses were grazing contentedly.

Our host, Costis Meimarides arrived wearing jodhpurs and black riding boots. He explained that he had rushed over from a competition twenty miles away where his team had just won first prize. His wife, Mara had prepared lunch for us and as we sat at table they told me more about their club and their training programme. After a lunch of quiche, lamb fricassee and a mixed green salad picked from a local garden he took me down to the riding club, about a kilometer away, to see the installations. The riders were absent that day because of various competitions and so we arranged to meet the next Sunday.

In the meantime word got out that Athina would possibly take part in the Athens Olympics. I confirmed in a press statement that a serious proposal had been made to the heiress and her father but that it was too early to know yet what would happen. I did not at this stage reveal the name of the club, which was the Attikon Riding Club, and told the reporters that we would talk to them after more was known of the proposal and the facilities.

The next Sunday I went with my daughter, Marina, to the Attikon Riding Club. Its activities were in full swing when we arrived. Riders were jumping hurdles, others were cantering round an adjacent paddock, a small group in single file were trotting out of the grounds to go on a cross-country jaunt. Various club guests, taking a more passive stance, lazed in chaises-longues on the raised terraces of the club house. They casually watched the more energetic participants out on the field.

My host, riding hard, had just completed a round of grueling obstacles which to me seemed alarmingly close to one another. Marina was delighted with the equine environment and left us to go to the stables to see the horses there.

It seems that anywhere there is a horse there will be an Englishwoman nearby. The Attikon Riding Club was no exception. Two English wives with sun-reddened faces, graying hair, and "sensible shoes" sat sipping tea while three men in riding britches sat on the terrace attended by a yappy Jack Russell terrier. Young girls with long legs and cropped hair busily adjusted harnesses and checked their horses before entering the riding area. The atmosphere at the club took me back to earlier days in colonial Kenya. I remembered the clubhouse at the Songhor Sports Club in Kenya, a small country club with an adjacent sports field a few miles from Lake Victoria. It was where we went on Saturdays to meet other farmers and owners of nearby plantations who had come to ride, to sit at the bar or to chase each others wives and daughters, enjoying life while day by day the last days of the British Empire were drawing to a close.

The Songhor Sports Club (in British East Africa all the European clubs were called either the "Sports Club» or the "Railway Club") held gymkhanas every month. As youngsters isolated on our farms and plantations during school holidays we looked forward to these occasions. It was an opportunity for our staff and us to see friends, the Readers, the Doenhoffs, the Martins, the Perry's, the Suttons, and the Macleod's whose children caught snakes which their mother stoically sewed up in burlap bags and sent to the Nairobi Snake museum. When we were teenagers we would often sneak off with the well-exercised, sun-browned freckle-faced daughters of our neighbours. We managed to do this unnoticed while their parents were busy talking cattle and sugar prices or were concentrating on attracting the attention of the African barman in his tall red fez to open yet another large bottle of Tusker or White Cap beer for them. The Attikon Riding Club outside Athens had something of the atmosphere of the Songhor Club, but here on the semi-rural outskirts of metropolitan Athens there was a more intense atmosphere. The casual sexual undertones of Africa were missing. The riders I now saw were training in earnest for their next competition while those couples present looked as if they had been stuck together with habit-glue for decades.

On this particular morning my host pointed out two young girls who were dedicatedly preparing to take place in the trials for the Greek national equestrian team.

The girls hoped to represent Greece in the 2004 Olympic Games. This was after all what I had come for, to see and gauge whether the club's proposal for Athina to join them for the Olympics was serious and whether it was viable.

In the meantime word came that Athina had just won second prize in Jerez in Spain at a show jumping event in which the Infanta of Spain, the King's daughter, had been placed eighth. Thierry called to tell me that Sandrine had done well too. Each of the girls now had a professional team to back them up. Thierry had bought them four competition horses each, and there were two full time female employees to look after the horses.

When news got out about the invitation for Athina for the Olympics there was of course great interest from the Greek public. People stopped me in the street to ask whether she would come and ride with the Greek colours. During Thierry's appeal case in 2001 the president of the court leaned forward to ask me in a low voice

"Will Athina come for the Olympics?"

It was a matter of national pride for the Greeks to see Onassis granddaughter compete in Athens in 2004. There were many difficulties. There was the distance of Athens from where Athina lived and the plethora of activities and obligations Athina had. We discussed the proposal in detail with Thierry who said that Athina should wait first to see how she would do in the Pan-European Equestrian Championships before replying. Neither he nor Athina wanted her to enter the Olympics just for the sake of entering. Athina was too competitive for that and was too proud not to want to win a prize. In the meantime Greece waited to see if its favourite daughter, watched by a billion pairs of eyes, would take the plunge and ride out onto the field wearing the national colours. She did do this later at a series of top equestrian events, but not in the Olympics.

As time passed it became apparent that Athina was not up to Olympic standard even though she was progressing well and was dedicated to her sport. After she left home and went to live with Doda the couple invested large amounts in horses and established their own company called A+D Horses. For Doda Athina's money was welcome as it gave him freedom and the ability to ride better horses. Soon after Athina applied in Athens for her name to be changed officially to Onassis, a move that was seen by many as the beginning of a return to her Greek roots. She registered to ride with the Avlona Riding Club, located 15 miles outside Athens. Registration with a riding club was a prerequisite for entering the Greek national team. Doda too applied for Greek citizenship, leaving his Brazilian stable mates in order to ride for the Greek team in the Olympics. Soon afterwards Athina took another step and decided to establish the Christina Onassis Equestrian Games which she would finance; the event was to be one in the circuit of the recently established prestigious Global Champions tour. Athina had by this time, with Doda, cut all ties with her father and they had established new contacts and alliances in Greece. It would soon become apparent whether their choices had been wise and whether their new friends could help them.

The question of Doda's application for Greek citizenship inevitably became associated with politics and with the question of the Onassis Foundation presidency rights of Athina. There was a hard core of opponents to Athina ever becoming president of the Onassis Foundation that had a strong political influence in Greece because of its scholarships, donations and ownership of media. Doda's move to become Greek ran into strong political opposition and when he went to see Prokopi Pavlopoulos, the Minister of the Interior about this, Pavlopoulos, a close friend of the Onassis Foundation said he could only get this if a large financial donation was made. Doda it was reported left the meeting in anger feeling that his wife and the Onassis family had already given enough money to the Greek state and that the demand for even more money in order to sway the minister to give Doda Hellenic citizenship was unacceptable. An Athens newspaper ran a small item predicting that Doda would never get citizenship from Mr. Pavlopoulos ministry because the minister had eaten lunch just three days previously at the Onassis Foundation office, the centre of opposition to Athina's plans to become president of her family Foundation.

Doda and Athina had the support for the moment of the powerful Mitsotakis political family with Dora Mitsotakis-Bakoyannis, the foreign minister, promising to help him get his citizenship, but she too failed. The lady minister, through her husband, Isidoros Kouvelos, the president of the Greek Riding Federation had asked me previously to set up a meeting in Paris with Athina and Thierry when Athina was still living under the same roof as her father in Brussels. Thierry typically had refused and the contact only happened when the Olympic Games came to Athens in 2004 by which time there had been a power shift in the Roussel family: Thierry was on his way out and Doda was taking charge.

In the run up to the Athens Olympics it became known that Doda would be riding with his old Brazilian team and Athina was expected to come and watch him compete. The Olympic Games organising committee made it known that tight security demanded than anyone wanting to go into the VIP or competitors' paddocks must have submitted their applications by a specified deadline. As the date approached I phoned Boislande and told them that Athina would have to hurry if she was to get her pass, but the deadline came and went. Some days before the Games I had a call from Isidoros Kouvelos who said that Doda had requested that Athina get a competitor's paddock pass. He explained that no one was being granted them after the deadline and could I call Thierry to ask him what he wanted Kouvelos to do. Thierry was travelling and when I managed to talk to him and explain the situation, saying that an exception could be made for Athina, he answered "Please tell Mr. Kouvelos not to give her a pass. She must have no special treatment because she has been acting like a princess after she left home and thinks she can do anything because of her money. I want her to go and watch the Games with the other spectators. She must not have special treatment!"

"Isidoros," I said, "Thierry say that you should not give Athina special treatment. She is to see the Games from the spectator stands."

Kouvelos mumbled "OK" and we hung up. Three days later he called to say that he had issued restricted security areas pass for Athina, against the rules. When I asked him why, he answered, "But she is Onassis' granddaughter!"

She had just proved that she *could* do anything "because of the money".

Doda for his part adapted quickly to his famous Greek heiress companion's lifestyle. During the Athens Olympic Games in 2004 where he was competing as a member of the Brazilian riding team he ignored the Olympic Village where hundreds of international athletes, including numerous world famous athletes, were housed, and used as his base a suite in the historic 5 star Grande Bretagne Hotel, the most prestigious hotel accommodation in the city. After giving up the modest apartment he occupied in Brussels when he first met Athina he was now living like an Onassis. The Olympic Village was for the athletic *hoi polloi* not for Doda. He had also requested, via Boislande, two bodyguards and a limousine before his arrival. Even Onassis did not have a bodyguard when he was in Greece. His Brazilian family stayed with him at the Athens hotel, but not Athina, who, spooked by the media, was watching the games on TV from Belgium, protected by her trusted and efficient chief bodyguard, Guy Merault.

"To live well one must live hidden"

Industrialist millionaire Henri Roussel to Athina Onassis' father Thierry when he was a boy

It was March 11th 2001. Thierry was back in Athens for the appeal he had lodged against the December 1998 decision which had sentenced him to a convertible jail sentence of 5 years for defaming the Onassis Foundation presidency. Thierry had already come to Athens for the case twice previously, and on both occasions it had been postponed, once because of a clerical strike in the courts and the other time because Professor Katsandonis was in the middle of a long trial in which the wife of a High Court judge had been imprisoned for a major land scam in which thousands of acres of wooded land on Mount Penteli in Athens had been sold off as plots.

Thierry had decided to stay in Athens over the weekend since his case would be starting on the Monday. I picked him up at the Hilton and drove him to my apartment near Mount Penteli for lunch. It was a chance for him to get away from hotel food and to relax.

When deciding what to feed him I knew we had to avoid peas. Thierry intensely disliked this common garden vegetable that had been the object of a major clash of wills between Thierry and his father Henri when Thierry was 8 years old. His father had said that Thierry would not get up from the table if he did not eat his peas. Thierry decided to show Henri what he was made of. He ate the peas, at his own pace, one by one, chewing each legume for minutes at a time. The battle of wills lasted for six hours with neither side giving up until Thierry had eaten the last pea on his plate. Father and son had both made their point. *Petits pois* were never again served to the stubborn young heir at any of the Roussel mansions ever again. Neither Roussel had backed down.

My wife Dimitra is generally considered by our guests to be a good cook and I have paid the price for her culinary dexterity by adding on extra pounds of weight over the years. Because of Thierry being permanently on a diet Dimitra had to reluctantly on this occasion constrain her culinary ambitions and Greek sense of hospitality. Greek hostesses never feel they have fed their guests enough if they do not bloat them with dish after dish and hand them something wrapped up in aluminium foil to take home with them as they leave the front door. It had been decided the previous day that fish was the answer. She prepared a light lunch of fresh *barbouni* - red mullet - and a Greek salad, which I knew Thierry liked.

During lunch Thierry seemed relaxed, for a change having put aside thoughts of the court case that would resume the next day. He reminisced about his childhood, telling us how he grew up with his grandmother when his parents separated. Henri Roussel, the father Thierry admired so much, had been a man of the world, relaxed in manner and a wonderful host for his guests. Thierry recounted how Henri often invited friends of all social classes to his 17,000 acre estate and chateau in Sologne. Some of his friends came to his farms in Kenya, to his mansions in Marbella and Ibiza and to his seafront villa at Kilifi, north of Mombasa. It was at Kilifi that Thierry and Christina would often come in with rucksacks on their backs after camping in the Kenya bush to stumble past a prime minister or a head of state.

Thierry told us how he had first met Niarchos, Onassis great rival and brother-in-law, at the Roussels' Sologne estate where Niarchos came to hunt. In the summer Thierry and his father would go to Niarchos' private island, Spetsopoula in Greece, on their yacht. It was during one of these visits to Greece that Thierry first met Onassis. He later visited him and Christina on Scorpios on several more occasions with Henri.

Valerie Giscard d'Estaing, the former French President, was a regular visitor to Sologne and to the Roussel beach house in Kilifi. Christina and Thierry had spent time there with the French president. What a disappointment it was then in November 2000 when Giscard, who knew of the dispute between his friend and the Onassis Foundation executives, thought it appropriate to come to Athens to receive a 250,000 dollar Onassis Prize from Papadimitriou. Journalists present noted that in his acceptance speech he did not once mention Christina, who had been the former president of the Onassis Foundation, nor did Giscard mention the name of the yacht on which he was a guest – the *Christina* – even though he recounted in some detail a cruise he had taken on the mega-yacht with Onassis. This small betrayal of family friends was a shift from old loyalties, but as someone pointed out if the ghost of Christina was in the ceremonial hall she would have seen that the auditorium which should have been packed on such an important national and international occasion was almost empty for Giscard. The front rows, reserved for dignitaries and members of parliament were almost empty too. The Greek political and social establishment had not come to the Foundation's ceremony, surely embarrassing the Onassis Foundation presidency in front of Kostas Stephanopoulos, the Greek president and their famous French guest. The prize-giving was attended by only a smattering of politicians and some friends of the Foundation. It was a long way from what Onassis had envisaged when he wrote in his will that he was leaving part of his fortune for the creation of a prize to be on a par with the Nobel prizes.

Commenting on this failure Papadimitriou, in an interview in March 2001, angrily remarked that the Members of Parliament he had invited five months previously had not bothered to phone to say they were not coming. It was possible that the public snubbing of the ceremony had in part to do with the verbal attacks and law suits against Onassis' granddaughter. Perhaps it was the disparaging remarks made in a Greek newspaper interview by the Onassis Foundation president about Alexander Onassis and Christina when he stated that Onassis did not have worthy heirs. The Foundation was reaping what it had sown.

During lunch Thierry continued to reminisce about his family. Henri Roussel had been his idol. Thierry admitted that he had been envious of his father, seeing a man who had devoted friends and a relaxed lifestyle that Thierry himself never managed to attain.

"It was always a fight for me," Thierry said, "From the time I was in school there was always someone wanting to challenge me. It changed my character."

Henri Roussel had lived a good life, with his wives and mistresses, his hunting and fishing trips. His one big mistake had been a business decision taken years earlier. Henri had not managed to convince his brother to merge their company Roussel Pharmaceuticals with the L'Oreal group when they were approached with a merger proposal by the owner of the cosmetic giant. L'Oreal is today France's largest company.

"It was a monumental mistake - one of the few my father made," said Thierry.

Looking at Thierry while he concentrated on his *barbouni* I wondered what his school life had been like. I could not imagine this man succumbing to authority and school discipline easily. Nothing had been written about his academic background. Papadimitriou I knew liked to project Roussel as man of no education, an ignoramus with few mental faculties and even less judgement. I knew that this was not so. Roussel had a degree in Economics though he never advertised the fact. Additionally Thierry was the man who had brought the Onassis Foundation presidency members to their knees on several occasions. The fight in which we had all taken part had managed to break an Onassis will in Switzerland. These achievements were not those of a man of little knowledge. I asked Thierry about his schooling.

"I went first to a private boarding school," said Thierry. "I was always rebelling and was constantly in conflict with the athletics master who liked to dress me down in front of the other boys. I never backed down, so one day he said, *"Okay, Roussel, into the boxing ring."* Of course he was much bigger than me but I was determined to defend myself. I stepped into the ring, with all the boys watching. The first blow to land on my face was so powerful that it knocked me out. That was the end of that match for me. I lost the fight but one day soon after the master slapped me outside the upstairs dormitory. I punched him in the face and he went down a long flight of stairs. I was kicked out," Thierry added with a sheepish smile.

"Then I was sent to the *Ecole des Roches*," said Thierry. I knew the school because my nephew Alexander was enrolled there. It was an exclusive boarding school attended mostly by the elite of France's prominent families and by foreigners keen to get the best of the French education system. The institution was the closest that France had to Eton or Le Rosey. I could not imagine Thierry fitting in there well.

"You are right, Alexis," he said.

Dimitra interrupted us to bring a selection of *petits-fours*. She knew that Thierry would not touch a normal-size slice of cake and had ordered a selection of tiny chocolate eclairs and miniscule tartlets with fresh strawberries and plums. Thierry, absorbed in his reminiscences of the Ecole des Roches, started eating the sweets, for once forgetting his preoccupation with his *silhouette*.

"When I was about fifteen I was in conflict with another master, not something unusual for me. This teacher appeared determined to break my resolve and was always trying to show me up in front of the other students. It was 'Roussel stand up' 'Roussel, what are you doing?' 'Roussel go outside'. For a whole term he kept badgering me about my hair. It was the time when long hair was a sign of rebelliousness and I had, provocatively, I must admit, come back to school with hair which was much longer than the other boys.

The master made me stand up in front of the whole school and told me off once again for my hair. After dinner I went back to the dormitory and with a pair of nail scissors I clipped off bits of hair until there was virtually nothing left. It was an absolute mess. I looked like rats had been chewing on my head. I took a razor, lathered my head and shaved off the rest of the hair left on my scalp. It was not a successful operation because I could not see what I was doing and kept cutting my head. I was bleeding all over the place, but I was resolved. I would show the teacher who Roussel was."

"The next morning when I walked into breakfast there was a gasp from the whole school. The master turned to see what the fuss was about and saw me standing in my usual place. Bald. My chalk-white head was covered with cuts and scars. The whole school started clapping."

"Was that the end of it?" I asked Thierry.

"No, there was more. Several of the other boys, impressed by my new look, followed suit and soon there were a gang of us with shaven heads. There was hell to pay that Sunday when we were allowed out. Irate mothers bringing back their shaven-headed sons on Sunday evening demanded to see the principal and the governor of the school. The mothers complained that they were paying heavy fees for a school that had made their children look like convicts."

Thierry carried this rebellious streak in him into adulthood, often flouting convention when he believed he was right, and always ready to take on the mandarins, whether they were a group of schoolmasters or the presidency of the Onassis Foundation. I had watched him many times and had seen him in action, but as there was less to rebel against now he himself had become bossy. Ironically his good manners today conceal what he has always fought against in others - an authoritarian streak.

As nature looks for a balance, I can say with a smile, that Thierry has finally met his match in Athina. Though seemingly docile when she was younger she is unbelievably stubborn when she thinks she is right. I had first seen this in a test of wills when we went to Scorpios. Thierry lost, and had asked for my intercession. Athina was as firm as a rock. We could not bend her will. This clash of personalities took a nasty turn when Athina turned against her family after leaving school to live with Doda when she was still seventeen.

After lunch I drove Thierry back to the Hilton. He was still reminiscing about his father. It was obvious that with all the turmoil in his life, the insults heaped on him by the former Onassis employees and the tens of legal fights he had been involved in for more than a decade, that had driven him to the brink of suicide three times, as he admitted to me one day at the Hilton, he was now reaching out to his past with a sense of nostalgia for those early days when his father was still alive.

Thierry remembered a story Henri had told him about Niarchos. Henri and Niarchos had planned to go on a hunting trip to a plantation of a friend who lived in a remote upcountry corner in West Africa. I think Thierry said it was in Cameroon. The two tycoons had rented the inland property for a month as there was considerable big game in the nearby forest and the hunting would be good.

"Stavros Niarchos and my father took their guns and equipment with them," recounted Thierry. "They drove for hours along a remote forest road through deep mud. On their arrival at their destination Niarchos, covered in mud and dust, went to have a shower, as did Henri. When they came out of their rooms, refreshed and clean, Niarchos asked where the pool was.

'There isn't one,' answered a confused African head boy.

'Hire a bulldozer tomorrow and build one, I will pay,' ordered Niarchos.

"Henri and Stavros went off into the forest the next day while the pool was being excavated. Within a week concrete had been poured and the pool was ready" recounted Thierry. "'Fill it up now,' Niarchos ordered the head servant."

'But, Sir, we do not have any water,' replied the African.

'Is there an airstrip near here?' Niarchos asked the African, who by this time must have surely been wondering about the sanity of these two rich Europeans.

'Twenty kilometres away, sir. At the missionary station.'

'Good,' replied Niarchos."

Thierry stopped for a moment when he heard his name mentioned on a news bulletin on the car radio, and then continued "Niarchos told the African to connect him via radio telephone to the capital city. He ordered several plane loads of crates of bottled mineral water for the pool. The next day truck after truck filled with cases of water brought by plane to the mission airstrip arrived at the isolated forest plantation house."

Thierry told me how a crew of African workers spent all day emptying bottle after bottle, crate after crate and truckload after truckload of Evian water into the newly-built swimming pool. In the afternoon Henri Roussel and Stavros Niarchos arrived back from the bush with their day's trophies and stopped by the pool which was now full.

"'Civilization at last' said Niarchos, stripping off his clothes and diving into the sparkling pool, closely followed by my father. Ah....*They* knew how to live," added Thierry wistfully, stepping out of my car and making his way towards the wide glass and marble entrance of the Athens Hilton.

A series of premature deaths, suicides and fatal accidents in the Onassis family and those near them has for years fed the myth that there is a curse that has followed the Onassis family from its early days in Asia Minor to Europe and now to South America. The "Onassis Curse" was never mentioned as such in the Roussel household and I debunked it whenever any journalist referred to it. When Athina grew up it seemed that the chapter with the string of deaths that had been a part of the Onassis dynasty's tragedy-ridden history had closed for good. It also appeared that the Onassis Love Triangle curse, whereby two generations of Onassis women, Athina's mother Christina Onassis and her grandmother Tina Livanos Onassis, suffered the presence of other women with whom their husbands maintained long standing affairs, some lasting for years. Tina Onassis had the soprano dive Maria Callas to contend with, while Christina reconciled herself with her husband Thierry maintaining a parallel relationship for years with the glamorous model Gaby Landhage who became his second wife and bore him three children. Is the Onassis Triangle Curse merely a coincidence of the past, or will it resurface for the third time to hurt Athina too? Only time will tell: as they say in Greece "Nothing under the sun remains secret forever"..

By 2005 Athina was independent, married, albeit without children after several years with Doda, and master of her vast inherited fortune. Since her coming of age fatal accidents had started to happen again. Two young women were killed riding a Roussel family-owned jet ski in front of Athina's seafront Ibiza mansion estate. More was to follow. Cibele Dorsa, Doda's former companion and mother of their daughter Vivienne committed suicide after sending a damning letter to the editor of the leading Brazilian lifestyle magazine CARAS (FACES) naming Athina and Doda. The letter was rife with accusation. As the last communication of someone about to die it did not help to dispel the existence of an Onassis curse.

Some time before she died Cibele had granted a telephone interview to a female journalist at the Greek television station STAR where she made it clear that she was distraught at having had to give up her daughter to Doda and Athina's custody. The STAR reporter asked her if Athina was going to adopt Vivienne and how Cibele viewed Athina and Doda bringing up her daughter.

"I wish (them) happiness, you know," answered Cibele, "I just want my daughter back. That is my business; the other things are not my business. If Athina is good for my daughter I like (it). I want my daughter here; I believe she belongs in Brazil."

To another Greek journalist, Athanasis Anezaki, from ALTER TV she said in a telephone interview, "Doda is always without money. His father sends him money."

The story of 17 year-old Athina meeting and falling in love with Alvaro Affonso "Doda" de Miranda Neto at the Pessoa Riding School is fairly well known by now. The young impressionable teenage Onassis heiress fell head over heels for the handsome Brazilian twice-

Olympic medallist at the riding school, and against her father's wishes she moved in to live with the older man. Doda had been living with Cibele Dorsa, the glamorous Cindy Crawford look-alike Brazilian model, actress and presenter at Radio Transamerica. When Doda left Cibele for Athina she went to the media and expressed her bitterness at having lost her companion of eight years saying he had left her for Athina's money. Dorsa said much more, that Doda used to laugh at Athina, remarking to Cibele that the then-chubby Greek heiress was "like an elephant". Cibele told the media that Doda was always short of money and that he did not even have a car. A search of the Belgian tax records would be enough to see if she was telling the truth about the state of Doda's finances when he met Athina or if she was being spiteful.

Doda took little notice of what Cibele was telling the press now that he was with the Onassis heiress and he did not look back. Soon afterwards he took Vivienne to live with him and Athina in Belgium. How they managed this and why a judge in Brazil gave custody to Doda is a mystery. Cibele clearly resented the loss of her daughter but started her life over again, this time in a luxury 7th floor flat in an apartment building called "The Flowers". She worked for a while as an actress appearing in several plays and found a new love, an older man with whom she appeared to have a measure of happiness and stability, despite the constant pain of the loss of Vivienne who now appeared in photos in the media with her arms around Athina's neck or sitting next to her. Worse for Cibele were press reports that Vivienne was looking up to Athina as her mother. Cibele's link to the Onassis family via Doda had brought her nothing but anguish and despair. She had lost her beloved long-time companion to the young heiress, her family had been broken up by the arrival of Doda's new love and Cibele had been forced by circumstances that she alluded to in her suicide letter to give up her young daughter because of a plan involving money.

Cibele seemed happy with her older companion and was slowly putting her life together when a car accident before dawn after a party killed her companion and seriously injured Cibele, causing her to be hospitalised for three months. Cibele though was a fighter and even this new loss did not break her spirit. Left with a son, Fe – Fernando - from a previous partner Cibele put together the pieces of her broken body and her life and started again. She also managed to write a book called "Men in Your Pocket".

She subsequently met and fell in love with a young television presenter, Gilberto Scarpa, a dashing-looking well-known TV personality. With him she seemed to be genuinely happy. He too was in love with her, something that showed in the photos and videos they posted of themselves on the internet after they made plans to wed. But it was not to be, and those who believe in an Onassis curse were not surprised to hear of another death when the news from Brazil came that 27 year old Gilberto had taken his life by jumping to his death from Cibele's seventh floor apartment in south Sao Paolo. Cibele ran down to the street to see Gilberto lying on his back with his eyes open and started speaking to him, convinced he could hear her. But Gilberto Scarpa was dead, his life snuffed out by the shame of a drug habit he could not beat. Pride had been greater than what he saw as the alternative - to live as an addict.

For Cibele this was the latest tragedy in a life turned on its head from the day that an Onassis had walked into it taking away her companion Doda and her daughter. A friend in Sao Paolo, the journalist and musician Harold Emert, had spoken at length with Cibele before Gilberto's death and she had poured out her heart to him.

"She is a decent woman. Alexis," Harold said to me the next day, "and she seems to be making a go of it."

But it had all been too much for Cibele. With Doda, Vivienne, her older lover and Gilberto gone her life was a deserted landscape. She was overtaken by loneliness and two months after Gilberto jumped from her apartment Cibele wrote a heart rending letter with her final thoughts and penned accusations about Doda. She then opened the balcony window and let herself fall to her death. It was a tragic end to the tragic life of a 36 year old woman who had struggled and had lost, beaten by circumstance, bad luck and by the Onassis millions. Like an injured butterfly she had spun down through the air, down seven floors to leave her broken mortal shell on the pavement as her soul broke free. Cibele left behind one of the most moving suicide letters ever; a letter that contained a heartfelt apology to her children and damning accusations about Doda and about Athina's money. If there was ever doubt about an Onassis curse behind the decades of tragedy woven into the lives of the Onassis family, Cibele's letter with its accusations sounded like a curse of the worst kind, one that the even the most callous of human beings would find difficult to ignore.

Doda's reaction to the suicide of his former partner and mother of their daughter was to deny any responsibility and to immediately have a Brazilian court issue an injunction against his name being mentioned in Cibele's letter which was published in CARAS magazine. The editor and staff at the magazine were furious with Doda for issuing the court order banning the printing of his name. The issue was already off the presses when the staff at the magazine had to go back and delete his name with a thick black line wherever Cibele had included it in her note. The ban also applied to CARAS' website. The magazine's editor told the press that it was the first time that censorship had been exercised on any article printed in his magazine and added that even in a dictatorship this would not happen.

Eight days after the ban the editor of CARAS won a court victory. His appeal filed before the Court of San Paolo was granted, ensuring the publication in full of the letter sent by the Cibele to the magazine before she committed suicide on the night of March 26.

CARAS wrote -

"Now, thanks to the court's decision, CARAS can again fulfil Cibele's last wish before dying. Read below the complete letter sent by Cibele Dorsa before she died."

(Excerpts from Cibele's death note) -

"Of all the men who passed through (my life) the one who harmed me most was undoubtedly Doda, father of the daughter with whom I will have no more contact. The man who did me the most good, when he was alive, was Gilberto.

Living without my two children and without the love of my life tears me completely apart, as if I had woken during heart surgery, I feel my heart being cut by an electric knife that never stops. I can not stand crying...It does not stop, ever! I can not stand to live or rather to survive. My food does not go down, I feel a lump in my throat, I'm getting thinner every day, I feel my skin peeling off my body. The question is, if I end my life, am I committing suicide?

... the death scene of my love (Gilberto) comes back to me constantly, I remember the body of Gilberto in the middle of the street, but his eyes were open and I thought he could hear me so I talked to him a lot ... I do not consider myself suicidal, I am suffering more pain now than when I had the car accident. Now there is no morphine, nothing to soothe the pain, nothing to stop this feeling of drilling in my chest. Moreover, Doda never seems to tire of humiliating me, he would not even meet (me). He was the worst man I ever met in my life, a wolf in sheep's clothing.

Fernando and Vivienne -

Forgive me, your mother, but loneliness is a terrible prison, it feels like I'm locked inside myself, I'm tired, I'm sorry but the lack of (having) you, I confess with Gilberto here it was easier to bear, I love him so much, I do not know how I can continue ... here at home it was cold... I'll find my love. You guys do not even need me. One day ask Carla your aunt or my uncle and know the whole truth. I love you guys and I'll be looking at you guys from up there ...

Vivi, we will meet each other in other lives. I never abandoned you. Your father made a millionaire's plan to take you away from me and I had no other option. Fernando) ditto ... I'll be rooting for you at football, in realizing their dreams...

Doda-,

...One day God will forgive you for what you did and do to me, with Athina and with children, try to be someone better, I'm sorry ... Athina will never know a real man, one love. I am suffering now, however, I was totally happy with Gilberto, a man of truth, who showed his face that did not lie, hid nothing and so it was until the end. He jumped off the building out of shame at having been defeated by drugs ... for shame.

Mother, Carla, Uncle, Father, Bruna, Maciel and Dantino-

Forgive me ... it did not work, I tried for almost two months but the pain is hell. I'm going alone... do not worry, I'm sure God understands someone who dies for love. Obsessed I'm not, I am very aware of what I'm doing, my life became a lie, and you guys know, I opted for the truth.

Cibele Dorsa

P.S. I want to be buried in the same grave as Gilberto. Please...I want my coffin on top of his.

***

The Onassis Curse - For those who are not superstitious and believe only in statistics I have drawn up a small table of untimely deaths, suicides and incidents connected to the Onassis family, and to those who had a connection to them. The rest of us need no convincing that there is indeed a century-old curse on the House of Onassis.

Smyrni – Asia Minor (Izmir)
1.October 1922 Alexander Onassis, uncle of Aristotle Onassis, is taken by the Turks, imprisoned and hanged.
2.October 1922 – Onassis 12 year old female cousin, forcibly taken by a Turkish officer from her mother's arms as the Onassis family were boarding a fishing boat to take them to safety in Greece. She was never seen again by her family. (Her story is in the chapter titled "The Other Onassis Sister")
3.1968 - Spetsopoula Island, Greece – Onassis wife's sister Evgenia Livanos-Niarchos dies of injuries and pulmonary heart

failure in a case that was investigated for several weeks by the Greek authorities.

4. 1973 – Nice, France - Onassis' Lear jet explodes in the air as it approaches Nice airport to pick up Onassis' son Alexander to take him to Paris. The two Kouris brothers, pilot and co-pilot of the jet, are killed.

5. 1973 - Athens Airport– Alexander Onassis, Aristotle Onassis only son and heir is injured on takeoff in a plane he is piloting. The controls of the plane have been switched. Brain-damaged Alexander dies in hospital when taken off life support systems at his father's request. A long investigation and court case results in a 'not guilty' verdict for those indicted. Aristotle Onassis was convinced until his death that his son was a victim of sabotage by his enemies.

6. 1973 – Halkiadakis, the detective hired by Onassis to investigate Alexander's death is found dead with a broken neck after his car is hit by a truck outside Athens.

7. 1974 -Paris – Athina "Tina" Livanos Onassis Niarchos, 45, mother of Christina Onassis and grandmother of Athina dies of a drug overdose.

8. 1977 – Paris – Maria Callas, 53, the opera singer, lover and long time companion of Ari Onassis dies alone in her apartment from a drug overdose.

9. 1988 – Buenos Aires – Christina Onassis, 38, mother of Athina and daughter of Aristotle Onassis dies in unexplained circumstances.

10. 1999 – Martha's Vineyard, Maryland, USA. John John Kennedy, 39, onetime step-son of Aristotle Onassis is killed with his wife Carolyn and her sister Lauren in a private plane he was piloting when it crashed into the sea in unexplained circumstances.

11. 2003 - Ibiza, Spain – 2 young Eastern European girls are killed in a collision while riding a jet-ski belonging to the Roussel family in front of Athina's villa "La Jondal".

12. 2006- Brazil - Cibele Doda is involved in a car crash. Her male companion is killed and she survives, spending 3 months in hospital.

13. 2011 Sao Paolo, Brazil – Cibele Dorsa's fiancée Gilberto Scarpa, 27, commits suicide by jumping from her 7th floor apartment balcony

14. 2011 Sao Paolo, Brazil – Cibele Dorsa, former long-time companion of Athina Onassis' husband Alvaro de Miranda Neto and mother of their child Vivienne commits suicide by jumping from her balcony after writing a suicide letter naming Alvaro and Athina Onassis.

Additionally, according to author Nicholas Gage, an unbaptised infant, Homer, born to Aristotle Onassis and Maria Callas, dies shortly after birth.

Those around families like the Roussels and the Onassis inevitably hear a plethora of stories. Some are true, some are not and some are apocryphal. I discovered that there were stories that I could never repeat because I would be violating a private confession or something said at a dinner table where I had been with the family. The following incident is about Thierry and Christina and was recounted to me by reliable family source who assures me that the incident is true.

Thierry's father Henri, having installed his wife and mistresses in his various chateaux and grand apartments, had a need for a more intimate place for his more private engagements. He maintained in Paris that most French of institutions, the *hotel particulier,* an apartment used by Frenchmen as a temporary love nest. Thierry, in his twenties, owner by then of a successful media services company and not to be outdone by his father, had his own *hotel particulier* next door to Henri's.

Thierry had knocked down the walls of two neighbouring apartments and joined them to create a large studio. This was a *hotel particulier royal.* Thierry then installed a state of the art stereo system and had a specially built two and a half metre square bed installed to have ample bed surface on which to entertain his girlfriends.

My story takes place after Thierry had begun his now well-known parallel relationship with Christina and Gaby. Both women knew of the presence of the other.

There was at that time rivalry as to which one would win the young Roussel for herself. Thierry had a system of making sure the women never ran into each other. One day when he was relaxing on his own the front door bell rang. He was startled because he always asked his female companions to phone before coming. He had no idea who was at the door when he went to answer it.

To his surprise, he saw it was Christina. She had arrived wearing a full length 200,000 dollar Russian sable fur coat. As she stepped into the *hotel particulier* and closed the door behind her, her coat swung open and Thierry saw that apart from a pair of long black silk stockings, she was totally naked. She had come across Paris at night in a taxi dressed in nothing except the fur coat and her stockings. Thierry was stunned and captivated by Christina's daring. For Christina Thierry was a prize that had to be won at any cost, and she used all her Mediterranean female guile to try and capture him.

Twice when I asked him about the incident, he refused to answer if it was true. The glint in his eye told me that the story was as I had heard it.

Scorpios – Mon Royaume Pour un Cheval!

In the idyllic picture-postcard bay of Nydri with its scattered wooded islets the familiar small red launch that belonged to Athina chugs across the shallow, turquoise-coloured straights to Scorpios, bringing supplies to the gardeners, engineers and domestic staff who are busy fastidiously maintaining the Onassis island. The gardeners nurse dozens of varieties of plants and thousands of multi-coloured flower buds have opened, creating a blaze of magenta, flame-red, coral-beige, and vanilla-white along the island's paths and terraces.

In a clearing by a small cement jetty the greenhouse's windows, broken by a recent winter storm, are being replaced. At the Pink House, shutters have been taken off their hinges to be sanded and painted once more to a brilliant white, before being re-hung on their brass hinges. The Scorpios shepherd is putting out feed for the sheep, the chickens, and the guinea-fowl in the complex known simply as "The Farm". It was here that Aristotle Onassis ordered piped classical music to be played to his cows because he had heard that this increased milk production. On the north-east end of the island in the cavernous engine rooms next to the administrative and staff building a mechanic has dismantled one of the two giant Mann generators to replace worn parts. Next door, in the laundry-room, maids in starched uniforms and aprons carry bundles of freshly-ironed sheets and curtains out to a waiting van. The crisp laundry will be taken to the five villas of the island. Beds, upon which famous and infamous people have slept, made love, stayed awake at night planning the political future of whole continents or, with the same attention to detail, pondered over the change of colour in the nursery of a New York apartment, will be made up. Former residents and visitors who stayed at these houses were so well known that their first names even today are enough to identify many of them to the public, Aristotle, Winston, Jackie, Tina, Thierry, Christina, Alexander and Lee. Names which, except for that of Thierry, are fixed in a past which is now long gone. They belong to a glamorous time that will never be forgotten.

Next to the manicured emerald lawns behind the long stone pier protecting the crystal clear turquoise waters of the yacht harbour small families of pheasants dodge in an out of the low rows of mauve bougainvillea hedges. Whenever a staff member approaches, the birds quickly disappear into the thick undergrowth among the dense blue pine and tall cypress trees which Onassis planted on Scorpios. Nearby, scattered ancient silver-green olive groves teeming with ring-necked doves and magpies guard over the immaculate narrow tarmac road which winds around the island from the harbour installations, past the Chapel, beyond the Farm, past pristine South Beach, hidden in a tiny cove marked only by two huge cypress trees, then on to East Beach, before winding over a hill to descend to the Pink House and the Master House. In another month summer will be here and Scorpios will be full of the sounds of cicadas and the staccato *tzzztt–tzzztt* rasp of rotating lawn sprinklers.

In the simple whitewashed Orthodox chapel near the main jetty four members of Athina's family —

young Uncle Alexander, Aunt Artemis, Grandfather Ari and Christina lie at peace in their marble tombs, their souls free of the golden but tragic era in which they lived. For Athina, their only descendant, a new day is starting somewhere in the world with her husband, Doda. Her former island home in Greece waited for her and her family, but the couple were never here together, never came to light a candle and hold a memorial service to the dead family members who gave them the money that has allowed them to rub shoulders with the Rothschilds, the Cashiragis, the rich and famous at the Athina Onassis Horse Show and at their Global Champions Tour venues, and to allow them to travel the world in their private multi-million dollar Gulfstream jet.

The white marble graves of Christina and Aristotle Onassis regularly have a small vase of freshly-cut flowers placed on them, not by Athina and her Brazilian husband, but by the house staff of Scorpios who maintained the island property in pristine condition in the absence of its former owner who preferred the paddocks of the international riding circuit to her private Greek island kingdom.

Up until April of 2013 the residents of Nydri and the people of Scorpios vainly looked forward to the tall deer-eyed daughter of Thierry and Christina returning to her fabled island. Suddenly there was yet another twist in the Onassis story when a Greek paper printed a story that Athina had sold Scorpios and the neighbouring island of Sparti to 24 year-old Ekaterina Rybolovleva, the good-looking daughter of a Russian oligarch, for 117 million dollars. For the Russian buyers it was a major coup. They had bought a legend, probably the best piece of holiday real estate in the world, and one that had been valued at 123 million dollars when Ari Onassis died 38 years ago. Kilometer-long forested Sparti Island, with its private harbour, hand-built stone ring road and an unfinished villa of 500m2 had been thrown in for good measure. After much media speculation the news of the transfer in ownership was confirmed by a press release in Moscow issued by the Rybolovlev family.

I once again received calls from the media wanting to know if it were true, and what I thought of the sale. I answered that, for me, and for almost every Greek, the sale of Scorpios Island was the closing chapter of a Camelot-like story of magic and hope. I had predicted several times in the past that Athina would sell the island, despite statements to the opposite by Athina, Doda and their associates. Sadly, I was right.

The iconic symbol of the fabled shipping Greek dynasty had been sold. It meant the end of the Onassis era. Greeks were disappointed that "their" Athina had cut her last ties with her past and with the cherished private island that Aristotle Onassis had loved so much, and where he, his son Alexander, Onassis' sister Artemis, and Athina's mother, Christina Onassis, are buried.

The new owners visited the island and Nydri village across the water on Lefkada island and impressed the locals with their generosity and promises of jobs. Generous donations were made to schools and medical facilities at Nydri. Now details about the owners became known. Dmitri Rybolovlev is a Harvard-educated Russian mogul who made a 9 billion dollar fortune in fertilizers and also owns the Monaco football team. He recently bought an 88 million dollar apartment in New York for his daughter and a house in Palm Springs for 100 million. Soon the new owners started major renovations to make Scorpios the sparkling jewel it once was. Young Ekaterina has the means and enthusiasm to bring life back to the island and possibly even to create a legend of her own. For the residents of the small resort of Nydri the arrival of the Russians with big plans and the potential to economically rejuvenate the area is a welcome bit of news in the middle of the worst crisis Greece has seen for generations.

Inevitably the sale raised questions about the state of Athina and Doda's finances. She had already sold her mother's famed chalet Villa Crystal in St. Moritz, had rid herself of the landmark Glyfada seaside plot on the Athens Riviera where the Onassis family villas had stood. She had also auctioned off her mother Christina's legendary jewels, inherited from her grandmother Tina Onassis Livanos, and Athina had sold off other properties. Scorpios, was the last to go with its five villas, including the Pink House, the beloved residence of Jackie Onassis where I and my family had also had the good fortune to spend memorable days.

Like all fairy stories, the tale of the Onassis family appears to end here, with no heir to carry the name and fortune after Athina. The last vestiges of the fortune are passing into the hands of lucky buyers as Athina Helene Onassis de Miranda, the last of the Onassis line, who was once "our Athina", gives priority to her equine interests and her handsome Brazilian horseman husband. It is true that she has done well in the Longines GCT competition she helped found and that she is now among the top ten riders, ahead even of Doda and of recent Olympic Gold medalists. She has hired the world's premier coach to work for her at her stables, hires helicopters to ferry him to and from the venue, and has spent millions on the best horses and facilities that money can buy through her company A+D Horses owned by her and Doda. In the end though it is her Onassis determination that has seen her rise, year by year, to the top ranks of the world's show jumpers. But the question of her Onassis family legacy and how she has handled it has divided public opinion and that of those close to her. Many have publicly criticised her for selling Scorpios to Ekaterina Rybolovleva and for her lack of sentimentality in parting with this part of her heritage, for the cash, but Onassis himself was notoriously unsentimental in matters of money. In this, his granddaughter may have turned out to be even more of an Onassis than anyone could have predicted some years ago.

Many will insist that it is her right to do what she wants with her inherited fortune, while others claim that the money came with historical family and patriotic obligations. In any case Greeks are understandably sad and disappointed to see a fabled chapter of their recent history ending, while the words of Shakespeare's *King Richard the Second* inevitably come to mind-

"A Horse! A Horse! My Kingdom for a Horse!"

The End

Printed in Great Britain
by Amazon.co.uk, Ltd.,
Marston Gate.